Studies in Sociology

Edited by

PROFESSOR W. M. WILLIAMS
University College, Swansea

8

A SOCIOLOGY OF ORGANISATIONS

A SOCIOLOGY OF ORGANISATIONS

J. E. T. Eldridge
Professor of Sociology, University of Glasgow

A. D. Crombie
Australian National University, Canberra

LONDON · GEORGE ALLEN & UNWIN LTD
RUSKIN HOUSE   MUSEUM STREET

First published in 1974

© George Allen & Unwin Ltd. 1974.

ISBN 0 04 301070 9 hardback
ISBN 0 04 301071 7 paperback

Printed in Great Britain
in 10 point Plantin type
by Alden & Mowbray Ltd
at the Alden Press, Oxford

ACKNOWLEDGEMENTS

We should like to thank the editor of this series, Bill Williams, for his well directed advice and comment whilst the book was in draft form. Naturally we remain responsible for what now appears. We should also like to thank Margaret Hall and Dinah McConville for their skilful and speedy typing of the manuscript. Finally, we record our special thanks to Rosemary Eldridge and Marjorie Crombie for their positive encouragement and help whilst this book has been in preparation.

CONTENTS

PART I INTRODUCTION

I

A Sociology of Organisations?

Consider the following story invented by Alasdair MacIntyre: 'There was once a man who aspired to be the author of the general theory of holes. When asked "What kind of hole—holes dug by children in the sand for amusement, holes dug by gardeners to plant lettuce seedlings, tank traps, holes made by roadmakers?" he would reply indignantly that he wished for a *general* theory that would explain all of these. He rejected *ab initio* the—as he saw it—pathetically common-sense view that for the digging of different kinds of holes there are quite different explanations to be given: why then he would ask do we have the concept of a hole?'[1] This cautionary tale was originally directed at political scientists who offer general theories of modernisation, urbanisation or some such all-embracing concept. It might have been directed with equal force at certain species of organisation theorists. Certainly one does not venture far into the literature on organisations before discovering papers like: 'Foundations of the Theory of Organisation'; 'The Structure and Function of Organisation'; 'Some Ingredients of a General Theory of Formal Organisation'; 'Towards a Theory of Organisations.'[2] At the same time one cannot help noticing the bewildering

[1] A. MacIntyre, 'Is a Science of Comparative Politics Possible?', *Against the Self-Images of the Age* (Duckworth, 1971), p. 260.

[2] P. Selznick 'Foundations of the Theory of Organisations', Joseph A. Litterer (ed.), *Organisations: Systems Control and Adaptation* (Wiley, 1969), Vol. 2, pp. 358–68; J. Feibleman and J. W. Friend 'The Structure and Function of Organisation', F. E. Emery (ed.), *Systems Thinking* (Penguin, 1969), pp.

array of treatments from different disciplines and from the interface between disciplines which occur when organisations are actually described and analysed. Take, for example, the very large interdisciplinary reader, edited by James March, *Handbook of Organisations*.[3] It is basically an attempt to represent the state of play in organisational analysis at the time of compilation and without doubt many of the individual contributions are of great interest. But the overall impression is of a babel of voices. The opening section is enigmatically labelled 'Foundations'. It consists of social psychological papers on leadership, decision-making, and small group studies together with a sociological discussion of social structure and organisations. But it is extremely difficult to see what these papers are the foundations of: certainly not a general theory of organisations. Following a relatively brief section on methodologies (including a paper by Scott of particular interest to the research sociologist)[4] the third and major section of the book is entitled 'Theoretical-Substantive Areas'. This includes papers on decision-making, communications and interpersonal relations in organisations not noticeably dissimilar to those treated under 'Foundations'. It also includes a valuable paper on the comparative method in organisational analysis which might well have been treated under the methodology section.[5] Alongside papers such as these however are two other kinds. There are a series of papers which group discussion around 'common-sense' labels such as prisons, schools, trade unions, political parties, hospitals and business organisations. In addition there are contributions which have to do with particular kinds of theorising, namely management theory and economic theories of organisation. The final section of the book cryptically labelled 'Applications' has to do with the problem of implementing change in organisations: a number of strategies are reviewed which themselves reveal different levels of interest (the individual, the group, the organisation) and also different theoretical perspectives. Of course, if one applies what one has discovered about organisations to 'the real world' then the implication is that one's knowledge is practically relevant to the affairs of men and as such a prescriptive element is built in: you must do x, y and z if you would achieve a successful/efficient/happy/healthy/rational organisation.

30–55; T. Parsons 'Some Ingredients of a General Theory of Formal Organisation', Joseph A. Litterer, op. cit., pp. 197–213; P. Drucker 'Towards a Theory of Organisations', *The Age of Discontinuity* (Heinemann, 1969), pp. 233–61.

[3] James G. March (ed.), *Handbook of Organisations* (Rand McNally, 1965).

[4] W. Richard Scott 'Field Methods in the Study of Organisations' in March, op. cit., pp. 261–304.

[5] Stanley H. Udy, 'The Comparative Analysis of Organisations' in March, op. cit., pp. 678–709.

Now those who implicitly advocate a general theory of organisations (at least in programmatic terms) tend to do so on the grounds of its (ultimate) practical relevance. Further, such a general theory will need to be interdisciplinary. The eclecticism of March's *Handbook of Organisations* is but a stage towards a unity of language, theory and purpose: a harbinger of a prescriptive discipline of organisations. The sense of this is well represented in a comment by Parsons:

'There are many insights which social scientists have developed in this field which can be highly useful to the practical administrator here and now. But the field is one of immense complexity at the scientific level and is only at the beginning of its scientific development. An immense amount of work will be required before we can have anything that deserves to be called a theory of formal organisation. We have, however, made some very important beginnings. For administrators, the great importance of social science theory lies in the future when these beginnings will have grown into a mature science.'[6]

It will be noticed that in this context, Parsons writes of social science, rather than any particular discipline within the social sciences. He might presumably have been more catholic in his advocacy, as some organisation theorists are, by including production engineering, cybernetics and ergonomics. But in any event the single discipline is seen as a collaborator in a greater enterprise. It should not escape our attention however, that the nature of this enterprise is to develop a unifying conceptual framework: 'Modern organisation theory represents a frontier of research which has great significance for management. The potential is great, because it offers the opportunity for uniting what is valuable in classical theory with the social and natural sciences into a systematic and integrated conception of human organisation.'[7] In other words in its developed form organisation theory is another discipline and in principle becomes subject to the same kinds of criticism as any other discipline might, notwithstanding its polyglot development. The search for conceptual unity may prove stultifying rather than liberating and the identification and handling of problems in the field standardised rather than innovating. The quest for scientific maturity might in fact end in stagnation. This leads us, not to doubt the usefulness of inter-disciplinary work in the analysis of particular problems, but to argue

[6] Parsons, op. cit., p. 213.
[7] William G. Scott 'Organisation Theory: An Overview and an Appraisal' in Joseph A. Litterer (ed.), *Organisations: Structure and Behaviour* (Wiley, 1963), Vol. I, p. 26.

that an economics, or a psychology or, in our case, a sociology of organisations has a claim to be considered in its own terms, rather than as some inferior species of activity the value of which is only to be measured in terms of its contribution to general organisation theory. Those who wish to make the intellectual pilgrimage towards a general organisation theory may or may not be chasing a will o' the wisp. They may be led to more and more rarefied abstraction in which, for example, general organisation theory is held to be derived from a general systems theory. That is not our purpose, although it is necessary to consider various kinds of systems analyses in the context of a sociology of organisations.

We have suggested that the rationale of committed organisation theorists is that *ad hoc* collections of papers such as those represented in March's *Handbook of Organisations*, should be regarded as stepping stones towards a general theory. It should, however, be noted that even within a single disciplinary framework, readings on organisations have this same *ad hoc* feel. This we think to be true of Etzioni's reader on complex organisations which nevertheless contains many excellent papers.[8] This should give us cause for reflection. The problem one confronts is that separating off sociological studies from other studies of organisations, in so far as that is possible, does not reveal a particular kind of conceptual unity (although some sociological imperialists are not beyond trying to impose it). What we discover is that sociologists study organisations (variously defined) for different thematic and theoretical reasons. Part of what we have in mind here may be encompassed in the distinction between formal and substantive theory put forward by Glaser and Strauss.

'By substantive theory we mean that developed for a substantive, or empirical area of sociological inquiry, such as patient care, race relations, professional education, delinquency or research organisations. By formal theory, we can mean that developed for a formal, or conceptual, area of sociological inquiry, such as stigma, deviant behaviour, formal organisation, socialisation, status congruency, authority and power reward systems or social mobility.'[9]

It is worthwhile pausing here to notice some of the implications this distinction has for Glaser and Strauss. We may enumerate them:

1. One may attempt a comparative analysis between or among groups

[8] A. Etzioni, *A Sociological Reader on Complex Organisations* (Holt, Rinehart & Winston, 1970).
[9] See B. G. Glaser and A. L. Strauss, *The Discovery of Grounded Theory: Strategies for Qualitative Research* (Aldine Press, 1967), p. 32.

in a substantive area. The focus is on generating a specific substantive theory.

2. One may attempt a comparative analysis of different substantive cases all of which are defined as being within a given formal area. The focus here is on developing a specified formal theory.

3. One may offer modification or confirmation of an existing formal theory or reformulate the existing theory by the development of substantive theories in relevant areas.

The methodological stance adopted by Glaser and Strauss is fundamentally of an inductive kind. Rather than put faith in a deductive 'grand theory' from which hypotheses are logically derived and tested, the argument is that one should attempt a progressive build-up from facts to substantive theory and thence on to formal theory, which because of the way it is developed will be grounded in data. Such theories will be ever open to development and change by further substantive work.

Whether or not one accepts the whole Glaser and Strauss methodological package the distinction between formal and substantive theory does alert us to a problem inherent in discussing the sociology of organisations. What this comes to is that the organisation—or some segment, group or process within it—becomes the research site for many different kinds of study. Indeed as one checks back on the somewhat random list which Glaser and Strauss give to illustrate both formal and substantive theories in sociology, it is clear that the structure and processes of organisations are highly relevant study for practically all the examples cited. This perhaps helps to account for the somewhat untidy and arbitrary character of books on organisations—that is, those which attempt some sort of over-view.

But the Glaser and Strauss distinction does suggest for us a way forward:

1. We should be much concerned with indicating the state of play concerning formal theorising about organisations.

2. Since such formal theory is grounded on substantive theorising, we should draw attention to salient areas in which such theory has taken place. This enables one's understanding of organisations as entities to be developed.

3. Since organisations are research sites for other theorising of the formal and substantive kind, we should show a modicum of awareness of these concerns—the more particularly however as they potentially offer to contribute to formal and substantive theorising about organisations *per se*.

The Glaser and Strauss approach emphasises then that in the development of knowledge and theory there are various levels of sociological activity—the direct data collection and ethnographic work which form the basis for substantive theory and which in turn provides comparative statements from which formal theory may be generated. Moreover, sociological work not only operates at various levels but is many-sided:

'... besides ethnographic studies *multiple* substantive *and* formal theories are needed to build up, through discovering their relationships, to more inclusive formal theories. Such a call for multiple theories is in contrast to the directly monopolistic implication of logico-deductive theories whose formulators talk as if there is only one theory for a formal area, or perhaps only one formal sociological theory for all areas. The need for multiple substantive theories to generate a formal theory may be obvious, but it is not so obvious that multiple formal theories are also necessary. One formal theory never handles all the relevancies of an area and by comparing many we can begin to arrive at more inclusive, parsimonious levels of formal theory. Parsimonious grounded theories are hard won by this design.'[10]

Glaser argues that the logico-deductive theorist is at fault in that he engages in a premature parsimony of formulation. The concepts from which he begins are too hastily constructed and the deductions from the premises are too loose-fitting in relation to reality.

Interwoven as it were with the issues raised by Glaser and Strauss is the fact that within sociology there are competing orientations. The shorthand used to designate these differences may sometimes refer to key figures in the history of the subject—accordingly we may refer to Marxist, Weberian and Durkheimian perspectives. Alternatively we may refer to particular stances in sociology—for example structural functionalism and conflict theory. More recently a critical dividing line has been suggested between social systems theory and social action theory. What is implied here has been well expressed by Dawe:

'There are ... two sociologies: a sociology of social system and a sociology of social action. They are grounded in the diametrically opposed corners with two central problems, those of order and control. And, at every level, they are in conflict. They posit antithetical views of human nature, of society, and of the relationship between the social and the individual. The first asserts the paramount necessity for societal and individual well-being of external constraint; hence the

[10] B. Glaser, *Organisational Careers: a Sourcebook for Theory* (Aldine Press, 1968), p. 5.

notion of a social system ontologically and methodologically prior to its participants. The key notion of the second is that of autonomous man, able to realise his full potential and to create a truly human social order only when freed from external constraint. Society is thus the creation of its members; the product of their construction of meaning, and of the action and relationships through which they attempt to impose that meaning on their historical situations. In summary, one views action as the derivative of system, whilst the other views system as the derivative of action.'[11]

This kind of distinction has been articulated in the context of the sociology of organisations by Silverman.[12] And certainly the issues raised are ones we are very conscious of as authors, not least because we do not share the same perspective. However, rather than offering a social action text or a systems text we have seen our task as one of elucidating a range of sociological approaches and interests. In the nature of the case the account is not exhaustive but we have spread the net quite widely. We will indicate briefly what we have tried to do.

Part II, 'Organisations: Concepts and Classifications', explores the issue of taxonomies, first by pointing out the ways in which they are influenced by basic definitions of what an organisation is. The question then pursued is: what rationale is entailed in selecting certain elements, properties or characteristics as a basis for analysis? What is the nature of the labelling process by which we differentiate organisations from other social entities and then classify organisations in terms of their similarities or differences? On what grounds, if any, are we justified in doing anything other than common-sense labelling? What claims are made for some of the going typologies in the sociology of organisations? What assumptions are built in?

In Part III, 'Organisations: Missions and Cultures, the concept of organisation is further elaborated. The organisation is viewed as a particular kind of social system, one which is purposeful, and which is structured so as to facilitate the realisation of purposes. Purposeful behaviour of any sort entails a relation between the actor and the environment in which the properties of either may independently affect the courses of action chosen, and their outcomes. We give more attention than has often been the case to the characteristics of organisational environments and to the character of the choice situations confronting organisational leaders.

[11] Alan Dawe, 'The Two Sociologies', *British Journal of Sociology* (June 1970), Vol. XXI, No. 2, p. 212.
[12] D. Silverman, *The Theory of Organisations* (Heinemann, 1970).

In talking of organisational 'culture' we acknowledge also the individuality and uniqueness of the organisation as it results from the distinctiveness of the organisational choices that are made, in spite of similarities and continuities in structures and processes. The 'internal' characteristics of the organisation in action are discussed in the same contextualist frame of reference as the relations between the organisation and its environment—the understanding of particular parts and processes is sought in an exploration of the wider contexts in which they occur.

Part IV, 'The Organisational Phenomenon', concentrates in Chapter 6 on certain seminal themes which may be located in the writings of Spencer, Durkheim, Marx and Weber. After a period of neglect Spencer is now rather more widely read. We have tried to underline the sense which he obviously had of the growth of a society of organisations as a concomitant of industrialism and also the ambivalence which he manifested towards this development. Marx and Durkheim, one is surprised to discover, are somewhat ignored in discussion on the sociology of organisations. We hope at least in an indicative way to have remedied this. Weber, of course, in this field has the status of folk hero. Heroes exist to be challenged as well as worshipped. We suspect that Weber has suffered in both respects. The challenges have sometimes been ill-judged because of a tendency to take his statement on bureaucracy out of context and then 'prove' how wrong he was. The worship has obscured the contributions of other sociologists in this respect, notably, we would argue, Spencer, Marx and Durkheim.

Chapter 7 deals with continuities and cross-currents of sociological analysis and is derivative of much that is touched upon in Chapter 6. It is based upon three sensitising concepts which have guided sociologists: totalitarian, oligarchic and pluralist analyses of organisation structures and the relations between organisations. These raise questions about the kind of models entailed in employing such terminology, how far they fit with empirical reality and how this is to be explained.

The final part of the book has to do with political and ethical issues raised by sociological studies of organisations. We have paid particular attention to the critiques which categorise the sociologist as a mandarin within powerful organisations or as a servant of power. This leads us into a discussion of the client-researcher relationship and into an exploration of the role of the sociologist as a change agent. This has in turn involved us in a consideration of action research and the problems of commitment and evaluation which appear to be entailed. We have argued that embedded in such programmes are theories about how organisational change may be accomplished. The theories may relate to different levels—the individual, the group or the organisation—but they tend to be gradualist in form. The possibilities of more discontinuous approaches to change are however alluded to. In any event we emphasise that the issues of power and its distribution—both within organisations and in a society of organisations—can on no account be side-stepped.

PART II ORGANISATIONS CONCEPTS AND CLASSIFICATIONS

2

Defining and Labelling Organisations

(a) THE CONCEPT OF ORGANISATION

It may appear somewhat unnecessary to draw attention to the term organisation because we all have common-sense notions of what is entailed. Nevertheless definitions tend, if only in a preliminary way, to circumscribe the way subsequent study proceeds. Indeed we may note that certain aspects or elements tend to be highlighted by a definition such that a certain mode of inquiry or way of conceptualising a study of organisations may be implied.

A preliminary note on definition

OED definitions focus on the verb rather than the noun. To organise is to 'form into an organic whole', 'give orderly structure to: frame and put into working order, make arrangements for or get up (undertaking involving co-operation)'. It is clear from this that an activity involving deliberate intent on the part of the organiser is entailed and we may also register the use of the terms *order* and *co-operation*. This of course is a very formal definition in that it tells us nothing about the mechanisms, techniques or bases upon which order and co-operation are secured. This we will look at more closely in its own right. The definition which speaks of 'forming into an organic whole' has reference back to the noun 'organism' which in its turn is defined as 'organised body with connected interdependent parts sharing common life (material structure of) individual animal or plant; whole with interdependent parts compared to living being'. Here our attention is immediately drawn to the notion of *interdependence* and to the fact that the logic of analogy may apply: an entity is defined as an organism not necessarily because it is a living being but because it is *like* a living being. When therefore one speaks of an organisation or of an organised entity these definitions may be written in. What still remains to be supplied however is some statement about the elements that are defined as being interdependent—both what they are and what the supposed interconnections between them are. And if the biological analogy is propounded, then clearly one wants to know how the analogy is being applied and with what qualifications. The analogy, if employed, may well affect the language used to describe organisations. We might expect to encounter terms like: species, birth, growth, development, maturation, function, adaptation, competition, decay, death. Broadly it may be said that the OED statements are attempts to offer definitions in terms of the formally essential nature of organisation (providing we recognise that it is not logically necessary to link the activity with a biological analogy) rather than in terms of any classificatory or even enumerative definitions. An enumerative definition in which we say that A, B, C and D are organisations only serves some illustrative guiding function unless it sets out to be exhaustive. To offer an enumerative definition in the case of organisations would in any practical sense appear to be impossible. When we turn to classificatory definitions we may recognise that there are: (*a*) classifications which seek to separate the concept organisation from other concepts with which the writer thinks it may be confused; (*b*) classifications which seek to differentiate between organisations with reference to one or more criteria.

Usually we need to go on to ask questions about the basis and object of the classificatory system. Having ascertained that, one may at a later stage raise questions about the utility of the classification or perhaps the consistency with which it is applied.

On differentiating organisations from non-organisations

Caplow defines an organisation as 'a social system that has an unequivocal collective identity, an exact roster of members, a programme of activity and procedures'.[1] The term 'social system' is itself defined as 'a set of persons with an identifying characteristic plus a set of relation-

[1] T. Caplow, *Principles of Organisation* (Harcourt, Brace & Court, 1964), p. 1.

ships established among these persons by interaction'[2] and what is entailed here is the notion that an organisation is a *particular kind* of social system. He argues, for example, that racial or ethnic groups are cases of social systems which are not organisations because they have no programmes. It would be preferable to say that they do not *necessarily* have a programme. It is also suggested that social classes are not organisations because their collective identities are not unequivocal and their rosters not exact. Leaving on one side the perennial knotty concept of class, we should at least recall that class organisations in the form of trade unions or political parties are not entirely unknown and this is somewhat blurred by Caplow's formulation. Cliques and play groups are not organisations according to Caplow because they lack collective identity. Again, however, one has reservations since the existence of such groupings may well be recognised by the membership and by many outsiders. In the main here we are suggesting that there are ambiguities which emerge when one looks at the examples Caplow gives to distinguish between organisations and non-organisations. Basically this is brought out by questioning the way Caplow applies the criteria of differentiation, not by criticising the criteria themselves. One might however query that element of the definition which speaks of an exact roster of members. Many large religious denominations, do not, one may suppose, have exact rosters of their membership—the quality of the figures being much affected by the efficiency and regularity with which local churches keep records.[3] Yet large groupings of this kind are certainly considered fodder for students or organisations and are indeed subsequently listed by Caplow as such.

What is implied in Caplow's appraisal is the idea that one can empirically identify social systems as organisations or non-organisations by reference to certain characteristics whose presence or absence can be ascertained. In principle one may further refer to these criteria to make additional classifications of types of organisations but we postpone a discussion of the point.

Parsons also writes of the organisation as a particular kind of social system, namely one which is 'deliberately constructed and reconstructed to seek specific goals or values'.[4] In giving illustrations of what he has in mind Parsons refers to government departments, business firms, universities and hospitals. It is a type of collectivity which, he maintains, can be differentiated from local communities, regional subsocieties and,

[2] ibid., p. 1.
[3] See for example, Benson Y. Landis, 'Confessions of a Church Statistician', in Louis Schneider (ed.), *Religion, Culture and Society* (Wiley, 1964).
[4] T. Parsons, *Structure and Process in Modern Societies* (Free Press, 1960).

on a smaller scale, from friendship cliques, informal work groups and the like. Parsons's approach leads him to suggest possibilities of classifying types of organisations by relating them to different kinds of goal or function. To this point we shall have to return. For the moment, however, we observe that again the distinction between organisation and non-organisation is not altogether convincing. If one is to go along with the usage of groups seeking goals it is not clear, say, that informal work groups do not sometimes do this: for example, the goal of output control. If it be held that the *specificity* of goal attainment is the decisive criterion, then one may entertain doubts as to whether the empirical cases cited by Parsons really match up to this—as opposed to the possibility that a multiplicity of goals may be embodied in organisational activity, so much so that only by straining credibility or by speaking with great vagueness could one refer to *the* organisational goal.

Etzioni supports Parsons's definition of organisation and uses similar empirical examples to indicate what social units are included and what excluded.[5]

He further suggests three defining criteria of organisations: (*a*) the division of labour, power and communication . . . responsibilities are deliberately planned with the intention of realising specific goals; (*b*) there are one or more power centres which control the total organisation in the pursuit of specific goals; (*c*) there is a concern with personnel which may be reflected in such activities as recruitment of members, removal of unwanted members, and re-allocation of tasks among membership.

In seeking to differentiate in this way Etzioni makes it clear that the difference between organisations and other social units is one of degree rather than one of rigid demarcation:

'Other social units are marked by some degree of conscious planning (e.g. the family budget), by the existence of power centres (e.g. tribal chiefs), and by replaceable membership (e.g. through divorce), but the extent to which these other social units are consciously planned, deliberately structured and restructured, with a membership which is routinely changed, is much less than in the case of other social units we are calling *organisations*. Hence organisations are much more in control of their nature and destiny than any other social grouping.'[6]

Despite the plethora of specialist writing on organisations, in our view one of the most useful attempts to distinguish organisation from other social units is that of MacIver and Page as discussed in their

[5] A. Etzioni, *Modern Organisations* (Prentice Hall, 1964).   [6] ibid., p. 3.

introduction to sociology.[7] There use is made of the term 'association' as a social group which exists to pursue particular purposes and interests:

'Associations develop as means or modes of attaining interests. An association is likely to be formed wherever people recognise a like complementary, or common interest sufficiently enduring and sufficiently distinct to be capable of more effective promotion through collective action provided their differences outside the field of this interest are not so strong as to prevent the partial agreement involved in its formation. This principle holds for the formation of a family, a business firm, a church, a union, a club, a professional society, and even . . . a political state.'[8]

We can see from the illustrations given at the end of the definition that the concept is more comprehensive in coverage than that of Caplow, Parsons or Etzioni. MacIver and Page do differentiate between primary group associations and large associations and the latter category has much in common in terms of empirical reference to the concept of organisation as elaborated by the other writers we have cited. The concept of association is set against two other group concepts. First, there is the notion of interest-conscious unities without definite organisation. Thus social class or ethnic group categories may be of this order —but MacIver and Page are careful to note that associations based on class or ethnic interests may in fact arise. Secondly, there is the concept of community as a territorial unit. It is observed that one can have a number of associations within a single community. Associations as interest groups suggest a narrower base of allegiance and membership than communities. Nevertheless it is recognised that associations may become communities because, for various reasons, practically the whole of life may be encompassed in certain kinds of associations, as in the case of a trading company or military outposts, prisons, convents, monasteries and, in certain rural situations, the family. This kind of overlapping, however, perhaps only serves to draw our attention to the character of some associations which becomes of relevance when differentiating between kinds of association. MacIver and Page neglect to point out that the relation between community and association does not simply imply the possibility of several associations in one community. It may entail the existence of associations which impinge upon a community but are not contained by it, as in the case of a large business corporation with segments in different communities (either local or national).

[7] R. M. MacIver and C. H. Page, *Society* (Macmillan, 1957).   [8] ibid., p. 437.

The other important point about MacIver and Page's definition is that it does not include the notion of goal. Rather the emphasis is upon interests. Their subsequent classifications are much conditioned by this. Although there may be practical difficulties in deciding what constitutes the dominant interest of an association at any given time, and although interests may change over a period of time, what is implied is that some interests may be shared so that one may perhaps be able to speak of common goals, but other interests may be congruent—such that individuals also have separate interests which can be met in the association. A man plays in a football team perhaps to keep himself fit, but he may also share the interest with other members of wanting success for the team. That is not all, however, since conflicts of interest may also appear in organisations:

> 'Like the greater communal manifestation of social cohesion—class, ethnic and racial groups, a crowd, as well as community itself—the unity of the association is imperfect and unstable, representing what it endures, the victory of integrative over disintegrative processes. A study of the conflict and harmonies of interest that appear within the life of associations could be for the student an excellent preparation for the investigation of that greater unstable equilibrium which is the social order itself.'[9]

Although planning and conscious pursuit of aims are especially written into the notion of organisation as against other social groups and categories, we see here that associations also *share* with other groupings conflict as a part of their social life. This in itself provides some precaution against an over-smooth view of the organisation as an orderly goal-seeking entity.

It is a little surprising that, while Max Weber is one of the most widely cited writers in discussions about organisations, these invariably refer to what he wrote on bureaucracy, not his direct comments on the concept of organisation. He defines the concept as follows:

> 'A social relationship which is either closed or limits the admission of outsiders will be called an organisation when its regulations are enforced by specific individuals. . . . Whether or not an organisation exists is entirely a matter of the presence of a person in authority, with or without an administrative staff. More precisely it exists so far as there is a probability that certain persons will act in such a way as to carry out the order governing the organisation; that is that persons are present who can be counted on to act in this way whenever the

[9] ibid., p. 449.

occasion arises. For purposes of definition it is indifferent what is the basis of the relevant expectation, whether it is a case of traditional, affectual or value-rational devotion (or) . . . a matter of expediency. . . . So long as there is a probability of such action, the organisation as a sociological entity continues to exist in spite of the fact that the specific individuals whose action is orientated to the order in question, may have been completely changed. The concept has been defined intentionally to include precisely this phenomenon.'[10]

We note in anticipation that the concept of organisation is certainly not a synonym for bureacracy.[11] Whereas we have seen that Caplow, Parsons and Etzioni define organisation as a kind of social system and MacIver and Page as a kind of social group, for Weber it is treated as a kind of social relationship. This is the term employed to denote the existence of a probability that between two or more persons there is a meaningful course of social action. By pointing to the significance of an individual's social behaviour, Weber is wanting to avoid the reification of a collective concept like organisation, state, church and so on.

This contrasts markedly with the idea of organisations having goals or even interests. Rather it is a question of certain individuals issuing orders and being obeyed. Hence the question of authority is a central element in the definition, and attempts to differentiate between types of organisation clearly will go back to the bases of authority. In addition, however, the notion of probability offers a range of actual possibilities from high to low and writes into the definition the idea that organisations may vary from stable to highly unstable. Finally we can see that, whilst wishing to avoid the danger of reification, Weber does allow for the changing personnel in an organisation, hence the continuity of an organisation is not *ipso facto* dependent upon certain individuals. What matters is whether or not the defined social relationship exists at any given time. Whether this form of methodological individualism can be sustained is one of the questions which we consider at various points in the present volume.

(b) LABELLING ORGANISATIONS

(i) *Common-sense labels*

Terms like school, trade union, church, army, political party, are examples of the common-sense way in which we differentiate between organisations. In employing these terms in everyday conversation we

[10] Max Weber, *Economy and Society*, G. Roth and C. Wittick (eds) (Bedminster Press, 1968), pp. 48–9.

[11] For a discussion of Weber's treatment of bureaucracy see below pp. 143–149.

all think we know what we are talking about—the terms are indeed part of our stock of knowledge which serves to make communication possible. The term 'school' *obviously* has different connotations from the term 'trade union'. It is so obvious that we take it for granted. The sociologist can properly make it part of his business to reflect on the way people parcel the world up into working concepts. But that in a sense is only a point of departure and leads us to make the following points.

1. The labels are manifestly meant to apply to the real world. They refer to actual entities, sets of activities in which various physical resources are being used. Yet the labels are abstractions for all that. One could rarely, if at all, give an elaborate and accurate (let alone total) description of the activities entailed. The abstraction is a simplification about what is going on in the real world. Although we may enter into conversations in which we tacitly assume that we all use the same label in the same way, that is share the same simplifications, it does not always work out like that. Sometimes, of course, the participants in the discussion may not realise that they mean different things when they use a particular term, in which case we would describe them as talking past each other. More often than not, however, comes the realisation that one does not mean what the other means when he uses the collective label.

2. There is the problem of grossness in employing common-sense labels. The term gang, for example, can apply to a wide range of organised activities—from children's peer groups to adult racketeers; the term army ranges from small private mercenary groups to a large publicly financed army with nuclear weapons at its disposal. Sometimes we conduct common-sense refinements to deal with this kind of problem— we may distinguish between, say, comprehensive, public and grammar schools, between Congregational and Anglican churches, between white collar and manual workers' trade unions, or between Labour and Conservative parties. Hopefully this makes for greater clarity in discussion. In everyday conversation it allows us to compare and contrast types of school, types of trade union, types of political party and so on which we may evaluate from various standpoints and pronounce judgement upon. At one level of concern the sociologist cannot ignore such distinctions, since they structure the terms in which debates are conducted, problems defined and sometimes decisions taken. But even the more refined common-sense label cannot be taken as a final resting place.

3. From time to time we discover that common-sense labels break down. Is scientology a religious organisation? Is the British Medical Association a trade union? Such questions can provoke great contro-

versy. A legal judgement may sometimes be called for—and although this may be highly important in terms of the constraints laid upon, or possibilities opened up to the organisation subsequently—such a judgement does not automatically draw into unity conflicting opinions. We may notice here that a legal judgement is itself a form of labelling which goes far beyond common sense. It is precisely the inadequacy of common sense which presents the need for more systematic clarification with reference to appropriate legal criteria as a basis for differentiation. This leads us to anticipate our later discussion to point out that there may be modes of systematic clarification other than legal which also go beyond common sense. We shall indicate below some of the criteria which may be employed and the rationale which informs them.

4. Common-sense labels (even when they are refined) can be hindrances as well as aids to understanding organisations. They might disguise both the similarities and differences between organisations which other approaches might bring to the surface. The labels Congregational and Anglican, for instance, suggest two churches with differing doctrinal emphases and contrasting views about the nature of church government. Yet an investigation which seeks to look behind the labels may discover similarities in the way decisions are actually taken. Moreover a little more than common sense is required to explore whether certain kinds of churches, schools, unions, political parties share certain characteristics despite their differing spheres of activity. It is certainly part of the sociologist's task to sensitise us to and explore such possibilities. At the simplest level this may take the form of carefully noting specified empirical facts about particular organisations. At a more complex level the concern may be with the properties or characteristics of organisations in and through which common-sense abstractions about organisations are replaced by the analytical abstractions of the social scientist.

(ii) *Labelling with reference to specific organisational elements*
Assuming the information is available and made accessible, it becomes possible to point to the extent to which particular organisations incorporate facts of a quantifiable and concretely verifiable character. We have in mind what Stinchcombe has termed natural variables.[12] Such variables exist independently of an investigator studying organisations and, depending on his purposes, he may or may not choose to take account of them. Some of these variables are of a dichotomous kind: one may, for example, classify members of an organisation by

[12] A. L. Stinchcombe, *Constructing Social Theories* (Harcourt Brace, 1968).

sex. Others may have a range of values which may be read off, for example, the number of people who are members of an organisation, the age distribution of membership and duration of membership in the organisation. Clearly it is possible in principle to monitor particular organisations over specified periods of time with reference to such data and to compare them with other organisations.

There are a number of points which this kind of labelling procedure draws to our attention:

1. Although they are natural variables the relevant data are not always easy to obtain and one cannot always accept official documentation as the final word, as to what the facts really are. Certainly claims by organisations concerning the size of their membership cannot always be taken at face value.

2. Sometimes studies of organisations take place with cut-off points which are much affected or even determined with reference to such variables. Thus one may choose to look at single-sex organisations, young people's organisations, organisations with short duration membership, and so on.

3. For some purposes it is a particular natural variable—its constancy or its change—which becomes the focus of study, the thing which is to be explained. One might ask, for example, how is the observable growth in membership size or the changing sex composition of an organisation to be explained.

4. The examples of natural variables we have cited apply, as it happens, to all organisations (and indeed to other groups), but some natural variables may only have reference to particular organisations. The materials and resources used by different organisations clearly vary enormously in kind. This may mean that for some purposes one uses a limited natural variable and applies it to organisations in which the variable is located—say, for example, the number of books purchased by a library, or the amount of money spent on lathes by an engineering firm. For other purposes, simply to identify the fact that some natural variables are located in some organisations and not in others may provide one with a clue to the explanation of possible differences in social behaviour. The substantive concern of the librarian buying books is obviously different from the substantive concern of the manager buying lathes: yet we may also note that the example we have cited relates to the activity of buying, so that some basis for the comparison of an activity in disparate organisations remains a possibility.

5. Some natural variables have a slightly less simple character than any we have so far discussed. This is where an index is utilised. For

example, some business organisations calculate their direct labour costs as a ratio of total costs. For some purposes, comparing particular organisations with reference to this economic indicator, may be helpful. In so far as they exist independently of the investigator such variables are still properly described as natural. Nonetheless there is an element of construction about them and, in the example we have used, one should recognise definitions and practices underlying costing procedures can vary enormously. Even at this raw empirical level therefore, an element of social definition enters in by virtue of the fact that certain basic data about the organisation are being manipulated in a technical way. Clearly, verification of the data is more than simply checking out on the facts. One cannot assume consensus either within or across organisations about the kind of calculations involved. If, on the other hand, the researcher attempts some kind of standardisation and reworks the data to improve on the consistency of the measure, then the variable can no longer strictly be treated as natural.

6. The natural variables so far discussed relate to data which organisational leaders or administrators may well have an interest in collating. There may, however, be natural variables which for all practical purposes are ignored by members of an organisation, but are utilised by students of organisations. For example, communication between members of an organisation may be considered in terms of natural variables which treat of the method, frequency, direction and duration of contacts. One is thinking here of the overt aspects of interaction not the meaning which is attached to it. How effectively one may utilise such natural variables is partly a technical question of methodology, but will also vary considerably, one may reasonably suppose, with other organisational characteristics—for example size and secrecy.

We conclude this section by noting that there is a large universe of natural variables which the student of organisations may take into account. Whether and how he makes use of them will obviously be connected with his interests and will be conditioned by research practicalities. We are not at this stage focusing on problems of explanation. Suffice it to mention here that the exploration of relationships between natural variables in one or more organisations can be involved. The relationship between organisational size and membership interaction is a case in point.[13] Caplow, for example, argues that although the evidence is incomplete there is a tendency for the size and stability of organised groups to be correlated. Part of his evidence rests on the

[13] See W. H. Kephart, 'A Quantitative Analysis of Intergroup Relationships', *AJS* (August 1950), Vol. LV, No. 6, and Caplow, op. cit., pp. 29–36.

observation that 'since the number of relationships in an organisation increases much faster than membership size, large organisations have a much denser network of relationships than have smaller organisations of the same general type'.[14]

(iii) *Labelling with reference to specific organisational characteristics*

In writing of organisational elements we pointed to natural variables (whether dichotomous or continuous) which are, so to speak, empirically already available for an investigator to utilise. In referring to the possibility of labelling organisations with specific characteristics, we have in mind the fact that the investigator may construct his own categories for classificatory purposes. The possibilities are endless—what the investigator actually does will depend partly on his problems and partly on his imagination. But they are not all of the same order:

1. He may simply 'tidy up' a natural variable, as for example, when all the possible readings on organisational size are reduced to 'large', 'medium', and 'small'.

2. He may take cognisance of a number of natural variables (possibly simplifying them *en route*) which appear to him to have a family resemblance and subsume them under one general category. For example, if one wished to categorise organisations with reference to their administrative form, one might draw attention to a number of elements, such as the number of different job titles and distribution of personnel between them; the line-staff ratio; the method, frequency and direction of communication within the organisation; the span of control; and so on.[15] We have already seen that some natural variables are only applicable to particular kinds of organisation. In this case we see that some of the items mentioned do not look to be generally applicable and this can indicate built-in limitation to their use.

3. He may combine natural variables (again possibly simplifying them in the process) to form particular analytical categories. So one might, say, take the number of organisational members and attendance at meetings convened for members and construct a category of commitment to the organisation. The questions which lurk in the background here are: (i) How far can these concepts be made operational that is, susceptible to measurement? (ii) How generally applicable are they, given the natural variables from which they are derived? (iii) Are there many natural variables which one might use for looking at, in this case, commitment to organisations?

[14] op. cit. p. 34.
[15] See Tom Burns ,'The Comparative Study of Organisations', in V. Vroom (ed.), *Methods of Organisational Research* (Pittsburgh University Press, 1967).

4. He may combine or cross-classify analytical concepts to construct new categories. For example, Etzioni takes the concept of power and the concept of involvement (with the organisation) and links them together to form the concept of compliance relationships. In this case the procedure entails differentiating between types of power (coercive, remunerative, normative) and types of involvement (alienative, calculative, moral) which by cross-classification admits of nine potential forms of compliance relationships.[16]

Organisational properties

In his essay 'Continuities in the Theory of Reference Groups in Social Structures',[17] R. K. Merton outlines a provisional list of group properties. Twenty-six properties are listed:

1. Clarity or vagueness of social definitions of membership in the group.
2. Degree of engagement of members in the group.
3. Actual duration of membership in the group.
4. Expected duration of membership in the group.
5. Actual duration of the group.
6. Expected duration of the group.
7. Absolute size of the group, or of component parts of a group.
8. Relative size of a group, or of component parts of a group.
9. Open or closed character of a group.
10. Completeness: the ratio of actual to potential group members.
11. Degree of social differentiation.
12. Shape and height of stratification.
13. Types and degree of social cohesion.
14. The potential of fission or unity of a group.
15. Extent of social interaction in a group.
16. Character of the social relations obtaining in a group.
17. Degree of expected conformity to norms of a group: toleration of deviant behaviour and institutionalised departures from the strict definition of group-norms.
18. The system of normative controls.
19. Degree of visibility or observability within the group.
20. Ecological structure of the group (i.e. spatial distribution of members in the group).
21. Autonomy or dependence of the group.
22. Degree of stability of the group.

[16] A. Etzioni, *A Comparative Analysis of Complex Organisations* (Free Press, 1961). See also below pp. 45–47.

[17] in, R. Merton, *Social Theory and Social Structure* (Free Press, 1957).

23. Degree of stability of the structural context of the group.
24. Modes of maintaining stability of the group and of the structural context.
25. Relative social standing of groups.
26. Relative power or groups.

Concerning this list we may observe first that it contains a mixture of items, some of which are examples of what we have termed organisational elements, others of organisational characteristics. Accordingly, some of them are easily identifiable properties like absolute size of the group, others are complex analytical abstractions like social cohesion. Secondly, we may note that the properties relate to different levels of interest: some to group structures (e.g. 7, 9, 11, 12, 20), some to group processes (e.g. 13, 18), some to relationships within the group (e.g. 15, 16, 17), some to the relationships between parts of a group (e.g. 7, 8, 14), some to the group *vis-à-vis* other groups (e.g. 8, 25, 26) and finally some to the character of the environment in which the group exists, with which perhaps not strictly a group property is viewed in relation to the way it impinges on group structure and process (e.g. 23, 24). Thirdly, some of these properties are discernible with reference to more or less objective facts or phenomena (e.g. 7, 11, 15, 20), others rest in part on the subjective judgements of group members (e.g. 2, 4, 6, 16) and still others take their meaning from the conceptual framework in which they have been placed by the sociologist (e.g. 18, 23, 24).

As Merton points out, there is widespread disagreement as to which group properties provide the basis for the most instructive classifications and the list he provides gives some sense of the diversity of interest evident in sociological work on groups and organisations. Such a list may prompt one to point to omissions, or to relatively neglected categories, or to consider the kinds of relationships which may be posited between group properties. The main justification claimed by Merton, however, for such a list is that 'it provides a point of departure for "experimenting" with alternative classifications, rather than adopting *ad hoc* classifications evolved for a momentary purpose'.[18] It is, for him, the necessary groundwork which has to be covered as a prelude to the establishment of explanations of the social. In other words, it is a step towards the construction of sociological theories.

(v) *Pure type labels*
The use of ideal or pure types is of course properly associated with Weber:

[18] ibid., p. 325.

'It is important to realise that in the sociological field as elsewhere, averages, and hence average types, can be formulated with a relative degree of precision only where they are concerned with differences of degree in respect to action which remains qualitatively the same. Such cases do occur, but in the majority of cases of action important to history or sociology the motives which determine it are qualitatively heterogeneous, Then it is quite impossible to speak of an 'average' in the true sense.'[19]

Because of this, Weber argues, it is necessary for the sociologist to construct ideal types that define the meaning of social action in a pure form. These are scientific constructs which are unlikely to be treated in their pure form in the real world: 'The more sharply and precisely the ideal type has been constructed, thus the more abstract and unrealistic in this sense it is, the better it is able to perform its functions in formulating terminology, classifications, and hypotheses.'[20]

This form of labelling is employed by Weber in differentiating between organisations. Drawing on the examples he gives we may make the following points:

1. Quite frequently one pure type is presented as the polarised dichotomy of another. For example, the distinction is made between an autonomous and a heteronomous organisation: the first referring to an organisation which has been established on the authority of its own members, and the second referring to an organisation which has been established and imposed on the membership by an outside agency. Other examples are the contrasts between voluntary and compulsory associations and between administrative and regulative order in organisations.

2. There is a tendency to offer a generic ideal type and then further ideal types within the general case. Thus a ruling organisation is defined as one in which members are 'subject to domination by virtue of the established order'.[21] Within that definition a contrast is drawn between political and hierocratic organisations: the first referring to an organisation where 'existence and order is continuously safeguarded within a given *territorial* area by the threat and application of physical force on the part of the administrative staff',[22] and the second referring to an organisation 'which enforces its order through psychic coercion by distributing or denying religious benefits'.[23] Further differentiations are then made between types of political and economic organisation.

3. Particular organisations may be defined in a way which utilises

---

[19] *Economy and Society*, op. cit., pp. 20–1.   [20] ibid., p. 21.
[21] ibid., p. 53.   [22] ibid., p. 54.   [23] ibid., p. 54.

a number of ideal types. The definition of the modern state is a good example:

> 'It possesses an administrative and legal order subject to change by legislation, to which the organised activities of the administrative staff, which are also controlled by regulations are orientated. This system of order claims binding authority, not only over the members of the state, the citizens, most of whom have obtained membership by birth, but also to a very large extent over all action taking place in the area of its jurisdiction. It is thus a compulsory organisation with a territorial base. Furthermore, today, the use of force is regarded as legitimate only so far as it is either permitted by the state or prescribed by it.'[24]

Labelling of this sort, therefore, is of a heuristic kind: to some extent it certainly makes use of common-sense labels but is more self-consciously precise in the attempt to minimise ambiguity. It enables one to look at an actual organisation by referring back to a battery of ideal type categories (and if necessary constructing further types as an aid to understanding). Some of the types relate to structures (rational, legal and patrimonial bureaucracies), others to forms (consensual and imposed order); some refer to universal processes (power and control), others to historically specific items (the modern state); and finally some are geared to substantive areas (economic, political, ecclesiastical) but are formulated in a more precise way than common-sense usage.

[24] ibid., p. 56.

3

Types of Organisations

Exploration of some of their shared properties leads us to view organisations as purposeful social systems which are characterised by a functional division of labour with respect to the ends of the system as a whole. But it is perhaps the differences among organisations that are striking—differences not only in their goals or functions, but in their technologies, their structures, systems of authority, and so on. Unable to say much that is both useful and true with respect to all organisations, and sensitive to the limitations of generalising from case studies of single organisations or parts of organisations, a number of organisation theorists have concentrated instead on generating typologies of organisations which will allow us to make systematic comparisons between different *classes* of organisations and perhaps venture into the construction of theory of the 'middle range'. This is the explicit aim of Etzioni, whose typology is described below. A further alternative is the approach that is taken in the recent book of Blau and Schoenherr,[1] who study and compare the properties of a very large number of organisations in order to illuminate the relationships between structural properties such as size, differentiations, formalisation of rules, bureaucratic rigidity, complexity and so on. The use of a typology may be thought of as a variant of this comparative method in which variations in organisational characteristics are related to a classificatory variable, on the basis of which different types of organisation have been identified.

We have already noted that sociologists make use of the methodological devices of ideal types and extreme types, as well as the better understood classificatory types. Ideal types, as we have seen, are usually associated with the work of Weber, and in particular his formulation of the concept of bureaucracy. Extreme types consist in the

[1] P. Blau and R. Schoenherr, *The Structure of Organisations* (Basic Books, 1971).

37

description of polar cases at the ends of a continuum along which in principle all examples of the phenomena under investigation may be ordered. Jung's extroversion-introversion scale, and the distinction between mechanical and organic solidarity made by Durkheim are examples that are familiar to social scientists. Classification is based on the selection of a central variable with respect to which the universe of the phenomena concerned may be subdivided. This classificatory concept should refer to an attribute or characteristic that is found in all members of that universe and should be precisely and unequivocally defined, so that any given member can be placed into one and only one of the classes delimited by the concept. In fact these strict logical requirements are seldom met.

Here we intend simply to outline some of the more influential typologies and to try to indicate some of their strengths and weaknesses. It has to be remembered of course that the construction of a typology, however elegant, is not an end in itself. It is valuable to the extent that it suggests new hypotheses to guide inquiry, and directs attention to relationships not previously observed. For the purposes of exposition only, we note that typologies themselves may be put into different classes according to the type of variable on which the typology is based. Thus Silverman has distinguished between environment-input typologies, environment-output typologies, and typologies based on intra-organisational factors.[2] We will consider typologies based on functions (Katz and Kahn, Tavistock, Blau and Scott), technology (Woodward, Blauner, Thompson), regulation (Etzioni), and structure (Ackoff, Vickers). We will also consider total institutions as a type of organisation.

(a) TYPOLOGIES BASED ON FUNCTIONS

Katz and Kahn's identification of four types of organisations, based upon the 'geno-typic function' that is performed, is the clearest case of a functionalist typology. Genotypic function refers to the type of activity in which the organisation is involved as a subsystem of the larger society, and the four types are productive or economic, maintenance, adaptive, and managerial-political. The exemplar of each of these types is, respectively, the business enterprise, the school, the research institution, and the state. They argue as follows:

'. . . for a society to endure there must be economically productive activities which meet basic needs and provide basic services. There must be a central set of values and norms with socialising agencies to

2 D. Silverman, *The Theory of Organisations* (Heinemann, 1970), pp. 14 ff.

inculcate these belief systems and to provide general and specific training for social roles. To ensure some viable integration or compromise among organised groups and interest publics there must be an authoritative decision-making structure for the allocation of resources. Finally in an advanced society specialised agencies develop for the creation of knowledge and for fostering artistic endeavour. These major tasks are distributed among organisations which generally specialise in a single function but make supplementary contributions in other areas.'[3]

Their work is clearly related to and draws from the general theory of Talcott Parsons, and the organisational typology sketched by him, which differentiates organisations according to the needs of the larger system that they satisfy—adaptation, goal attainment, integration, or pattern maintenance.[4] They thus share the same weaknesses of this high level theorising, in particular that the role of deliberation and purposefulness is given little weight when organisational behaviours are interpreted in terms of the system needs they meet. As a methodological tool for the development of organisational theory the categories are at too high a level to be able to promote insights into the internal functioning of organisations.

Acknowledging that division by genotypic function leaves fairly crude categories, they discuss a number of 'second order' characteristics, such as the nature of the through-put, the type of commitment and involvement, and the kind of organisational structure. This allows more subtle distinctions to be made, but at the cost of some loss of coherence. It is of interest, however, that one of these second order characteristics—'transformation of objects versus molding of people'—is the basis of a distinction between types of organisations produced by working in a quite different tradition of systems theory.

From work begun at the Tavistock Institute in London the distinction has been developed between socio-technical and socio-psychological systems, or organisations. The socio-technical system concept was developed initially from a series of investigations in the coal mining industry to draw attention to the fundamental interdependence of the social and technological systems in production enterprises.[5] In the process of systematically applying the concept of open system

[3] D. Katz and R. L. Kahn, *The Social Psychology of Organisations* (Wiley, 1966), p. 113.

[4] T. Parsons, *Structure and Process in Modern Societies* (Free Press, 1960).

[5] E. L. Trist and K. W. Bamforth, 'Some Social and Psychological Consequences of the Longwall Method of Coal-getting', *Human Relations* (1951), 4; E. L. Trist *et al.*, *Organisational Choice* (Tavistock, 1963).

in the investigation of enterprises, Emery and Trist write as follows:

'The technological component has been found to play a key mediating role and hence it follows that the open system concept must be referred to the socio-technical system, not simply to the social system of an enterprise. It might be justifiable to exclude the technological component if it were true, as many writers imply, that it plays only a passive and intermittent role.... There is, on the contrary, an almost constant accommodation of stresses arising from changes in the external environment; the technological component not only sets limits upon what can be done, but also in the process of accommodation creates demands that must be reflected in the internal organisation and ends of an enterprise. Study of a productive system therefore requires detailed attention to both the technological and the social components.'[6]

Subsequent application of essentially the same conceptual framework in the investigation of institutions whose main purpose is the processing of people rather than things, suggested that in such cases it is not primarily the nature of the technology, or the physical apparatus that constitutes the critical boundary condition with which the social system is correlated, but the characteristics of the individuals that are to be acted upon. Thus in describing his research in a prison, Emery writes:

'The key to the difference would seem to be in the obvious and indisputable fact that one is primarily concerned with things, and the other with human beings. The prison achieves its institutional ends by doing certain things with and to its inmates. It must therefore give primary consideration to the psychological properties of the inmates, because these make some measures effective and others non-effective. These common psychological properties constitute the key boundary conditions of the prison—they are an essential part of the prison, and yet they must, in large measure, be treated as a "given", i.e. as existing and obeying laws and influences that are independent of the wishes of prison administrations.... Basically, the prison is one of the class of socio-psychological institutions. It differs from hospitals—medical and mental—and from religious, educational and political institutions in that it is based on doing something against the wishes of its inmates, and usually against their interests.'[7]

[6] F. E. Emery and E. L. Trist, 'Socio-technical Systems' in C. W. Churchman and H. Verhurst (eds), *Management Sciences, Models and Techniques* (Pergamon, 1960), Vol. 2, pp. 86–7.

[7] F. E. Emery, *Freedom and Justice within Walls* (Tavistock, 1970) p. 2.

This distinction, unlike most of the others we refer to, developed out of active engagements with organisations of varying kinds, and issues from the orientation of action research. In the case of production enterprises, many other theoretical traditions have distinguished between the social system and the technical system. The Tavistock tradition has been distinctive in insisting that neither system has a necessary causal primacy in determining the effectiveness and other characteristics of organisational functioning, but that the state of each system jointly determines organisational outcomes. This being so, active interventions must be directed to their joint optimisation. This stands in contrast both to the prescriptions of the human relations theorists, who have emphasised the social system in interpreting organisational effectiveness as a function of the quality of social relations at work, and the technological determinists, who have persistently interpreted organisational structure and behaviours in terms of the nature of the technology employed. The work of Woodward and Blauner, discussed below, belongs more to this tradition.

Blau and Scott's is one of the best known typologies, based on the criterion of *cui bono?*—the identification of the prime beneficiary of the organisation's existence.[8] Four categories of persons potentially benefit from what the organisation does—members or rank and file participants, owners or managers, the clients or 'public in contact', and the public at large. One of these categories they say, may usually be identified as the prime (though seldom the only) beneficiary, and the four corresponding types of organisations are (a) mutual benefit associations; (b) business concerns; (c) service organisations; and (d) commonweal organisations. Some of the examples they give of each type are (a) political parties, unions, clubs, professional associations; (b) industrial firms, wholesalers and retailers, banks, insurance companies; (c) social work organisations, hospitals, schools; and (d) military services, police and fire departments, internal revenue departments. They suggest that each type of organisation tends to confront differing characteristic dilemmas:

> . . . the crucial problem in mutual benefit associations is that of maintaining internal democratic processes—providing for participation and control by the membership; the central problem for business concerns is that of maximising operating efficiency in a competitive situation; the problems associated with the conflict between professional service to clients and administrative procedures

[8] P. Blau and W. R. Scott, *Formal Organisations* (Routledge & Kegan Paul, 1963).

are characteristic of service organisations; and the crucial problems posed by commonweal organisations is the development of democratic mechanisms whereby they can be externally controlled by the public.'[9]

A weakness of this schema is that it is not adjusted to the real complexity and heterogeneity of the outputs of many kinds of organisations—a university or a publishing house for example—which often makes it very difficult in practice to determine how benefits are distributed. It has been pointed out too that there are often quite significant discrepancies in response to such questions as which group benefit most according to the *official* purposes of the organisation, which group *actually* benefit most, and which group *ought* to get most of the rewards? These are important questions open to empirical inquiry, and the answers may tell us more about the dynamics of organisational life.

(b) TYPOLOGIES BASED ON TECHNOLOGY

The kind of technology used has been employed as the basis for differentiating among organisation by at least three well-known organisational writers—Joan Woodward,[10] Robert Blauner,[11] and James Thompson.[12] In the framework of organisational sociology, Woodward's typology is narrow in scope, deriving from a comparative study of 203 British manufacturing firms. An initial division into ten categories of production system was aggregated into three larger technological divisions, forming a crude scale of technical complexity—small batch and unit production, large batch and mass production, and process production. Factor found to be associated with increasing technical complexity were decreasing labour costs, increasing ratios of indirect labour, administrative and clerical staff to hourly paid workers, increasing proportion of graduates among supervisory staff, and widening span of control of the chief executive. Other factors first increased and then decreased in association with the shift towards greater technical complexity. Woodward concludes:

'. . . technical methods were the most important factor in determining organisational structure and in setting the tone of human relationships inside the firms. . . . It appeared that different technologies imposed

[9] ibid., p. 42.
[10] J. Woodward, *Management and Technology* (HMSO, 1958); *Industrial Organisation: Theory and Practice* (OUP, 1965); (ed.) *Industrial Organisation: Behaviour and Control* (OUP, 1970).
[11] R. Blauner, *Alienation and Freedom* (University of Chicago, 1964).
[12] J. Thompson, *Organisations in Action* (McGraw-Hill, 1967).

different kinds of demands on individuals and organisations, and that these demands had to be met through an appropriate form of organisation.'[13]

Blauner defines technology as 'the complex of physical objects and technical operations (both manual and machine) regularly employed in turning out the goods and services produced by an industry'. Whereas Woodward is mainly interested in the structural correlates of technological variation, Blauner's is a study of alienation and freedom—he is principally concerned in other words with the consequences for the individual and his job of different technical systems. He is concerned to explain the 'uneven distribution of alienation among factory workers in American industry'. His is not a full-blown typology—in particular he makes no claim for the exhaustiveness of the categories that he isolates. These are: (a) craft technology—exemplified in the printing industry; (b) machine minding technology—examplified in textiles; (c) assembly line technology—exemplified in the motor car industry; and (d) continuous process technology, for which the chemicals industry is the exemplar. These four types are also representative of stages in the historical trend towards increasing mechanisation, with the craft technology of printing and the continuous process production of chemicals representing the two poles, and with the other two as intermediate types. When alienating potential is plotted against these different levels of technical complexity, the result is a U-curve, with alienation lowest in craft industry, increasing to its highest level in assembly line production, and declining again for continuous production. While these conclusions are of interest, his analysis as a whole is, like Woodward's, inclined to the deterministic with respect to the influence of technology, rather underplaying the autonomy of the social system and the impact of strategic organisational choice. He writes:

'Variations in technology are of critical interest to students of the human meaning of work because technology, more than any other factor, determines the nature of the job tasks performed by blue-collar employees and has an important effect on a number of aspects of alienation. . . . Since technological considerations often determine the size of an industrial plant, they markedly influence the social atmosphere and degree of cohesion among the work force. Technology also structures the existence and form of work groups, in this way influencing cohesion. Even the nature of discipline and supervision to some extent depends on technological factors. And technology largely determines the occupational structure and skill

[13] Woodward (1958), op. cit.

distribution within an enterprise, the basic factors in advancement opportunities, and normative integration.'[14]

Of these 'technology' typologies, that put forward by Thompson is conceptually the richest.[15] His study is concerned with organisational strategies for coping with the contingencies posed by technology and environment, and explores patterns of organisational design and structure, methods of co-ordination, decision and control in relation to different types of technology and different levels of environmental complexity. In examining the implications of the degree of stability and heterogeneity of the environment, as well as the nature of the technology, he escapes from a rather narrow concern with technology alone as a causal variable. His distinction between (a) long-linked (b) mediating, and (c) intensive technologies, is much wider in scope than those previously considered, being used by him in the analysis of instrumental organisations of every kind—governmental, military, educational, and medical, as well as manufacturing.

The long-linked technology is characterised by serial interdependence between tasks or processes, and is epitomised in the assembly line. Mediating technology is represented in the operations of organisations such as insurance companies, post offices, and employment bureaux, whose primary function entails 'the linking of clients or customers who are or who wish to be interdependent'. Organisations with intensive technologies are those which draw upon a variety of different techniques for the purposes of effecting a change in some specific object. Sometimes the object is human, as in the case of schools and hospitals—sometimes it is not, as in the case of the construction industry.

The long-linked technology can be most fully exploited when applied to the turning out of a single, standardised product, so that the resources needed at the various stages of the transformation process may be used to capacity, and deficiencies in the production cycle swiftly recognised and corrected. Organisations founded on a long-linked technology characteristically seek to come to terms with the significant contingencies affecting their operations by strategies of vertical integration—extending their domains so as to include within their boundaries important sources of uncertainty. Such integration can extend both backwards and forwards—to handling their own input and output problems. Thus major US oil companies have integrated forward from refining into marketing, and backward by acquiring control of shipping and crude oil supplies.

[14] Blauner, op. cit., p. 8. For an extended critique of Blauner's study see J. E. T. Eldridge, *Socioligy and Industrial Life* (Nelson, 1973), pp. 183–95.
[15] Thompson, op. cit.

With mediating technologies major complexities derive from the need to process in standardised ways the various requirements of different kinds of external agents, and to carry out this processing very extensively. Organisations operating such technologies enlarge their capacities to cope with task contingencies by increasing the size of the population that they serve. Thus the effectiveness and stability of banks and airlines is very much a function of the extensiveness of their operations. An insurance company must find poolers of risk 'to avoid the possibility of any one loss destroying the coverage of the others'.

The intensive or 'custom' technology demands for its successful operation the availability of an appropriate range of skills, resources and capacities and an effective system for determining which combination of these will be most effective for the transformation of a particular object. When the object worked on are people, the organisation has to come to terms with the fact that such people can, and are likely to take an active role, and correlate their behaviours to what the organisation does in ways that may impede organisational effectiveness. Uncertainties of this sort, Thompson suggests, are typically countered by the organisation seeking to incorporate the object to be transformed, placing it within the boundaries of the organisation. For people-processing, or socio-psychological organisations, this strategy is epitomised in the case of 'total institutions' such as prisons, mental hospitals, and military induction centres, where 'inmates' are almost totally encapsulated.[16] Another example is the tendency for firms acquiring complex electronic or other equipment to ingest at the same time a team of experts from the company producing the equipment.

(c) A TYPOLOGY BASED ON REGULATION

Thompson's classification and the concept of technology upon which it is based are intended to be of value in interpreting the interdependencies between environmental forces and organisational structures and strategies, and it is not surprising that his categories have relatively little bearing upon the finer texture of group and individual experiences in organisations. The adoption of this focus is the special virtue of the typology adopted by Etzioni,[17] which chooses as the central classificatory variable the structural-motivational relationship of 'compliance'— 'a relationship consisting of the power employed by superiors to control

[16] E. Goffman, *Asylums* (Penguin, 1968). For further discussion see below, pp. 52–56
[17] A. Etzioni, *A Comparative Analysis of Complex Organisations* (Free Press, 1961).

subordinates and the orientation of the subordinates to this power'. Compliance is made up of the two elements, power ('an actor's ability to induce or influence another actor to carry out his directives or any other norms he supports') and involvement ('the cathectic-evaluative orientation of an actor to an object, characterised in terms of intensity and direction'). He distinguished three types of power, corresponding to three different kinds of means that are employed to make subjects comply: coercive, remunerative, and normative. Coercive power is based on the use or the possible use of physical force, detention, restriction of activities, etc.; remunerative power is based on control over material resources and rewards through the distribution of wages, commissions, fringe benefits, etc.; normative power rests on 'the allocation and manipulation of symbolic rewards and deprivations through employment of leaders, manipulation of mass media, allocation of esteem and prestige symbols, etc.[18] He also distinguishes three types of involvement, representing increasing degrees of commitment on the part of members: alienative, calculative, and moral. Cross tabulation of of the types of power and involvement gives Table 3.1.

Table 3.1

| | | Kinds of involvement | | |
		Alienative	Calculative	Moral
Kinds of power	Coercive	1	2	3
	Remunerative	4	5	6
	Normative	7	8	9

According to Etzioni, the three 'congruent' types represented by boxes 1, 5 and 9 are empirically far more common than any of the other types, and this is so because the 'effectiveness' of organisations is maximised when the type of power used and the type of involvement felt are thus in congruence. These three organisational types are coercive, utilitarian, and normative organisations. Organisations which are predominantly coercive include concentration camps, prisons, mental hospitals; those which are predominantly utilitarian, relying on rational legal authority and the use of economic rewards are exemplified in business and industry; and normative organisations which depend primarily upon the value of membership and intrinsic rewards are represented by churches, colleges, professional associations, voluntary and mutual benefit associations. The remaining six types may occur, but are always tending to develop towards one of the congruent types, either by changing the basis of involvement or the type of power which predominates.

[18] ibid., p. 5.

His exploration of these types is explicitly intended to make a contribution to 'middle range' theory of organisations, by filling in the 'lamentable hiatus' between case studies of single organisations and abstract generalising about all organisations. It is distinctive in its concern with power and psychological variables pertaining to members' orientations.

(d) TYPOLOGIES BASED ON STRUCTURE

These typologies, together with a number of others, have been subjected to a good deal of discussion and elaboration in the literature. We intend to outline two further typologies, those of Ackoff and Vickers, which, though they make important and useful distinctions, have not yet been given the same attention.

The classificatory variable used by Vickers concerns the way in which organisations generate the resources needed for their survival and growth—the sources from which they receive their primary support. Selection of the source of inputs as the basis for classification presents an interesting contrast with Blau and Scott's *cui bono* criterion, which differentiates among organisations rather on the basis of the destination of outputs. Vickers has distinguished between user-supported, public-supported, member- and donor-supported, and endowment-supported institutions. The major categories are the first two, and the distinction between them is a response to some important inadequacies in the traditional and influencial distinction between public sector and private sector organisations, which has become misleading with the development of mixed economies and the welfare state.

'Some institutions in what is commonly called the public sector, such as the railways and the post office, are user-supported, though others, such as the hospitals are public-supported. In any case it is misleading to describe as "private" a sector consisting of autonomous corporations which perform so many public functions, and some of which are publicly controlled and even publicly owned.[19]

User-supported institutions, therefore, are those which recover their costs from individual consumers of goods or services offered on a market, and public-supported institutions those which recover them from public funds, generally through rates and taxes. The distinction between public and private sectors is still useful however, for public corporations, even when user-supported (as in the case of the coal,

[19] G. Vickers, *Freedom in a Rocking Boat* (Allen Lane, 1970), p. 44.

railway and power industries in Britain), are more closely subject to political control of their affairs than are private corporations. The differing character of user and public-supported institutions exercises a critical influence over mechanisms for the production and distribution of wealth in society:

> 'The user-supported section of our economy is free to accumulate profits and increasingly finances itself out of these accumulations. These undertakings are still judged primarily by the criteria appropriate to investments. . . . The public-supported sector is still widely regarded as living as a parasite, or perhaps a predator, on the user-supported sector. It abstracts money from the user-supported sector and uses it to provide those goods and services, including government, which the current ethos or the legacy of history regards as impossible or unsuitable to be paid for by the users.'[20]

Other kinds of undertakings are maintained by the gifts or subscriptions of those who support their objects. These are member-supported when they exist for the benefit of their supporters, and donor-supported when they exist for some other purpose. The member-supported institution is typified by the trade union, the professional association, and the club, and naturally corresponds quite closely to Blau and Scott's mutual benefit association. Compared to the other types its membership is more homogeneous and its purposes more limited, so that those on whom it places demands are better able to assess what its services are worth to them and to their fellow members. Of the final category, endowment-supported institutions, charitable foundations, the colleges of the older universities, and the established Church are the most familiar examples. Endowment is defined as the legal right to enjoy the current revenues derived from past accumulations of wealth. Clearly very many institutions derive some measure of support from such a source. In fact, as Vickers puts it, 'hybrid types abound and multiply', so that in most actual organisations a mixture of the types of support is found. Universities, for example, are generally dependent in various measure upon public monies, students' fees, and benefactors.

However, it is often the case that an organisation depends primarily upon one particular type of support, and Vickers is chiefly concerned to draw attention to the implications this may have for policy-making. Fundamentally, the different sources of support imply different degrees of dependence by those in control of an institution on those whose support is critical, and also qualitatively different kinds of dependence. The type

[20] ibid., p. 44.

of support needed also has a critical bearing on the potentialities that an organisation has for growth, and the kinds of pressure towards or away from growth that it can be expected to experience.

The typology proposed by Ackoff[21] is based on the concepts of geneity and nodality, and has been taken up in Ackoff and Emery[22] and Crombie.[23] Geneity refers to the relations between a system or organisation and its parts. The homogeneous organisation is one which has greater control over its members than they have over it—the members function so as to serve the organisation's objectives. The heterogeneous organisation is one whose members have greater control over it than it has over them—the organisation exists to further the objectives of its members.

In a homogeneous organisation large numbers of persons are required to limit their possible behaviours to those which have been calculated by others to be effective in producing the ends sought by the organisation. Their possible range of responses must therefore be constrained in some way. In various circumstances this may be achieved by coercion, persuasion, the manipulation of incentives, the voluntary compliance of individuals in support of the organisational 'ideology', and so on. The essential point is that for a group of people to pursue effectively the objectives of the larger system of which they are part, the potential variance in their purposeful behaviours has to be reduced. Organisational control refers to the characteristic ways in which human behaviour in organisations is limited and rendered sufficiently predictable for their separate functions to be consistently connected within a functional division of labour. With respect to the behaviours of their members therefore, homogeneous organisations are *variety decreasing*.

While homogeneous organisations use their members as instruments, heterogeneous organisations are used by their members as instruments. For an organisation to function so as to increase the possible courses of action and expand the range of goals available to its individual members, it must be responsive to their will, and not impose its own objectives upon them. In order to serve the ends of their individual members such organisations have to be aware at every stage of what these ends *are*. This type of awareness has typically been sought through such mechanisms as the market place, the ballot box, censuses and surveys, the actual participation of members in decision-making, and the like. When an organisation functions as an instrument for individuals,

[21] R. L. Ackoff, *A Concept of Corporate Planning* (Wiley, 1970).

[22] R. L. Ackoff and F. E. Emery, *On Purposeful Systems* (Tavistock, 1972).

[23] A. D. Crombie, *Planning for Turbulent Social Fields* (Unpublished PhD thesis, Australian National University, 1972).

enabling them to do things through belonging to the organisation that they would not otherwise be able to do, the organisation is *variety increasing* with respect to members' behaviours.

Examples of organisations which tend to be predominantly homogeneous in character are corporations, prisons, army units, and ships. On the other hand, political parties, universities, clubs, and communities are predominantly heterogeneous.

Nodality refers to the way in which authority is distributed within the organisation. A uninodal organisation has a hierarchically structured authority pyramid capped by a specific sub-system which functions as an ultimate decision-maker, and which also, as a consequence, carries the final responsibility for what the organisation does. This sub-system which may be an individual or a group (in the latter case, the 'dominant coalition'), is able to resolve disputes among decision-makers at any lower level. A multinodal organisation has no such ultimate decision-maker, so that making decisions about the organisation as a whole requires a certain level of agreement between two or more relatively autonomous decision-makers.

Table 3.2. ACKOFF'S TYPES OF ORGANISATION

	Uninodal	*Multinodal*
Homogeneous	corporations army units prisons ships	multinational corporations coalition governments
Heterogeneous	clubs professional associations political parties	universities employers' confederations congresses communities

Homogeneous organisations

A number of critical problems derive from the organisational requisite for obtaining and maintaining the participation of members, and a sufficiently high level of involvement by them for the organisation to achieve its objectives. Either the members must be coerced in some way, or there must be a favourable balance of rewards to induce them to stay. The use of coercive means for obtaining participation is generally unstable in the long run, and with the progress of industrialism has given way to the manipulation of monetary and psychological rewards, as advocated, for example, by the Scientific Management and the Human Relations Schools respectively. In homogeneous organisations other than those based on coercion, members have to be compensated for the reduction of variety in their behaviour. Etzioni's typology, which we have already discussed, is especially useful in drawing attention to a number of the issues involved for organisations in managing compliance. Planning for a homogeneous system involves identifying a set of goals for the system which are compatible with the state of its environment, and with which the goals of its individual members can be reconciled.

Heterogeneous organisations

A number of critical problems for heterogeneous organisations relate to the mechanisms by means of which the members can make their goals known, and to the adequacy of organisational resources for helping them to achieve these goals once they have been articulated. Demands for the 'democratisation' of universities, political parties, professional associations, schools, and a host of other institutional domains have become more pervasive and more persistent during the last decade or so, and there is currently a great deal of experimentation going on in all kinds of institutional settings to find ways of supplementing or replacing the traditional mechanism such as the ballot box and the laws of supply and demand. Various strategies for consultation, participation, and 'power to the people' are beginning to emerge.

A related difficulty that is also characteristic of heterogeneous organisations concerns the tendency of those responsible for the day-to-day running of the organisation to subvert its actual *raison d'être* by formulating and defining goals for the organisation itself which conflict with its ability to serve its members' interests. The professional staffs of powerful motorists' associations have in the past shown themselves vulnerable to such goal displacement. In this regard the conception of the organisation as a *resource* is quite critical. So long as the organisation remains a resource for the benefit of its members it can be variety increasing. As soon as it attempts to use its members as resources for its own ends it becomes variety reducing. Planning for a heterogeneous organisation entails firstly that the needs and goals of the individual members find expression, and subsequently that these ends are reconciled amongst themselves and with the constraint of being part of a system in a particular environmental setting.

Uninodal organisations

The problematical consequences of uninodality for the organisation relate on the one hand to the quality of the ultimate decision-maker, and on the other, to the ability of the membership in some respects to keep this decision-maker under control. This latter problem is of course especially relevant to the *heterogeneous* uninodal organisation. The key consequence for planning is that the institutional leader or dominant coalition in general has to be in agreement with planning decisions that affect the state of the organisation as a whole.

Multinodal organisations

In organisations that are characterised by a multi-centred allocation of authority, many of the key problems are to do with the reconciliation of the judgements and the aspirations of the various relatively autonomous decision-makers. In order for things to get done, and for the organisation as a whole to fulfil its mission, some mechanism for resolving disputes has to be developed. There has to be some agreement concerning both the relevant 'courts of appeal' (precedent, seniority, constitution, etc.) and the appropriate means for working towards solutions (bargaining, compromise, arbitration). Planning for a multinodal organisation requires a minimal level of shared understanding of, and commitment to the plan amongst the independent decision-makers.

(e) TOTAL INSTITUTIONS AS A TYPE OF ORGANISATION

The concept of total institution, elaborated by Goffman, draws attention to a variety of organisations which have a number of common characteristics.[24] Its encompassing power over the individual member is elucidated by Goffman in the following way:

'A basic social arrangement in modern society is that the individual tends to sleep, play and work in different places, with different co-participants under different authorities and without an overall rational plan. The central feature of total institutions can be described as a breakdown of the barriers ordinarily separating these three spheres of life. First, all aspects of life are conducted in the same place and under the same single authority. Second, each phase of the member's daily activity is carried on in the immediate company of a large batch of others all of whom are treated alike and required to do the same thing together. Third, all phases of the day's activities are tightly scheduled, with one activity leading at a prearranged time into the next, the whole sequence of activities being imposed from above by a system of explicit formal ruling and a body of officials. Finally, the various enforced activities are brought together into a single rational plan purportedly designed to fulfil the official aims of the institution.'[25]

Organisations which may closely approximate this ideal typical

[24] See Goffman, op. cit.   [25] ibid., p. 17.

delineation include: orphanages, homes for the blind and the old, hospitals for the physically or mentally ill, prisons, concentration camps, barracks, ships, boarding schools, work camps, colonial compounds, convents and monasteries. Goffman emphasises the idea of a relatively small administrative group supervising a much larger group of 'inmates'. Staff surveillance is aimed at achieving compliance with the administration's sense of order and any deviation is liable to encounter punishment. The list of organisations which may take on the character of total institutions is sufficient to dictate that their aims may vary considerably. They may be concerned with education, training, religious purification, 'effective' protective custody and so on. But they share in common the fact that official definitions of the situation are highly significant for staff and inmates:

> 'It is widely appreciated that total institutions typically fall considerably short of their official aims. It is less well appreciated that each of these official goals or charters seems admirably suited to provide a key to meaning—a language of explanation that the staff, and sometimes the inmates, can bring to every crevice of action in the institution. Thus, a medical frame of reference is not merely a perspective through which a decision concerning dosage can be determined and made meaningful; it is a perspective ready to account for all manner of decisions, such as the hours when hospital meals are served or the manner in which hospital linen is folded. Each official goal lets loose a doctrine with its own inquisitors and its own martyrs.'[26]

Those in supervisory positions may or may not live their whole lives in total institutions: where they can return to the outside world after completing a period of work, a 'spell' of duty, then the social split between staff and inmates is more clearly marked and in this sense one may talk of the binary character of the institution.

In Goffman's approach to understanding total institutions the emphasis is, first, on the way in which authority is wielded—its assault on the 'self' of the inmate, his sense of personal identity, the process of regimentation in and through which individuality, freedom of action and expression are stifled and punished when observed. To recognise the power of the administration is to face the question, how can the inmate survive psychologically or physically? Manifestly not all do. What adaptive mechanisms may be employed? How do people 'makeout' in situations which not only have an instrumental formal organisation to accomplish their ends, but which also place them typically in a

[26] ibid., pp. 80–1.

highly visible context which heightens the opportunity of surveillance ?

To approach an explanation Goffman writes of primary and secondary adjustments to the organisation. (These are concepts which in fact have application to all organisations but are of critical significance in the study of total institutions.) Primary adjustments relate to the individual who accepts and conforms to the official definition of his situation in the organisation. He co-operates with the administration on its terms and from the point of view of authority is seen and treated as a 'normal' member. Secondary adjustments have to do with 'any habitual arrangement by which a member of an organisation employs unauthorised means, or obtains unauthorised ends, or both, thus getting around the organisation's assumptions as to what he should do and get and hence what he should be'.[27] It should be noted that where organisations with strongly developed patterns of secondary adjustments that breach the official organisation goals arises, individuals may want to make further adjustments if they do not wish to identify with these emerging activities. A clear example is presented in the case of the growth of a policing system of controlling inmates in a concentration camp from among the inmates. This had been officially forbidden but in time came to be accepted. Prisoners then had to cope with this by making primary or secondary adjustments. To use the term primary and secondary adjustments is not then to accept a static definition of the organisation and its activities. Indeed, as the above illustration suggests and as Goffman is careful to point out, 'organisations have a tendency to adapt to secondary adjustments not only by increasing discipline but also by selectively legitimating these practices, hoping in this way to regain control and sovereignty even at the loss of some of the participant's obligations'.[28]

Two kinds of secondary adjustments are elaborated by Goffman, those which are disruptive in relation to the existing organisation— inmates may be planning to abandon or radically restructure the existing organisation—and those which are contained—in which adjustments

Table 3.3.

Level of Adjustment
to Total Institution

Type of *Adjustment*	Primary		Secondary	
	Individual	Group	Individual	Group
Contained	1	2	3	4
Disruptive			5	6

[27] ibid., p. 172.   [28] ibid., p. 178.

are made within the on-going life of the organisation and may in a sense contribute to its maintenance. If we remind ourselves that primary and secondary adjustments may be individual or collective affairs it is possible to codify this in Table 3.3.

In his own work, and with a wealth of examples, Goffman focuses upon secondary adjustments of a contained kind (categories 3 and 4). Again the emphasis (although not exclusively so) is on the adjustment processes of inmates rather than staff. In principle, the latter may also exhibit secondary adjustments since it does not follow that they will wish to pursue official goals in all times and places. So the thrust of Goffman's work is on the 'practices' of hospital underlife and on the ways in which patients 'work' the system.

It should be pointed out, however, that Goffman's reasons for focusing attention on the total institution are more than a matter of ethnography. At least three things may be noted:

1. It can be used to illuminate the concept of self.
2. It can inform us on the question of social control in total institutions, notwithstanding their different substantive goals.
3. By taking an organisation in which extreme deprivation of things that are taken for granted in many situations occurs, it can teach us something about life and the mechanisms which operate in all formal organisations.

Much of this strategy is summarised in the following comment:

'The study of underlife in restrictive total institutions has some special interest. When existence is cut to the bone, we can learn what people do to flesh out their lives. Stashes, means of transportation, free places, territories, supplies for economic and social exchange, these apparently are some of the minimal requirements for building up life. Ordinarily these arrangements are taken for granted as part of one's primary adjustment; seeing them twisted out of existence through bargains, wit, force, and cunning, we see their significance anew. The study of total institutions also suggests that formal organisations have standard places of vulnerability, such as supply rooms, sick bays, kitchens, or scenes of highly technical labour. These are the damp corners where secondary adjustments breed and start to infest the establishment.'[29]

If people sometimes 'fight back' in total institutions—with great ingenuity because of their limited opportunities—then this suggests something important is being highlighted in the study of social relations.

[29] ibid., p. 268.

Moreover, although total institutions may incarcerate the individual, control is not a one-way matter of staff over inmate. And although Goffman scrutinises contained secondary adjustments most closely he is aware of the dynamic possibilities within a situation:

'Inmate control of staff in total institutions takes traditional forms, for example: arranging for "accidents" to occur to a staff person, or the massed rejection of a particular item of food, or the slowing down of work production, or the sabotaging of plumbing, lighting, and communication systems, all of which are readily vulnerable to inmate action. Other inmate actions on staff may take the form of "collective" or individual teasing and more subtle forms of ritual insubordination, such as the military technique of saluting a troublesome officer from too great a distance, or with too much precision, or with too slow a tempo. A staff threat to the whole system of undercover arrangements may be answered with extreme action such as strikes or riots.'[30]

[30] ibid., p. 263.

PART III ORGANISATIONS:
MISSIONS AND
CULTURES

4

Organisations and Their Missions

Most of the important thinkers who have contributed in the last 200 years or so to the interpretation and understanding of society as a whole have had to concern themselves more or less directly with the changing nature and dimensions of the organisational phenomenon. Many of them, much closer than us to the period of industrial take-off, saw or sensed the accelerative thrust of new science-based technologies and the rapid multiplication of work organisations implied in this. Today, the proportion of work in the industrial societies (other than the domestic work of housewives—though we can expect some changes here) that is not carried out by formal organisations is negligible, and the remnants of individual craft labour, subsistence agriculture, and to a lesser extent, self-employment, remain as reminders of our pasts.

The dramatic increase in the numbers, size and importance of organisations during the last two centuries represents the evolution of a highly elaborated social division of labour, in which the tasks essential for the maintenance and development of society as a whole have become the responsibility of more and more specialised units. This is true not only of work organisations, though the effects here may be more critical. Voluntary and leisure organisations too have specialised their functions. In neither case however, would we want to suggest that this development is necessarily unlinear, because there are always efforts in some part of the social field directed towards arresting or reversing the specialising trend. Recently the preoccupation of educators with 'community colleges', and the current public interest in such ideas as community health centres and recreation complexes, are symptoms of this integrating force.

Efforts in our own time to counter the functional specialisation of organisations' tasks may be due to a growing appreciation that in many respects we have reached, if not gone beyond, the point at which such specialisation brings diminishing marginal returns, or a gross decrease in overall efficiency, for society as a whole.

We are concerned here simply to note that the industrial societies have had to come to terms with a world more and more filled by organisations, with more and more of its opportunities and threats regulated by them. Correspondingly, the primary social worlds of its members have been increasingly dominated and structured by the demands placed upon them as members of, participants in, or customers or clients of organisations of every sort, and as members of educational and work organisations in particular. Growing numbers of increasingly specialised organisations, existing at an important level of integration in the social field between the individual and the primary group on the one hand, and the total social system on the other, collectively exercise a critical role in the transformation and growth accomplished by the field as a whole, though it is a constant topic for debate as to which types of organisations play the leading role.

Some argue as to whether the acts of governments or of business—political institutions or production enterprises—are the more decisive. Jordan comments informatively on an earlier view:

'Marx reflected and expressed the conviction of his times that acts of government could have no lasting or profound consequences and that the decisive events took place at the level of economic and industrial organisation.'[1]

While many, and not only Marxists, would agree that production organisations still play the leading part, other argue that the consequences of the acts of governments have become more 'lasting and profound' as their administrative bodies have swollen and their special agencies multiplied. Among those who, unimpressed by this governmental sprawl, still feel that the course of society is critically determined by the nature of its production organisations, there are disagreements as to whether the primary, secondary, or tertiary sector is critical, with many

[1] Z. A. Jordan, *Karl Marx: Economy, Class and Social Revolution* (Michael Joseph, 1971), p. 55.

arguing that this is dependent upon the precise circumstances of any particular society.

Some, perhaps having a deeper faith in human nature, argue that the accomplishments of education or religious institutions are the decisive ingredients in a society's ascendance or decline, growth or stagnation, and look to the schools and universities, and the churches, as sources of moral and political leadership. Illich's incisive critique of educational organisations is interesting in this context in maintaining that the impact of the *school* in modern society has been decisive—decisively bad. He concludes:

> 'The New World Church is the knowledge industry, both purveyor of opinion and the work bench during an increasing number of the years of an individual's life. Deschooling is, therefore, at the root of any movement for human liberation.'[2]

It would seem to be quite widely agreed however, that these socialising organisations are in general subordinated, in the amount of effective influence they wield, by the power enjoyed in the governmental and business spheres. More challenging are the arguments of those who maintain that controlling influence over the direction of societal development does not reside with organisations of any particular type but rather with an elite of powerful groups and individuals drawn from the apex regions of *all* organised and institutionalised spheres—military, political, commercial, religious, professional labour, and so on. The argument between the 'elitists' and the 'pluralists'—those who maintain that power is effectively centralised in society, and those who believe it to be dispersed among many centres that counterbalance one another, has very many facets. Discussions concerning the part played by formal organisations however, cannot fail to take account of the trenchant critique put forward by C. Wright Mills:

> 'The power elite is composed of men whose positions enable them to transcend the ordinary environments of ordinary men and women; they are in positions to make decisions having major consequences. ... For they are in command of the major hierarchies and organisations of modern society. They rule the big corporations. They run the machinery of the state and claim its prerogatives. They direct the military establishment. They occupy the strategic command posts of the social structure, in which are now centred the effective means of the power and the wealth and the celebrity which they enjoy.'[3]

[2] Ikan D. Illich, *Deschooling Society* (Calder, 1971), p. 47.
[3] C. W. Mills, *The Power Elite* (OUP, 1959), p. 34.

(a) THE ORGANISATION AS AN ENTITY

These well-known facts of the growth in numbers and influence of formal organisations in modern society, and the debate over which domain of organised activities—production, governmental, educational, or some other—now constitutes the leading part in the development of such societies, provides us with the context for focusing on the organisation itself as a unit, or more particularly, as a purposeful agent in the social field. In this way, by considering some of the characteristics of organisations as entities, and elucidating the sense in which they can be said to 'act', it may be possible finally to throw some light back into these 'high-level' problems of the effects of organisational activities within the whole social field.

Organizations, like other kinds of social groups, have some properties that one can get to know about without knowing anything about the properties of its members. Such factors as the length of time an organisation has existed, its location and size, its prestige or reputation, its capital assets, its profitability and so on are of this sort, and have been called *global* properties. Knowledge of such properties as these may give us important and useful insights. The most important and obvious of these properties however is that the organisation *does*. Does it manufacture electric motors, does it provide insurance, does it administer government health policy, does it sell goods, and if so what kind? The question of how knowledge concerning the functions of innumerable organisations is unequally acquired and disseminated, may be of considerable interest in itself. Commercial organisations, offering saleable goods and services perhaps have the greatest interest in promoting such knowledge about themselves, but public agencies too are increasingly engaged in advertising their distinctive competences. Here we are concerned simply to draw attention to the very considerable amount of useful information it is possible to have about organisations as such before we know anything about the characteristics of its individual members.

Granted the observability of such global properties, we generally infer that an organisation has acted (or behaved) when we observe changes in these properties over time. When an organisation shifts, entirely or in part, to a new location, when it expands in size or its output increases, when it takes on a new function or exhibits a new expertise, we are entitled to say that the organisation has acted. In the outpourings of the mass media a very high proportion of the 'news' refers to acts taken by organisations. A union has decided to go on strike, a national bank announces an increase in its lending rate, a government department has conducted a survey, a university has appointed a new vice-chancellor. In saying that an organisation acts we mean not only that something about it or its relations with other bodies has changed but that this observed outcome could have been different. The union might have decided *not* to strike—perhaps to operate a go-slow instead; the lending rate might have been lowered; a different appointment might have been made by the university, and so on.

This amounts to saying not only that organisations act, but further, that they act *purposefully*. In fact this property of purposefulness has been a central concern of organisation theorists, who have identified here the distinctiveness of organisational life and filled many pages with discussion of the origins and nature of organisational goals. We say that an individual or a group (including therefore organisations) is purposeful if it is capable of exercising *choice* with respect to both the ends that it seeks and the means that it employs. This in turn implies a certain liberation or independence from the environment, for an agent with these capabilities is able to pursue the same end in many different states of the environment, or to pursue a series of quite different ends while the relevant environment remains constant. In the midst of advancing secularisation churches have persisted with their ancient mission, while universities may quinquennially cut off, redirect or start new research activities in ways not enforced by their environments —such bodies are behaving purposefully.[4]

One of the reasons why there has been so much confusion over whether organisations 'act', whether they can be said to have goals apart from the goals of their members, and whether or not saying that they have entails 'reification' or the positing of a 'group mind', is because the *parts* of organisations, the individual members, are themselves purposeful. Now while it may be possible to analyse and interpret events such as the signing of a labour-management contract, a nation's declaration of war, the doubling of the number of beds in a mental hospital, in terms of the properties and behaviour of individuals, this is not essential to knowing what has happened, nor to predicting some of the consequences. The existence of a contract tells us that the parties to it have made a choice that, if adhered to, will have the effect of guiding their future behaviours in some direction rather than others.

We will, in the next chapter, want to concern ourselves with the very important matters of the relations between the organisation and its parts, and the relations among the parts themselves, and we do not

⁴ See R. L. Ackoff and F. E. Emery, *On Purposeful Systems* (Aldine Atherton, 1972).

intend to imply that these factors are at all lacking in significance for what an organisation is or does. We affirm however, that the properties and behaviours of the organisation itself represent a meaningful and necessary level of analysis in understanding organisational behaviour. The remainder of this chapter constitutes such an analysis.

(b) ORGANISATIONAL GOALS

Organisations exist for particular reasons and survive only so long as they are able to generate some product that can be exchanged for the resources necessary to acquire new inputs, and to maintain themselves in operating order. They are not necessarily deliberately set up to pursue a specific goal or goals, as some writers have stated, although this may be the case. To understand why an organisation chooses to 'earn its living' in one way rather than another, and why it may sometimes change from what it is doing to doing something else, it has been found useful to use the concept of organisational goal. We have argued that organisations 'behave', and that they behave purposefully. In other words organisational activities are in their cumulative effects directed towards the creation or maintenance of certain states of affairs in the future. For a viable organisation, the stream of activities that it evinces are not capricious and unrelated, but are activities that have been calculated to be effective in producing particular desired outcomes, the most fundamental of which is the very survival of the organisation.

Many writers on organisations have failed to illuminate the real contentiousness and variability in organisational goal-setting. The behaviour of rats in mazes has been taken as the paradigm of rational goal-seeking behaviour. It is not usually found necessary to question the goal of a hungry rat or the status of food in its environment, before we set about observing what it does and explaining this.

Let us adopt the unconventional course of thinking about organisational goals from the environment 'inwards'. (In so doing we preview the subsequent discussion of organisational environments.) Some time ago, in a seminal paper, Chein suggested that many psychologists have tended to take the existence of goal objects (objects or situations which can serve as need satisfiers) for granted, and they have shown little interest in examining various environments, as such, from the point of view of what they offer by way of goal objects and/or noxiants ('noxiants' are objects or situations which can produce pain or unpleasantness).[5] Much the same can be said of organisation theorists,

---

[5] I. Chein, 'The Environment as a Determinant of Behaviour', *Journal of Social Psychology* (1954), 39, p. 120.

though as we shall show later, this situation is changing. The social field that is occupied by organisations is not a homogeneous space. It is differentiated in particular by uneven distributions of opportunities and threats, across the field and through time.

At the present time, for example, the dominant public issues that have been put before us have created a climate which has made possible the identification of a number of functions not presently being adequately performed, or not being performed at all, and have created a high probability that organisations moving into these areas can do so profitably; research institutions specialising in the identification, measurement and treatment of pollutants, and the manufacturers of anti-pollutant devices and pollutant-metering equipment; producers of small, 'clean'-engined cars; consultant organisations in urban planning. Clearly problems exist for all such enterprises, but they are called forth now and supported by value shifts at the level of the social field which make new resources and courses of action available for the carrying out of such functions. Similarly, the unfolding web of developments in Great Britain in the last decade or so has proved supportive to the emergence of such varied institutions as 'polytechnics', nuclear power stations, and racist organisations. On the other hand, this same pattern of development has proved inhibitive to some sorts of organisations, for which opportunities decline and survival becomes a real issue. The nationalised rail and steel industries for example have as their critical problems how to minimise the social costs of cutting back their operations. Churches and corner shops have been put on the defensive, while leisure organisations and supermarket chains ('hypermarkets' too now it seems!) have gone on expanding.

Our view is that the display of purposefulness must be seen as a *relationship*, between the 'actor' and the changing environment that action must be correlated to. One of the more important contingencies affecting organisational goal-setting is the *availability* of goal-objects— of opportunities both for supporting and amplifying existing relationships, and of forging new relationships in this environment. The tendency has been to present goal-formulation as an activity that takes place *in vacuo*, at a specific indentifiable point of time, and to think of goals therefore as 'things' that the organisation wants, which are relatively independent of the environment.

In this regard the distinction made by Thompson[6] between goals *of* and goals *for* an organisation is important and useful. Goals *for* an organisation are conceptualised as 'intended future domains', which may be held by individuals or collectivities in the organisation's

[6] J. D. Thompson, *Organisations in Action* (McGraw-Hill, 1967).

environment—non-members who actively seek to change the content or direction of what the organisation does. Goals *of* the organisation are the future domains intended by members of the dominant coalition within the organisation. Vickers cogently reminds us that the main energies in purposeful behaviours are in fact taken up with establishing and maintaining relationships, what he calls 'norm-holding', with various parts of the environment.[7] The vital business of the creation and regulation of these relationships is explored in more detail below, when we come to consider the nature of *strategic choice*.

What an organisation is actually doing now cannot easily be accounted for in terms of desirable states of affairs which lie in the future, without resorting to rather problematical teleological argument. This has proved fertile ground for disputes over the nature of organisational goals. Dealing with the purposeful behaviour of individuals, Lewin has accounted for the way in which the future exerts an influence over present behaviours in the following terms:

> 'The goal as a psychological fact undoubtedly lies in the present. It really exists at the moment and makes up an essential part of the momentary life space. On the other hand the 'content' of the goal . . . lies as a physical or social fact in the future. Indeed it may not occur at all. The nature of the expectation and the character of what is expected, in so far as they act as psychological conditions at the moment, naturally do not depend upon whether or not the event comes to pass.'[8]

Given that goals exert an influence over behaviours only in so far as they 'exist' for individuals as psychological facts, we are led to the view that the organisational problem is firstly for its leadership to project the organisation into its future, and then to put before its members appropriate statements and images of the relationships that this projection yields, so that they are imbued with a sufficient level of understanding and shared purpose for them to be able to jointly produce the relationships that are desired. In practice of course, it is often thought essential only to gain the commitment of the top echelons and key personnel to these goals, relying upon the structure of work situations, the administration of punishments and rewards, and the functioning of communication and authority systems to ensure that the activities of operative and officials conform to organisational objectives.

This leads us however to a further important distinction that has

[7] G. Vickers, *The Art of Judgment* (Chapman & Hall, 1965), p. 33.
[8] K. Lewin, *Principles of Topological Psychology* (McGraw-Hill, 1936), pp. 37-8.

been spelt out by Perrow, amongst others—that between *official* and *operative* goals, between what organisations say they do, and what they actually do.[9] This disparity varies enormously among organisations, and is sometimes, though not always, a legitimate cause for changes of bureaucratic cynicism or duplicity. While some organisations may find it beneficial to deliberately mislead with regard to what they are actually doing, others may simply be unaware, lacking self-consciousness, of the disparities between their stated and realised ends, *especially* where long time-lapses are needed to evaluate programme effects. The official goals are the statements of intent that are generally to be found in charters and constitutions, annual reports and other official publications, and the public utterances of officials. These statements, as Perrow points out, tend to be deliberately vague and ambiguous, reflecting the real need for manoeuvrability. They constitute interesting data from the point of view that they do usually reflect values that the organisation believes (or hopes) will be accepted as legitimate and supported. Operative goals are uncovered by careful observation and inquiry into the criteria that actually have influence in the choice among alternative courses of action by those who carry out the 'work' of the organisation. Such criteria are more often found implicit in the way things get done than explicitly recognised.

In his study of an employment agency for example, Blau found that the official goal of providing the best possible service to individual clients tended to be subordinated to the goal of maximising the number of job placements achieved, due to the fact that agency interviewers were rated according to the quantity rather than the quality of their work.[10]

Thus while official goals perform necessary functions for the organization by putting before its various publics the organisation's self-image, they are not very useful for analytical purposes. Acted upon in any way, they are conditioned by contingencies arising within the environment of the organisation itself. Internally, the needs of individuals and the emergent 'informal' social structure (which are to be discussed in the following chapter), are particularly effective in channelling energies along other than officially adopted lines. It is in the light of this seemingly inevitable conditioning that the concept of *operative* as well as official goals has to be grasped for an understanding of organisational behaviour.[11]

[9] C. Perrow 'The Analysis of Goals in Complex Organisations', *ASR* (1961), 26, pp. 854–66.

[10] P. M. Blau, *Dynamics of Bureaucracy* (University of Chicago, 1955).

[11] For an interesting and informative study of goal-formation and goal-displacement in voluntary organisations see David L. Sills, *The Volunteers* (Free Press, 1957).

(c) FROM FUNCTIONS TO IDEALS

At any particular time different parts of the organisation are likely to be engaged upon doing quite different sorts of things which vary enormously in their importance to the organisation as a whole. A school for example, may at one time be engaged upon installing new coathangers or bicycle stands, in having new classrooms designed and constructed, and in reorganising from class 'streaming' to a comprehensive system. A factory spends money on redecorating the works canteen, negotiating equal pay for female operatives, and on the acquisition of major new plant. Sociologists have tended to concur that the question of which individuals and groups advocate and defend particular goals, and with what intensity, is usually more revealing of organisational structure than analysis and classification of the substantive content of goals pursued. Managers of airlines, mines, factories, and retail chains tend to believe that their particular goals have a special influence over the problems they face until they come together for discussion in seminars or training groups.

Perrow has discussed six types of goals which are distinguished according to the criterion of whose point of view is being recognised—society, the customer, the investor, the top executives, or others.[12] Societal goals represent the macro level—the functions that organisations perform for the larger social system of which they are part. At this level Etzioni has distinguished three kinds of functions which he calls order, economic, and cultural, while Katz and Kahn, as we have seen, distinguish production, maintenance, adaptation, and managerial functions. While these authors, as we shall see in the next section, relate their typologies of organisations to the kind of societal goals performed, we are inclined to agree with Perrow that they tell us little about organisational functioning.

The remaining five kinds are output, investor, system, product, and derived goals. The referent for *output* goals is the public-in-contact, in the role of consumers of products or services and the categories used refer to the substantive content of what the organisation does—road transport, banking, retailing, education, and so on, conceptualised at varying level of generality. *System* goals pertain to the state or manner of functioning of the organisation as a whole, independently of what it actually does, and entail choices with respect to such matters as growth, stability, profits, market share, etc. *Investor* goals reflect the point of view of financial supporters and tend to be more narrowly economic

[12] C. Perrow 'Organisational Goals' in *International Encyclopedia of the Social Sciences* (Macmillan, 1968) 11.

than the other categories. The referent for *product* goals is the characteristics of the goods or services produced and the alternatives available have to do with such issues as quality versus quantity, variety, styling, uniqueness, and so forth. Finally the category of *derived* goals refers to 'the uses to which the organisation puts the power it generates in pursuit of other goals', and encompasses such options as pursuing political aims, community service, employee development, and so on. This final category reminds us that many of the effects of organisational actions may be incidental to the pursuit of its main tasks, but nevertheless of great significance for the individuals, groups, or community affected.

From our examples of the school and factory, and from Perrow's classification, it is clear that an important dimension for understanding the various courses of action that an organisation pursues at any one time is their relative importance, or centrality, with respect to the viability of the organisation as a whole. We propose to give some order to variations of this kind by firstly giving meaning to the notion of organisational mission, and then distinguishing between functions, goals, objectives, and ideals.

The nature of organisational mission lies in the answers to such questions as 'What kind of business are we in?' or 'What service are we trying to provide?', when these become the stimuli for self-inquiry. Thus we find organisations engaged in lending books to the public, educating children (or adults), producing motor vehicles, maintaining law and order, caring for the old and infirm, forecasting the weather, processing food, providing insurance, exploring space, and so on. Robert Townsend, the former Chairman of Avis Rent-a-Car tells us that it took six months to produce a definition of their business; 'renting and leasing vehicles without drivers'.[13] Reflecting on his years as Secretary of Defence Robert McNamara writes:

'Despite its awesome power and the world-wide sweep of its activities, the basic mission of the Department of Defence is simply stated. That mission is military security; or, more broadly, to maintain in constant readiness the military forces necessary to protect the nation from attack, keep its commitments abroad and support its foreign policy.'[14]

Selznick, who has given an important place to the concept of mission in his analysis of institutional leadership, emphasises that the mission of an organisation is not to be thought of as invariant, despite this high

[13] R. Townsend, *Up the Organisation* (Hodder-Fawcett, 1970), p. 118.
[14] R. S. McNamara, *The Essence of Security: Reflections in Office* (Harper & Row, 1968), p. 122.

level of abstraction. It is usually necessary for the leadership to engage in more or less continuous redefinition and recasting of the general aims of the organisation in the light of its internal state—the 'strivings, inhibitions and competences' existing within it—and the external expectations that decide what must be sought or achieved if the institution is to survive.[15]

It is well known for example that in the administration of prisons, there has been mounting pressure in the direction of redefining aims away from punishment and towards therapy. Prison governors and others involved in the actual deliberation of mission have to take account of the fact however that the pressures for such change come mainly from outside and from professionals within, with the rank-and-file prison officers typically in opposition. Similarly, organisations in primary industry, particularly those in mining and food production, have come under very strong pressures to redefine their general aims in terms of the protection and management rather than the exploitation of natural resources. The 1972–3 Icelandic 'cod war' between Britain and Iceland had this as at least one ingredient. The management of farms and forestry commissions, mines and fishing fleets, have had to take into account changing concepts and values to do with the maintenance of the earth's resources.

As well as being liable to shifts in emphasis, missions may expand or contract in response to changing opportunities and organisational competences. The role of the army in Western societies has been consolidated into more specialised functions in defence to the acknowledged primacy of missile bombardment in future conflicts among powerful nations. Great shipping lines too, have had to withdraw towards reliance on the holiday cruise business as jet aircraft have eaten into their transport function. On the other hand rapid urbanisation and the growing demands for co-ordinated development have enabled some firms to grow out of building houses, to developing estates, towards competence in planning entire communities. While organisational missions may be deflected or redirected, expand to encompass wider functions or consolidate into more limited ones, they can very rarely be changed altogether. It is usually easier to build a new organisation than alter the basic mission of an existing one.

The effective carrying out of the organisational mission entails the co-operative involvement of many different individuals and groups most of which have responsibility only for the carrying out of limited subgoals of the whole. The many disparate courses of action that go into the accomplishment of missions are typically parcelled out among

[15] P. Selznick, *Leadership in Administration* (Harper & Row, 1957), pp. 67–8.

specialised roles and sections. In understanding the relations among these diverse contributions we will draw a distinction between goals and objectives.

We propose to reserve the term 'goals' to refer to the relatively short-run outcomes of courses or cycles of activity whose characteristics can be known beforehand. In relation to the overriding purpose or mission, the attainment of goals entails a relatively short time span, has limited repercussions upon the carrying out of other organisational functions, and tends to be concerned with means rather than ends. The attainment of goals can generally be programmed. Objectives on the other hand, lie beyond the range of routine courses of action, and their attainment is far more contingent upon events occurring during the period allocated. The carrying out of objectives entails a relatively longer time span, affects a broader scope of organisational activities, and reflects concern with ends rather than means. A further characteristic of objectives therefore is that their accomplishment may involve the attainment of a succession of goals, achievement of each one in the series providing the starting conditions for the achievement of the next, with each step leading closer to the objective.

Goals and objectives are not defined absolutely therefore—they lie on a continuum along which ends sought increase in their importance for the organisation as a whole. A related feature of the shift from goals towards objectives is that the consequences of actions become more and more irreversible. Once acted upon, the decision to build new plant, for example, is more compelling and binding upon the organisation than a decision to provide a new canteen. This goals-objectives distinction correlates with the distinction usually drawn between tactical and strategic planning.[16] Goals and objectives do not complete the picture however. Beyond goals lie the *functions* or *tasks* that constitute the daily routine activities of the bulk of the membership, and beyond objectives, one enters the realms of *ideals*.

Functions or tasks are simply unit parts of the whole activity needed for the realisation of goals and objectives—they are the units of activity distributed among individuals that constitute their 'jobs'. These are the activities described in the functional charts of organisations and to which the society's specifically vocational education is orientated. A persisting major problem for organisations has been to find a way of 'decomposing' organisational goals such that the resultant tasks are neither too large nor too small, too monotonous nor too variable to be matched successfully with the capabilities and needs of individuals. It

[16] One of the most cogent accounts of these distinctions can be found in Russel L. Ackoff, *A Concept of Corporate Planning* (Wiley-Interscience, 1970).

is obvious also that the goals and objectives that an organisation *can* pursue are determined to a considerable extent by the skills and the capacities of the individuals whose services are needed.

Beyond objectives lie ideals. Emery and Ackoff have recently defined ideals as purposes that can never be attained, but which can be approached without limit:

'Many wise man have observed that there is more satisfaction in pursuing an end than attaining it; to play a game well yields more satisfaction than does winning it. Also, some have observed that the manager's and researcher's objective is not so much to solve problems as it is to create more challenging and important problems to work on by solving the one at hand. This is to say that the continuous pursuit of more desirable ends is an end in itself, and hence attainment of a specific end can be conceptualised as a means to such pursuit.

'Such observations suggest that a pervasive objective of man and the social systems of which he is part is the successful pursuit of increasingly desirable objectives. If this is so, then it is reasonable for man and the social systems of which he is part to formulate objectives that can be pursued without end but can be continually approached. . . . An end that satisfies these conditions is an *ideal*.[17]

Ideals supply the criteria for choosing among objectives, and for guiding the selection of the subsequent objective when one has been attained. Ideals do not seem to be essential to the functioning of organisations—indeed we can probably all think of examples of organisations that we would judge distinctively lacking in ideals. Without them however organisations are far more vulnerable to 'drifting' into their futures, to adventurism and expediency. Perhaps universities, their characteristic internal struggles and weaknesses notwithstanding, are one of the more familiar examples of ideal-seeking institutions, in that their activities are ultimately directed to pursuit of truth, an ideal that has given continuity to the activities of some institutions over several centuries. Ackoff and Emery suggest that the quest for truth is one of four fundamental ideals to which the institutions of contemporary society may be orientated:

1. The quest for Plenty: politic-economic functions.
2. The quest for Truth: scientific functions.
3. The quest for the Good: ethico-moral functions.
4. The quest for Beauty: aesthetic functions.

We must note finally the essential relativity of the categories of

[17] Ackoff and Emery, op. cit., p. 237.

function, goal, objective and ideal, and their interdependence. They are interdependent in the sense that the accomplishment of goals implies the performance of a number of separable functions, while objectives are reached by way of a series of goals, and the pursuit of ideals consists in the successive attainment of a series of objectives—a series that may be regarded as infinite. They are relative in the sense that the same intended course of action may have the status of a function from the point of view of the organisation as a whole, while it constitutes a goal for a particular department, and has the character of an objective for an individual member of that department.

(d) ORGANISATIONAL ENVIRONMENTS

When as social scientists we try to move towards an appreciation of the social world through an understanding of the purposeful behaviours of individuals and the social systems that they are part of, then our subject matter is principally events, activities, processes, and so on—changes in the state of such systems and their interrelations over time. In seeking understanding of actions and processes in the social world, we invariably refer to the *social structures* by which they are shaped and constrained. It is one of the fundamental axions of social science that the purposeful behaviours of individuals and groups are conditioned in many ways by the properties of the environing social system. In other words, events in the social world are determined both by the properties of behaving systems and by the properties of their environments, this being so whether the focal system be an individual, a group, or an organisation.[18]

In investigating purposeful behaviours and interpersonal relations in organisations it has traditionally been thought sufficient to refer them to the characteristics of the organisation itself as the more inclusive social structure, although sometimes the diffuse influences of culture and community setting have been taken into account.[19] If however, we want to focus on the organisation itself and try to understand its behaviour, then clearly we have to try to define, describe, and interpret the context in which it exists—the environment of the organisation itself.

It is surprisingly only rather recently that social scientists have turned their attention to the nature of organisational environments. Previously

[18] For the development of this point of view in the case of individual behaviour, see A. Angyal, *Foundations for a Science of Personality* (Commonwealth Fund, 1941); and Lewin, op. cit.; in the case of organisations see the collection by J. G. Maurer, *Readings in Organisation Theory: Open-System Approaches* (Random House, 1971).

[19] See for example J. C. Abeglenn, *The Japanese Factory* (Free Press, 1958); M. Crozier, *The Bureaucratic Phenomenon* (Tavistock, 1964).

organisations have either been studied as though they were closed systems, or the availability of goals and of the resources for attaining them has been taken for granted.

In the last decade or so more attention has been given to the environmental determinants of organisational functioning, and there is now a developing interest in the ecological dimension of organisational behaviours—the ways in which regulation can be achieved in *populations* of organisations. A possible danger is that the study of environments may simply be added to the study of organisations and the two investigated as quite separate domains demarcated by organisational boundaries. The present concern with the nature of organisational environments arose from the realisation that organisation and environment in fact actively interpenetrate one another in all sorts of ways, and that this interpenetration is essential to the organisation getting things done. If we take our primary task to be understanding social processes rather than explaining social structures, then we shall find more useful a view of organisations and their environments as being in many respects continuous—elements of each entering equally into the determination of organisational processes.

In the interpretation of the behaviour of individuals this is the view that is expressed by Kurt Lewin in his equation $b = f(p . e)$—behaviour is a function of the person plus his environment,[20] and in the rigorous exposition of a concept of life by Andras Angyal.[21] In Angyal's view, the life process goes on within the 'biosphere', and events or processes in the biosphere are determined in part by the organism and in part by its environment—in other words both *autonomously* and *heteronomously*. The interesting thing to examine is not where the organism ends and the environment begins, but to what extent a particular happening or class of happenings is determined by the properties of the system or organism (autonomously), and to what extent by the properties of the environment (heteronomously). Analogously, sociologists might find it fruitful to think of the realm in which social life takes place as the sociosphere (a term suggested by Boulding),[22] and seek to discover the degrees to which sociospheric events are determined by social systems or by their environments. At least we should appreciate that neither the organisation nor its environment may be fully understood apart from an understanding of the constant processes of interchange between them. The organisation itself is no more than a crystallisation of

[20] Lewin op. cit.
[21] Angyal, op. cit.
[22] K. Boulding, *The Impact of the Social Sciences* (Rutgers University Press, 1966).

formerly scattered elements of the environment—a regrouping of energies, and its maintenance entails the more or less constant ingestion of further parts of the environment—men, materials, information— and its subsequent enrichment with new or transformed products.

However we try to describe and understand the interactions of organisations with their environments, we need some way of conceptualising the environment. Here we intend to concentrate upon an elaboration of the typology of environments put forward by Emery and Trist[23] in the belief that it is at present one of the most fruitful frameworks for systematising our understanding of organisational environments.[24]

They present four ideal-type environments which are differentiated by qualitative dissimilarities in their 'causal texturing'. The causal texture of the environment is the way in which, independently of any behaving system, elements of the environment are interrelated with one another in ways that make some courses of action possible, but discourage others. It draws attention to the way in which properties of the environment itself condition the kinds of exchanges that can take place between an open living system and its environment. Their schema is at a level of abstraction at which it is relevant to the behaviours of all types of living systems, but we will here concentrate on its applicability to the behaviours of organisations. It is premised on the view that purposeful behaviours in the social field can generally be represented as movements towards, or strains away from, certain ends, objects, or situations, which can therefore be considered as either helps or hindrances to the survival of the individual or social system and to the performance of its functions. Environments are thus considered to be constituted of *goals* and *noxiants*, and they may be differentiated according to the pattern in which goals and noxiants are distributed (random-clustered), their kinetic properties (placid-dynamic), and whether or not a given array of these 'environmental relevancies' is shared by more than one system.

---

[23] F. E. Emery and E. L. Trist: 'The causal texture of organisational environments', *Human Relations* (1965), 18.1, pp. 21–31.

[24] This typology has been widely discussed in the literature. See in particular the work of S. Terreberry, 'The Evolution of Organisational Environments', *ASQ* (12/4/1968), pp. 590–613; W. H. McWhinney, 'Organisational Form, Decision Modalities and the Environment', *Human Relations* (21/3/1968), pp. 269–81; and D. R. Kingdom *Matrix Organisations* (Tavistock, 1973). Elaboration by the authors themselves may be found in F. Emery, 'The Next Thirty Years: Concepts, Methods and Anticipations', *Human Relations* (20/3/1967), pp. 199–237; and Emery and Trist, *Towards a Social Ecology*, Plenum 1972. For an alternative though similar appreciation of organisational environments see Thompson, op. cit., especially Ch. 6.

I   *Placid-random environment*

The simplest of the four types is that in which goals and noxiants are 'relatively unchanging in themselves and randomly distributed'—they do not occur in the environment in any meaningful or systematic patterns from the system's point of view. The type I environment corresponds to a flat surface over which an organism can move, which is bare apart from a number of widely scattered heaps of food. It corresponds also to the relevant environment of the 'flea-market' salesman. He is confronted by a market situation which is almost totally unstructured, so that the same sales approach is appropriate for all comers, and one 'mark' (customer) is as good as any other. The environments of some relatively simple organisms such as an amoeba or a human foetus seem to be of the placid-random type. Attempts to deliberately structure environments at this level for human beings have occurred in such settings as England's old-fashioned mad houses, and in concentration camps.

When environmental relevancies are randomised—the 'goods' to be approached, and the 'bads' to be avoided have a distribution that is unpredictable to the system, any behaviour is as good as any other— 'the optimal strategy is just the simple tactic of attempting to do one's best on a purely local basis'. Actions may be selected fortuitously which are conducive to success, but such rewards cannot be anticipated in advance. In the social world such simple environments do not occur naturally, for the processes of evolution upon which social life is ultimately dependent require a higher degree of differentiation than is offered by them. The examples that can be found of systems occupying such environments are generally 'instruments' or parts of higher order systems, which design and maintain controlled environments in which these special parts can be protected and buffered from potentially disturbing influences. Historically there has certainly been a tendency in work organisations to simplify to the greatest possible extent the work environments of the lowest echelons of workers by mechanising and routinising their jobs and removing authority and responsibilities to higher levels. We cannot find any examples however of organisations themselves existing in environments of such simplicity.

II   *Placid-clustered environment*

The second level of causal texturing differs from the random environment in that goals and noxiants are now clustered—they occur in patterned ways and with particular degrees of probability that are potentially 'knowable' by the system. Clustering is the most important identifying characteristic—the goals and noxiants are still relatively unchanging in themselves. If the random environment is exemplified in Petticoat Lane, the clustered environment corresponds more to the market situation of a country town general store. In this case it pays to differentiate among customers on such dimensions as regulars and passers, by debtors and creditors, big spenders and small spenders. Similarly, if the relevant environment for a person searching for shells on the sea-shore is a random environment, the relevant environment of prospectors searching for oil or minerals is typically clustered— the occurrence of mineral resources is known to be correlated with certain topographical and geophysical features. The environment of plants that are subject to the cycle of the seasons, and of human infants, seem to be environments of this type. The factors spawned by the industrial revolution are the best example of environments of this type that have been deliberately engineered for human being. Significant variety in the work situation stemmed mainly from fluctuations in the physical demands of production processes and the variable desirability of available tasks.

An individual or social system in an environment in which its 'need satisfiers' and those objects or situations which have detrimental consequences are regularly interdependent in temporal or spatial configurations, thereby giving rise to variations in the 'supportiveness' of different parts of the environment, cannot expect to survive in the long run by the use of purely chance behaviour or 'doing one's best on a purely local basis'. Clustering offers the possibility of improving upon purely chance behaviours. It is no longer the case that pursuit of the nearest visible goal is as good as any other action:

'To pursue the goal object that it can see, the goal object with which it is immediately confronted, may lead the system into parts of the field which are fraught with unseen difficulties. Similarly, avoiding a present difficulty may lead the system away from parts of the environment that are potentially rewarding.'[25]

Clustering calls for the use of strategy rather than just tactics. Actions selected do not need only to satisfy the immediate situational demands— they need to belong to some ordered series of actions that are calculated to lead towards the strategic objective. In clustered environments the strategic objective can be appropriately conceptualised in *locational* terms—it is defining and moving towards the optimal location in the environment. Thus for example, mineral prospectors with limited resources for surveying and drilling have literally to select the best locations they can on the basis of the surface and strata variations.

[25] Emery and Trist, *Towards a Social Ecology*, op. cit., p. 46.

Similarly, a wise fisherman knows which part of the river to drop his line in.

At the level of the social field as a whole, clustering is represented by the pre-industrial stage of development. Trist has characterised societies at this level of development in terms of the relations between *welfare* (well-being, continuing to function well, maintenance of the steady state) and *development* (progression, continuing to advance, attainment of higher order steady states), which refer to the static and the dynamic aspects of the socio-cultural system's regulation and adaptation. The relatively placid environments of pre-industrial societies are character-ised by self-regulating welfare processes, embodied in extended kinship systems, while development processes require an active intervention, and are called into being, when, for some reason the maintenance of welfare through kinship breaks down. The foreground in such societies is not occupied by masses of powerful competing formal organisations, but by the affective and localistic units of kinship and community, and the established traditional institutions of Church and State. Environ-ments of organisations in such environments are relatively stable and free of active challenges to survival, but nevertheless require: 'con-centration of resources, subordination to the main plan, and the develop-ment of a "distinctive competence" . . . in reaching the strategic ob-jective. Organisations under these conditions therefore, tend to grow in size and also to become hierarchical, with a tendency towards centralised control and co-ordination.'[26]

In some respects the environmental relevancies of the traditional farm correspond to this level of causal texturing—work is constantly organised and progress assessed in relation to the diurnal and annual cycles of light and darkness, sun, rain, and frost, and the effectiveness of farming is in some measure dependent upon the accuracy with which these variations can be anticipated and responded to. While the causal texturing of the field as a whole is transformed by industrialisation, some relatively small and simple organisations may continue to operate in sheltered enclaves of an environment that is only clustered—museums and art galleries perhaps, rural stores, some clubs and voluntary organisations. For organisations more typifying of industrial society it is usually only particular functions and not the organisation as a whole that confront these relatively simple environments. The customer- or client-serving sections of organisations such as banks, post offices, insurance offices, and so on often have as a major concern coping effectively with daily and seasonal fluctuations in the demands received

[26] Emery and Trist 'The Causal Texture of Organisational Environments', op. cit., p. 25.

for services—finding a level and flexibility in the provision of service at which customers can be satisfied without waste of resources.

III   *The disturbed reactive environment*

The type II environment represents a transformation of the random environment whereby goals and noxiants become clustered. The disturbed reactive environment is characterised by a second qualitative change—it is a clustered environment in which there is more than one system of the same kind—in which there are other systems performing the same function, and for which therefore, the same elements of the environment have relevance as goals and noxiants. From the point of view of an actor such environments can no longer be considered placid— it has active elements, and it is more appropriate to think of this and the succeeding type as *dynamic* environments. The type III environment corresponds to the typical milieu for mature human behaviour, and is described in the economist's theory of oligopolic markets. It is exemplified also in most forms of contests and games, in which competitors act within certain boundary conditions to manipulate a variety of objects or situations with the aim of maintaining precedence over the other. It is the state of affairs that exists when two or more fleets are fishing the same offshore waters, or a number of production enterprises seek to sell a similar product in the same market.

When the environment contains a 'competitor', adaptive behaviour needs to take into account the information that the competitor has of the distribution of goals and noxiants (clustering), and what its probable courses of action will be, as well as the distribution of goals and noxiants *per se*. 'Operations' supplant strategy. An operation is a 'planned series of tactical initiatives' that are calculated not simply to be adapted to the realisation of given ends, but also in the process to block or elicit certain courses of action that are available to the other systems. Although overall location in the field is still an important consideration for survival and effectiveness, the critical factor now tends to be 'capacity or power to make more or less at will, i.e. to be able to make and meet competitive challenge.'[27] In the simpler environments most of the important sources of variance may be coped with by the appropriate use of approach-avoid tactics, by hiding or hoarding. When the major sources of variance are other systems, then some active coming-to-terms between them is required. Adaptive behaviour requires not only that a system be able to select appropriate courses of action to enable it to move into and exploit the 'richer' parts of its environment, but also that, when challenged, it be able to reconsider its aims. Except when it

[27] ibid., p. 26.

is decided to fight to the death, strategies of bargaining, coalition, co-optation, or competition will tend to become prevalent.

At the social field level the type III environment corresponds to the more complex and dynamic environments of industrial societies. Such societies are characterised by the fact that it is now development that is maintained by self-regulating processes, embodied in the market system, and reflected in the replacement of kinship groups by production enterprises as the leading part. Under industrial conditions, as we know only too well, welfare increasingly requires active intervention as kinship systems are no longer able to cope. Welfare is a function of development. The dominant figural elements of the social field become formal organisations, production organisations in particular, and for each of them, their environment is increasingly constituted of other formal organisations.

It is organisational environments at this, the disturbed-reactive level, with which we are most familiar. It is also with environments of this type that most recent efforts at conceptualisation have been concerned. Emery and Trist suggest that the flexibility needed to cope with active causal agents in the environment encourages organisational decentralisation and places an emphasis on speed and quality of decision at the various peripheral points. Other writers have been more particularly concerned with interorganisational relationships. Dill[28] proposes the concept of *task environment* to refer to those parts of the environment which are relevant or potentially relevant to goal-setting and goal-attainment, and suggest that for enterprises such environments have four major sections—customers, suppliers, competitors, and regulatory bodies. Evan[29] advocates the transposition of role theory and proposes the concept of *organisation-set* as a step towards a theory of inter-organisational relations. Levine and White[30] adapt Homan's 'exchange' model to the analysis of relations among health organisations in a community. Guetzkow[31] identifies three classes of interorganisational interactions: those resulting from the interpenetration of groups (e.g. the overlap of unions and professional associations with work organisa-

[28] W. R. Dill, 'Environment as an Influence in Managerial Autonomy', *Administrative Science Quarterly* (1958), 2, pp. 409–43.

[29] William M. Evan, 'The Organisation-set: Towards a Theory of Inter-organisational Relations' in J. D. Thompson (ed.) *Approaches to Organisation Design* (University of Pittsburgh, 1966), pp. 173–91.

[30] S. Levine and P. E. White, 'Exchange as a Conceptual Framework for the Study of Interorganisational Relationships', *Administrative Science Quarterly* (1961), 5, pp. 583–601.

[31] H. Guetzkow, 'Reactions among Organisations' in R. V. Bowers (ed.), *Studies on Behaviour in Organisations* (University of Georgia Press, 1966).

tions); those deriving from the activities of specialised boundary-spanning roles (e.g. research groups, secretaries, legal advisers); and those deriving from supra-organisational processes, such as the activities of governments, regulatory bodies, professional bodies, and so on. Thompson and McEwen[32] outline four organisational strategies for coping with the reactive environment, which entail the surrender of successively greater amounts of autonomy in goal-setting competition, bargaining, co-optation, and coalition.

IV *The turbulent environment*

In the conceptual series elaborated by Emery and Trist, turbulent environments are, like type III environments, dynamic and clustered, but unlike the reactive environment, they are characterised by dynamic processes occurring in the field itself, and not simply in the actions of other systems. The turbulent environment represents a transformation of the third level of causal texturing—it is a disturbed-reactive environment from which dynamic field processes have emerged as an unintended result of the interactions of the constituent systems. A useful analogy in understanding how turbulence arises is the effect of a company of soldiers marching over a suspension bridge. They may set up a resonance which leads to the bridge's 'self-destruction'. If the type II environment corresponds to the circumstance of a single milling enterprise exploiting a forest for timber, and type III corresponds to the new state of affairs created by other milling enterprises beginning operations in the same locality, the turbulent environment corresponds to the situation that can arise if the competing systems over-exploit the available timber, encouraging soil wash and erosion, and making regeneration difficult if not impossible. The environment takes on its own dynamic.

We are increasingly alerted to the possibility that the continuous transformation of energy and the accompanying release of wastes into the atmosphere and water systems may result in accumulations of noxious substances up to a critical mass point, at which irreversible processes begin to take place in eco-system balances. The belief is currently gaining ground that with the drift towards post-industrialism in the most advanced societies, social fields too are becoming turbulent. Emery and Trist suggest that turbulence arises in organisational environments as a result of increasing reliance on research and development, the deepening interdependence between the economic and other facets of society, radical increases in the volume and speed of communi-

[32] J. D. Thompson and W. J. McEwan, 'Organisational Goals and Environments: Goal-setting as an Interactive Process', *ASR* (1958), 23, pp. 23–31.

cations, and the sheer growth of organisations and linked sets of organisations to the point that they are so large that 'their actions are both persistent and strong enough to induce autochthonous processes in the environment.

Concerning the transformation at the level of the social field as a whole, Vickers suggests that the onset of turbulence corresponds to the end of a period of 'free fall'—the explosive expansion beginning with the industrial revolution that changed a rural into an urban way of life, and released several critical rates of change:

> 'Populations began to multiply faster; individuals began to produce and consume more, to travel and communicate more, to expect and demand more. As a result they began to depend more on each other and, soon, to get more and more in each other's way; but these consequences were noticed only later, because the explosion began in a world so underoccupied and so underdeveloped that for a time each change could excite itself and the others without breeding limitations. This is what I call the time of free fall.'[33]

More recently he writes of 'Freedom in a rocking boat—changing values in an unstable society', and warns that the whole social system has become 'self-exciting', threatening all its members with the danger of becoming 'ecologically trapped'.[34]

Alvin Toffler's analysis of 'superindustrial society' leads him to the view that members of the most advanced industrial societies, in which experiences and relationships are increasingly characterised by transience, novelty and diversity, are becoming more and more vulnerable to 'future shock'. Future shock is the disease of change, referring to the psychological bewilderment and disorientation that may affect individuals, groups and entire cultures when the rate of change in their environments outstrips their adaptive capacities:

> 'The acceleration of change in our time is itself, an elemental force. This accelerative thrust has personal and psychological, as well as sociological consequences ... unless man quickly learns to control the rate of change in his personal affairs as well as in society at large, we are doomed to a massive adaptational breakdown.'[35]

Emery and Trist believe that social fields are becoming turbulent in those parts of the industrialised world which are now drifting into

---

[33] Geoffrey Vickers, *Value Systems and Social Processes* (Tavistock, 1968), p. 52.

[34] Geoffrey Vickers, *Freedom in a Rocking Boat* (Allan Lane, 1970).

[35] Alvin Toffler, *Future Shock* (Bodley Head, 1970), p. 4.

post-industrialism. In such fields welfare and development become interdependent functions. In particular, accelerating rates of change mean that development becomes a *prerequisite* for the welfare of sub-systems, otherwise they are left behind and rendered obsolescent, falling into states of 'ill-fare'. The increasing interdependence among sub-systems has the consequence that the ill-fare of relatively few sub-systems, especially if they occupy strategic positions, can be critical for the larger system. 'The meta-problems created in this situation pass the limit within which autoregulative processes can adaptively operate with respect to either welfare or development, so that an active role becomes generally required.'[36]

The emergence of dynamic processes in the field itself means for the constituent systems a gross increase in their area of relevant uncertainty —the causal complexity of the environment is such as to render un-predictable, and to a degree uncontrollable, the effects of system actions and interactions. In such environments it does not seem possible for individual systems to formulate courses of action that would have a worthwhile probability of enabling them to maintain a level of efficiency in the performance of their function in the long run. Neither tactics, strategy, nor operations can be relied upon in a situation in which dynamic disturbances originate not only from competing systems but from the round or the medium in which they operate. When instability and complexity of environmental connectedness are ubiquitous there is unlikely to be any location in the field that remains benign more than transiently. Neither is the mobilisation of power, and the capacity to move more or less at will, likely to be of much use in the long run when it is not a question of subordinating other systems but of bringing order to the ground upon which they interact. It seems unlikely for example that government decrees and the threat of sanctions represent viable solutions to the problems of environmental degradation, industrial relations, or inflation.

The dominance of heteronomous events at this level suggests that a population of purposeful systems can best come to terms with turbu-lence by entering into joint, collaborative searches for solutions, premised on the recognition that their most significant problems are common problems. Unlike the disturbed-reactive environment, which requires some coming to terms between similar systems whose fates tend to be negatively correlated, the turbulent environment requires some coming to terms between both similar and dissimilar systems whose fates are to a significant degree *positively* correlated. Emery and Trist have suggested that if there is a mechanism for coping with

[36] Emery and Trist, *Towards a Social Ecology*, p. 130.

turbulence it is likely to be 'the emergence of values that have overriding significance for all members of the field':

> 'So far as effective values emerge, the character of richly joined, turbulent fields changes in a most striking fashion. The relevance of large classes of events no longer has to be sought in an intricate mesh of diverging causal strands, but is given directly in the ethical code. By this transformation a field is created which is no longer richly joined and turbulent but simplified and relatively static.'[37]

The latest organisational literature abounds with fragments of strategies for coming to terms with the challenges of the turbulent world that is coming into existence. We will return to the problems of organisational adjustments to such environments.

(e) INSTITUTIONAL LEADERSHIP AND STRATEGIC CHOICE

We have tried to describe some of the defining characteristics of organisations, and have discussed a number of important distinctions that have been made among different types of organisations. We arrive at the view, to be elaborated in the following chapter, that organisations are to be understood as purposeful social systems which are characterised by a functional division of labour with respect to the outcomes that are sought. We have drawn attention also to the importance of organisational environments as an independent source of relevant uncertainties, threats and opportunities, and discussed some important differences in the degree of environmental uncertainty that different organisations, or different parts of the same organisation may have to adapt to. We now need to discuss the critical role played by organisational leaders in mediating between the organisation and its environment.

After a long period in which organisation theorists failed to take the role of the environment into account at all, preferring to work with simplified 'closed system' models, we now have to acknowledge the danger, recently emphasised in an important paper by Child, that the causal significance of organisational environments as a determinant of structure and effectiveness may easily be overstated. While organisations of different kinds and of different sizes vary enormously in their overall degree of autonomy or dependence with respect to the environment, it is generally the case that an organisation's leading decision-makers are able, by the exercise of critical judgement and strategic choice, to

[37] Emery and Trist, 'The Causal Texture of Organisational Environments', p. 28.

deliberately shape and modify the nature of organisation-environment interdependencies. Galbraith's important analysis of industrial society underlines for example, the way in which large business corporations are able to manipulate and create product demand (Galbraith: 1967). Child argues that businessmen, educators, and union officials may influence their environments in lesser ways by choosing when to enter what markets, setting admission standards, determining recruitment policies and so forth. 'Some degree of environmental selection is open to most organisations, and some degree of environmental manipulation is open to most larger organisations. These considerations form an important qualification to suggestions of environmental determinism.'[38]

In his excellent, short study of 'leadership in administration', Selznick puts the view that leadership is 'a kind of work done to meet the needs of a social situation'.[39] As such it is neither equivalent to high office, prestige or authority, nor is it indispensable, though only organisations facing 'routine' and predictable environments can afford to go leaderless for long. Thompson,[40] sceptical of the survival of the single 'all-powerful chief' in today's complex organisations identifies the locus of such leadership with the organisation's 'dominant coalition'.

According to Selznick, the institutional leader is primarily 'an expert in the promotion and protection of values'. The key tasks of leadership are the definition of institutional mission and role, the institutional embodiment of purpose (i.e. building the mission into the organisation's social structure), the defence of institutional integrity, and the ordering of internal conflict. The default of leadership may be manifested in the failure to set goals, which permits the organisation to 'drift', or the failure to convert members to chosen goals, so that they 'enjoy only a superficial acceptance and do not genuinely influence the total structure of the enterprise'.

'Leadership creates and moulds an organisation embodying—in thought and feeling and habit,—the value premises of policy. Leadership reconciles internal strivings and environmental pressures, paying close attention to the way adaptive behaviour brings about changes in organisational character. When an organisation lacks leadership, these tasks are inadequately fulfilled, however expert the flow of paper and however smooth the channels of communication and command.'[41]

The basic point to be made is that it is not appropriate for organisa-

[38] John Child, 'Organisational Structure Environment and Performance—the Role of Strategic Choice', *Sociology* (1972), Vol. 6, No. 1, p. 4.
[39] Selznick, op. cit., p. 22.　　　[40] Thompson, op. cit.　　　[41] ibid., p. 62.

tion theorists simply to describe the internal structures and processes of organisations, and the nature of their environments, then to seek relationships between organisational and environmental factors. We have to be fully aware that individual leaders or members of the dominant coalition have the capacity to exercise strategic choice and to deliberately modify organisation-environment interrelationships, either by modifying the environment itself, or by altering the technology, structure, size, or human relationships of the organisation.

'. . . Environmental conditions cannot be regarded as a direct source of variation in organisational structure, as open system theorists often imply. The critical link lies in the decision-makers' evaluation of the organisation's position in the environmental areas they regard as important, and in the action they may consequently take about its internal structure.'[42]

The earlier discussion of organisational environments indicated that the difficulties experienced by leaders in what Vickers has called 'appreciation'[43] and policy-making are to an important extent a function of the causal complexity of the environment. In non-competitive environments in which goals and noxiants, opportunities and threats, are clustered together, the leaders' concern must be, figuratively speaking, to place his organisation in the right place at the right time. This is a typical concern for health and welfare organisations, seeking to match limited resources to complex patterns and syndromes of pathology, which vary in their geographical and temporal distributions.

The additional uncertainties created by the presence of other organisations competing for access to the same scarce resources, or success in the same 'market' mean that the organisational leadership has to address itself also to the problem of consolidating organisational capabilities and power in order to retain the capacity to move more or less at will and be able to adjust successfully to as many of the courses of action available to competitors as possible. Turbulent environments place even greater demands upon the vision and creativity of leaders, and yet in her analysis of the evolution of organisational environments Terreberry concludes that:

'. . . both the theoretical and case-study literature on organisations suggests that [they] are increasingly finding themselves in environments where the complexity and rapidity of change in external interconnectedness gives rise to increasingly unpredictable change in their transactional interdependencies. This seems to be good evi-

[42] Child, op. cit., p. 10.   [43] G. Vickers, *The Art of Judgment*.

dence for the emergence of turbulence in the environments of many formal organisations.'[44]

The evidence available to us today suggests that the problem of successful organisational adaptation to turbulent environments still awaits solution. Apprehending qualitatively new levels of uncertainty and complexity in the relevant environment, organisational leadership may opt for lines of least resistance, and adapt passively by artificially restricting their attention to limited areas or facets. Or, and perhaps more commonly, organisations fail to perceive a *qualitative* change, and respond to the turbulent environments as though they were simply a more complex disturbed-reactive environment. This issues in the quest for more power and enhancement of existing capabilities, strategies which may be successful in the short run, but which become identifiable in the long-run as maladaptations such as synoptic idealism, authoritarianism, or evangelicism.[45]

[44] S. Terreberry, op. cit., p. 598.

[45] A. D. Crombie, *Planning for Turbulent Social Fields* (Unpublished PhD thesis, Australian National University, 1972).

5

Organisational Cultures

When we focus upon the structure and development of whole societies, organisations may be regarded as parts of a more inclusive system, and their aggregate effects upon this larger system explored. Or, as we have seen, it is possible to focus upon the organisation as the unit of analysis, and the way in which the characteristics of the organisation as such vary with the character of the environment and influence the organisation's effectiveness. A third perspective is that which focuses on the *parts* of the organisation, and the relationships of dynamic interdependence among them whereby the organisation as a whole can be maintained, and some at least of its purposes attained. The first, macro-sociological perspective, and to a lesser extent the second, necessarily ignore much of the finer texture of the social life *within* organisations in concentrating upon the more general global properties and the mutual influences of organisations and the social structure. It is this finer detail concerning the ways in which individuals have to co-operate, form groups, distribute and accomplish tasks, and so forth, that now has to be considered. The subject matter is organisational process—the dynamics of co-operative relations among aggregates of people to get particular tasks done.

(a) ORGANISATIONAL SPACE

Katz and Kahn have used the term *organisational space* to refer to those parts of the social field in which social activities are governed by the characteristics and demands of organisations:

> 'By organisational space we refer to the locus of the various organisational activities and the behaviour distances between members in carrying out their many organisation-related tasks. . . .

. . . Organisational space is the social transformation of physical or objective space that provides the topography of the organisation.'[1]

Like the concept of social space from which it is derived, organisational space is multidimensional and its boundaries are therefore composite. In the first instance it tends to be approximately bounded by the physical location and structure of the premises or plant, and by the time periods within which this physical space is occupied by the organisation's members. The organisational space for a retail store corresponds at a first approximation to the periods during which the store premises are occupied by the staff. In addition there are certain times when legal boundaries become the most significant, as when the passage of laws and decisions of the courts bring new definitions to the rights and responsibilities that inhere in the relations amongst such groups as proprietors, employees, customers and clients, and to the nature and the extent of the authority that the organisation may exercise.

From the point of view of the social sciences however, it is the way in which social space is *perceptually* bounded and differentiated that is usually of the greatest significance. From this point of view organisational space comprises areas of activity which are socially recognised as being within the jurisdiction of the organisation, and over which it therefore has authority. When an individual joins and begins to get accustomed to an organisation, he begins to learn the limits of the legitimate demands that may be made upon him in terms of his time and effort, and the responsibility that he has to bear. By such means organisational space is collectively defined in the perceptions of organisation members.

The theoretical relevance of the concept of organisational space, which has been relatively little explored, derives from its obvious connection with a number of concepts in field theory. It belongs to the same conceptual paradigm as the concepts of *social field*, *behaviour setting* and *life-space* which similarly have as their referents social and psychological regions and forces.[2] The life-spaces of organisation members are conditioned and structured basically by the fact that obligations are incurred to be in certain places at certain times, engaged on specific activities. The life-space may be more specifically conditioned by the properties of the various behaviour settings that exist within the organi-

[1] D. Katz and R. L. Kahn, *The Social Psychology of Organisations* (Wiley, 1966), pp. 63–4.
[2] On these concepts see J. F. Brown, *Psychology and the Sycial Order* (McGraw-Hill, 1936); R. G. Barker and H. F. Wright, *Midwest and its Children* (Row, Peterson & Co., 1955); and K. Lewin, *Principles of Topological Psychology* (McGraw-Hill, 1936).

sation space. A behaviour setting is a particular place-thing-time constellation, a non-psychological context or milieu, to which standard behaviour patterns are regularly connected. As we have seen, organisational space itself is connected into the more inclusive realm of the social field.

The concept of organisational space therefore directs attention to the fact that there are other parts of social fields in which individuals are implicated, and in which different sorts of behaviour are called forth. Family, community, crowd, gang, friendship group, and so on, designate other settings in which distinguishable social structures and processes are manifest. Our understanding of internal organisational processes may be increased not only by considering different types of organisations, but also by exploring the differences and the similarities between patterns of organisational behaviour and patterns of behaviour in other spheres. This point of view has not been fully explored by social scientists, due to the tendency to emphasise the distinctive purposefulness of organisations, and the unusual importance attached by them to efficiency and rationality of actions. Some writers have nevertheless appreciated the value of using our knowledge of other domains to illumine our view of organisational behaviour. Selznick argues, for example: '. . . in attempting to understand large and relatively enduring organisations we must draw upon what we know about natural communities'.[3] In doing so, he says, we are led to consider such matters as the development of administrative ideologies, the creation and protection of elites, and the emergence of contending interest groups.

(b) ORGANISATIONAL CULTURE

Just as every individual's life-space—the combination of his personal characteristics and the 'world as it is to him', is different, so too we expect to find that every organisational space that we look into is unique. While the uniqueness of individuals is expressed in their *personality*, the individuality of organisations may be expressed in terms of their differing *cultures*. The concept of culture is more commonly used to refer to the individuality of larger-scale social systems, such as societies or ethnic groups. In using it now to refer to the individuality of organisations, the main difference to note is that organisational cultures do not have the same all-inclusiveness and self-containment that distinguish societal cultures, and assimilation into them is never so complete. It is as well to note however, as studies such as Goffman's analysis of 'total institutions' and Whyte's diagnosis of

[3] P. Selznick, *Leadership in Administration* (Harper & Row, 1957), p. 13.

'organisation man' indicate, that under certain conditions organisational cultures may in fact come to dominate member's existences.[4]

Culture therefore is a characteristic of all organisations, through which, at the same time, their individuality and uniqueness is expressed. The culture of an organisation refers to the unique configuration of norms, values, beliefs, ways of behaving and so on that characterise the manner in which groups and individuals combine to get things done. The distinctiveness of a particular organisation is intimately bound up with its history and the character-building effects of past decisions and past leaders. It is manifested in the folkways, mores, and the ideology to which members defer, as well as in the strategic choices made by the organisation as a whole. The individuality, or cultural distinctiveness of an organisation is attained through the more or less constant exercise of *choice*, in all sections and levels. The importance of choice in this regard may be better appreciated by comparing organisations with other complex self-regulating mechanisms.

A machine is a more or less complex organisation of identifiable parts that act together under certain circumstances to produce particular outcomes. Some machines are able to correct their mistakes as they go along and to improve their performances over time. However, it is generally agreed that unlike human beings, machines do not have personalities (the anthropomorphism of errant lady computers is usually appreciated as such), nor do groups of them in automated plants or automatic telephone exchanges develop a culture. The organisational complexity and self-regulatory powers of ant and bee colonies are even more incredible and perhaps more comparable to systems of organisation in human society and, yet again, we are not inclined to ascribe to individual colonies distinguishing cultural attributes.

The distinctive characteristic of organisation at the social level is the availability of *choice*, and it is due to this factor that we are able to discern personality differences among individuals but not among machines, and to describe the distinctive cultures of organisations but not of ant colonies. More specifically, organisations are able to make choices concerning the outcomes that they will seek to attain (profits, a more healthy community, the legalisation of homosexuality) and the various ways of combining personnel, technologies, and raw materials in order to realise these outcomes. Even organisations with identical missions tend to devolve upon quite unique solutions to the problems of acquiring, combining, and making use of their resources.

[4] E. Goffman 'The Characteristics of Total Institutions' in A. Etzioni (ed.), *Complex Organisations* (Holt, Rinehart & Winston, 1962), pp. 312–40; W. H. Whyte, *The Organisation Man* (Penguin, 1960).

In an enduring organisation the distinctiveness of this solution is likely to be adhered to, defended, and progressively systematised as an important 'invisible asset', even in the face of evidence that a differing solution would more nearly maximise the values that it seeks. Unlike the machine and the ant colony, the human organisation experiences considerable leeway in how its functions may be performed. In the absence of determinative mechanisms for matching organisational means to organisational ends, the solutions that it continuously arrives at are nevertheless not random or capricious, but reflect a certain organisational 'style'. The character of organisational choice is one of the major manifestations of organisational culture.

That variances of this sort in the behaviours of organisations exist, and that they have quite tangible effects for the individuals that come across them need not be laboured. Universities in general have common purposes, and have equal access to what knowledge there is concerning the most appropriate ways of pursuing these. The differences among the 'Oxbridge' universities, the 'Redbrick' universities, and the 'Plate Glass and Aluminium' universities are nonetheless evident and important—they have quite different 'characters'. It is not difficult to think of other cases of organisations seeking similar outcomes, which have equivalent resources, and yet which develop organisational 'styles' which are quite dissimilar.

(c) ORGANISATION AS AN OPEN SYSTEM

Organisational space is not of course an amorphous zone of free activity for those who move within it—in fact it is usually quite the opposite. As Katz and Kahn point out, at an elementary level it is structured along the dimensions of territory, status, power, and function. Members are separated and made interdependent according to the functions they perform and the locations in which they are performed, and according to positions occupied in the status and power hierarchies.

The difficulties of understanding what goes on inside organisations begin with the appreciation that organisational space is highly differentiated and characterised by a considerable degree of structural complexity. With the investigation of any phenomena that manifest 'organised complexity', there are invariably many different points of entry, and thus it is that a number of different schools of thought have built up as a result of concentration upon particular dimensions of organisational functioning that have from time to time been given primacy in the study of organisational behaviour.

A number of approaches differing in what they conceive as the central or leading element have been outlined by Pugh for instance, who distinguishes management, structural, group, individual, technology, and economic theories of organisational behaviour.[5] The reality is that all organisations are repeatedly being required to solve certain kinds of problems. Individuals have to be recruited, retained, and persuaded to behave in ways that serve the organisation's ends; tasks have to be defined and arranged, allocated and re-allocated amongst workers; work conditions and systems of rewards and sanctions have to be devised and maintained to facilitate performance and retain support; channels of communication among disparate parts have to be forged and made to work; and so on. Although there may be disputes about their relative usefulness, there is no question that the interpretation of such complex wholes can be approached intelligibly from each of the perspectives that Pugh outlines, and perhaps others.

The important point is that these are simply different *perspectives*, and one expects to find that any fairly sophisticated observer will come to appreciate the other facets, from whatever standpoint his inquiry begins. The management theorist may be biased towards the belief that the quality of managerial decision-making, and thus the ability of management, is the determining criterion of organisational success. He cannot ignore the fact however that managers are just part of a complex structure which they are unable to change at will, and which they may be unable to change hardly at all. The contributions of management to what the organisation can achieve are constrained in particular by the economic requirements of efficient performance, and by the technology that is available to the organisation. It becomes clear also that the manager's potential influence over the life of the organisation is circumscribed in important ways by the psychological properties of the individuals that he manages and the characteristics of the social groups that these individuals form. This is especially true of course of 'people-processing' organisations.

Let us take as another example, those whose orientation derives from concern over the nature of the individual, and the way in which the organisation affects him. Some psychologically orientated investigators have premised their involvement in the study of organisational behaviour upon a humanistic concern over the creation of conditions appropriate for the growth of the individual. Observation of the sources of satisfaction and dissatisfaction for the individual invariably shows that the nature of the task he has to carry out and the relations he has with

[5] D. S. Pugh, 'Modern Organisation Theory', *Psychological Bulletin* (1966), 66, pp. 235–51; reprinted in M. Gilbert (ed.), *The Modern Business Enterprise* (Penguin, 1972), pp. 76–104.

others in the workplace are of considerable importance. These factors are dependent upon the nature of the technology in use and the structure of work group relations, which are in themselves subject to some extent to managerial control and modification. Again, the structure of the organisation as a whole—its size, degree of complexity, formality, and so forth—and the economic exigencies it has to meet, have effects upon the individual's conditions of work, and need to be taken into account in a full exploration of the impact of the organisation upon the individual.

Inquiry beginning from each different perspective leads, potentially at least, to the uncovery of a wide array of factors that go into the organisation in action. At some stage analysis leads to consideration of component parts, designated by such terms as technology, tasks, authority systems, jobs or roles, group, manager, worker, and the structural configurations into which these are arranged, referred to by such concepts as centralisation, formality, complexity, and flexibility. Another group of common terms refer to the various consequences or outcomes of organisational activity—productivity, efficiency, satisfaction, conflict, and so on. The insight that has become the basis of the involvement of the social scientist in the study of organisations is the recognition of the regular and patterned interdependence of these factors. While disagreements persist over which are the more important factors to investigate, the nature and the order of particular interdependencies, the way in which regulation of the whole system of interdependencies is achieved, the view of the organisation as a set of elements that are interrelated with one another in regular and patterned ways is one that is now very widely shared. It is the uniqueness of this 'whole system of interdependencies' in every particular case, determined as it is by history and habits, personalities and power struggles, that we have referred to as the *culture* of the organisation.

The establishment of this important insight in the sphere of organisational psychology has been lucidly stated by Schein. He observes that the first interest of psychologists in organisations was in connection with the assessment and selection of individual workers, a function which was aided by the progressive improvement in their capacity to measure those characteristics that were required by the organisation. Subsequently, they became involved, with engineers, in problems of designing and organising work itself (job analysis, time and motion study). With the closer study of workers it became apparent that their effectiveness was further dependent upon the system of rewards and punishments created by organisations in order to motivate the behaviours they required, and inquiry extended to the influence of such factors as pay and promotion, and reprimands. The more detailed examination of motivations in turn revealed that a worker's relationships to other workers made more of a difference than had traditionally been assumed, and attention was focused on the processes of group formation and the functions of group loyalties.

'It was in the study of worker motivation, incentive systems, personnel policies, and intergroup relations that the organisation as a total system first began to come into focus . . . the deeper psychologists delved into the behaviour of individuals within organisations, the more they discovered that the organisation is a complex social system which must be studied as a total system if individual behaviour within it is to be truly understood.'[6]

A similar point of view had been expressed earlier by Woodward, who after commenting upon the increasing attention being given to observation and experiment by organisation theorists says:

'Even more important from the point of view of ultimate theory-building is the fact that the various schools of thought are all beginning to see themselves as concerned with the study of systems. This means that whether the approach is basically mathematical, psychological, sociological, or economic, the starting point is the identification of a system and the questions subsequently asked are very much the same: what are the objectives and strategic parts of the system under review and how are these parts interrelated and interdependent? One result of this is that those concerned with the study of organisation are beginning to develop a common language, on whatever discipline their work is based.'[7]

The appreciation of this significant and wide-ranging mutual interdependence of intra-organisational phenomena has been formalised in recent years by the development of the concept of the organisation as a system, or more particularly as an 'open' system, and the concept has proved a useful way of approaching the complexity of organisation behaviour. A system is simply a set of interrelated parts, each of which is related to every other part, and this notion has been employed for a very long time by the natural sciences. The solar system and the clock are the archetypes of systems in this simple sense. The attempt to investigate the organised, dynamic complexity of biological, psycho-

---

[6] E. H. Schein, *Organisational Psychology* (Prentice-Hall, 2nd edn, 1970), p. 3.

[7] J. Woodward, *Industrial Organisation: Theory and Practice* (OUP, 1965), p. 251.

logical, and social phenomena by means of a similar concept made it necessary to distinguish between closed and open systems, between those which are able to regulate themselves, differentiate, and grow, by means of exchange processes with their environments, and those which, unable to import energy from their environments, are subject to irreversible increases in entropy—the tendency towards completely random distribution of their elements.

The archetype of the open system is the simple organism, and the human organisations that we are interested in are very complex examples. They nevertheless share the same defining characteristics, in particular that they are able to consume energy (of which information is a kind) from their environments, which is transformed and passed into the environment again, with part of it being used up in the maintenance and internal elaboration of the system itself. An open system has the capability therefore of maintaining itself in a steady state while doing work, because it has properties that enable it to maintain a favourable energy balance and to constantly process the energy that is acquired.[8] Thus it is that open systems present to the observer two basic facets—an anatomy and physiology, or in the case of social systems, structure and process. The biologist's image of the existential form of the organism as a dynamic one, expressed in the precept, 'the organism is a process' has its counterpart in the social sciences: 'a social system is a structuring of events or happenings rather than of physical parts, and it therefore has no structure apart from its functioning'.[9]

(d) DIMENSIONS OF ORGANISATIONAL INTEGRATION

To conceptualise the organisation in action as an open system is of course no more than a starting point in the investigation of organisational behaviour, and as such only one of a number of possible starting points. Whatever the ultimate value of a consistent systems theoretic interpretation of organisations may be there is wide agreement with the general point of view that the elements and processes of the organisation are mutually dependent upon one another in such ways that a particular part or process cannot be separated and understood in isolation, but has to be viewed in the context of the whole. The factors

---

[8] On the systems point of view in social science see C. W. Churchman, *The Systems Approach* (Delacorte Press, 1968); W. Buckley, *Modern Systems Research for the Behavioural Scientist. A Source Book* (Aldine Press, 1968); F. E. Emery, *Systems Thinking* (Penguin, 1969).

[9] Katz and Kahn, op. cit., p. 31.

that typically demand the attention of both practitioners and social scientists are the various consequences or outcomes of organisational functioning—productivity or effectiveness, job satisfaction, morale, interpersonal and intergroup conflict, absenteeism, membership turnover, growth, profitability, and so on, in so far as these are measures of the effects of the organisation's existence. As with the exploration of particular personality traits manifested by individuals, there is nowadays a widespread expectation that investigation of a particular organisational outcome will lead into an appreciation of the dynamics of the whole organisation.

This conception of the organisation as an open system has been found by many writers to be a useful way of outlining and interrelating the phenomena of organisations in action. In following the same course it may first be of some value to refine the open system concept by specifying the dimensions along which open systems become organised, and by exploring briefly the characteristic sorts of problems that occur along each of these dimensions in the case of formal organisations. Living systems which manifest purposeful behaviour have, in order to maintain themselves successfully, to become integrated in the three dimensions of their depth (or 'vertical' dimension), their breadth (or lateral dimension), and the dimension of progression (Angyal: 1941). The depth dimension is that along which basic aims or purposes are formulated, and find expression in the activities carried out. The breadth dimension refers to the lateral co-ordination of the many contributory parts and processes that go into the effort to realise these basic purposes, and the dimension of progression refers to the co-ordination through time of the separate but interrelated paths of activity, or means-end chains.

1. The depth or 'vertical' dimension of an organisation is that along which the basic aims and values that define the organisation's *raison d'être* find expression in specific courses of action. This is exemplified in the formulation and adoption of policies, programmes, procedures, and practices that represent the basic values and strategic commitments of the organisation as a whole—the inducement of behaviours at the 'surface', in the day-to-day organisation functioning, that are compatible with, and serve to further basic values that are embodied in the organisation. The organisation grows or matures in this dimension by pushing forward in both directions—enriching and strengthening the depth in the debate of basic philosophy and ideals, and in exploring new and more effective courses of action for the expression of these roots. Stagnation on these fronts on the other hand stifles vitality and creativity and stunts organisational growth.

The sort of organisational problems that occur in trying to achieve integration along this dimension (that is, trying to ensure that what members of the organisation are actually doing day by day corresponds with the fundamental policies of the organisation) occur principally in the difficulties and resistances encountered in translating ideals into policies, and policies into workable programmes. The tendency of authority hierarchies to rigidify into caste-like stratification systems, and other barriers to adequate line or 'vertical' communication of this sort belong in this category. Selznick has expressed very well the meaning of good integration along this dimension:

'Beyond the definition of mission and role lies the task of building purpose into the social structure of the enterprise . . . of transforming a neutral body of men into a committed polity. In this way, policy attains depth. Rooted in and adapted to the daily experiences of living persons, policy is saved from attenuation and distortion as lines of communication are extended.'[10]

Failure on the other hand, is measured in the number of policies and stated intentions that do not find any expression in actions, and the extent to which actions that *are* carried out fail to represent basic axioms and are instead the product of conformity, ritualism or idiosyncrasy. The various 'dysfunctions' of bureaucracy to which Merton, Blau, Gouldner and others have drawn attention mainly have the character of disintegration along this dimension. Coming to regard rules as ends in themselves, reacting to close supervision by withdrawal of effort, sabotaging quality of output in order to maximise quantity—such behaviours represent breakdowns in the implementation of organisational goals.

2. The breadth or lateral dimension of an organisation refers to the span of the many and various types of activities that are manifested by them, and the problem of integration in this dimension is the problem of co-ordinating such disparate courses of action in the direction of mutual consistency and ensuring at the same time that they support the achievement of the aims of the whole. Living systems adapt by internal differentiation, which enables them to contend with wider degrees of variance in their environments, but a necessary concomitant of the process of internal differentiation is the process of integration whereby specialised functions remain closely co-ordinated. In the case of organisations, differentiation takes the form of the division of labour, which can proceed successfully only so long as the activities of specialised departments, units, and jobs can be co-ordinated with one another. In the words of Lawrence and Lorsch:

[10] Selznick, op. cit., p. 90.

'Any complex social system, which is the basic way we conceive of an organisation, is made up of differentiated parts, the activities of which must be integrated into a unified effort if the organisation is to cope effectively with its environment.'[11]

It is necessary not only to maintain the compatibility of many different programmes and courses of action through the organisation. A further requirement is that there be some effective setting and shifting mechanism whereby various different constellations of skills, machinery, information and so on, can be brought together when new problems have to be faced by the organisation.

The generic type of problem in this instance is that of horizontal communication and the capacity at supervisory and managerial levels for relating the rates of progress in the various discrete sectors of activity, such that key resources approach full utilisation without giving rise to serious lags or gains in the output of particular subsystems. Lateral co-ordination of this kind is achieved by various mechanisms of record keeping, meetings of unit and department heads, specialised liaison activities, joint committees, and so on, which Lawrence and Lorsch have called 'integrative devices'.

Breakdowns occur on this dimension when particular individuals or functional subunits become out of touch with and non-responsive to those around them. Such dissociation may have the effect of increasing the autonomy and survival capacity of the particular parts, but this happens at the expense of the adaptive potential of the whole. It is not an uncommon phenomena of organisational life that departments or individuals will fight vigorously in defence of roles that have been made obsolete by overall developments. Good integration consists in the appropriate matching of organisational capabilities with the present and potential demands of the environment and adequate mechanisms for producing new configurations of capabilities in response to changing circumstances.

3. Finally, in organisations the dimension of progression refers to the *temporal* spread of the many different courses of action going on at a particular time, that constitute an 'activated' division of labour. It draws attention to the continuity and consistency of organisational actions and the means whereby many different streams of activity are monitored through time to ensure that they remain consistent with basic aims and that they are likely to produce the outcomes desired.

[11] J. W. Lorsch and P. Lawrence, 'The Diagnosis of Organisational Problems' in J. M. Thomas and W. G. Bennis (eds), *Management of Change and Conflict* (Penguin, 1972), p. 275. See also P. Lawrence and J. W. Lorsch, *Organisation and Environment* (Harvard Business School, 1967).

Continuity of this sort in the processes that contribute for example, to the weaving of cloth, the graduation of students, the production of motor cars, is accomplished by the programming of work flows, the co-ordinating functions of supervisors and managers, formal job specifications and operating rules, by some measures of value-sharing, and increasingly, by formal organisational planning. The increasing complexity and lengthening time spans of organisational actions in every sphere has lead to greater reliance upon planning in general, and much greater use of specialised techniques of programmed budgeting, production scheduling, market research, research and development, and so on.

Breakdowns of integration on this dimension are manifest in the blocking or diversion of progress in certain of the means-end paths of which the overall organisational effort is constituted. The progress of one class in a school may be held up by lack of a teacher; a section producing one component of a manufactured product may fail to produce sufficient good quality parts; a department of a large administrative organisation may lose sight of the original goals and come to define and serve goals of its own. The result in each case is a segmentation of the organisation's capabilities and decreasing overall effectiveness.

We may use these categories to describe the way in which, for example, an army combat unit is held together. Basic induction training and subsequent socialisation has the effect of instilling into the combat soldier certain values and beliefs concerning the purposes of the enterprise he belongs to and enabling him to choose appropriate courses of action almost spontaneously under certain conditions (depth dimension). Any specific action that his unit is engaged in entails the formulation of strategy and tactics to guide the unit's actions, including the design of contingency plans to accommodate alternative possible responses of the enemy. Shared understanding and acting out of such plans contributes to integration in the dimension of progression. Finally, there is continuous need for co-ordination among the specialised parts of such a unit, so that the various capabilities for machine gun or mortar fire, reconnaisance or signalling, and so on, can be effectively managed (lateral dimension).

Organisations of every sort are required in some way to attend to the problems of translating aims into actions (depth), guiding different courses of action towards the overall goal (progression), and managing the lateral co-ordination of organisational subunits (breadth). Because these dimensions are but facets of a complex, dynamic whole, it is to be expected that a breakdown of integration in any particular dimension will tend to impair, or at least place extra demands upon integration in the other dimensions.

(e) ORGANISATIONS IN ACTION

We come to the view therefore that an organisational culture is a dynamic, complex system, characterised by constant adjustments in its internal relations, changing relations with elements in the environment, and increasingly required to adapt to changes taking place in the relations among the elements of the environment themselves. This complexity is such that inquirers have been able to apprehend such systems from a number of quite different perspectives; each contributing a unique emphasis. The sociologist undoubtedly benefits if he is able to appreciate the perspective of information- and decision-theorists, of psychologists and anthropologists, economists and political scientists and so on, but his particular contribution has to do with understanding the organisation as a purposeful social system, and being able to interpret the activities of organisations and the relations between organisations and their human parts, at the level of social reality.

Here, we will briefly explore organisational life from four different starting points: organisational structure, the technology or technical means, the individual in the organisation, and organisational regulation or control—each of which represents a major dimension in any attempt to understand the organisation as a whole. In discussing these four dimensions and exploring the relationships amongst them, we hope to be able to chart the most important problems and issues in organisational functioning and show their relationships to one another.

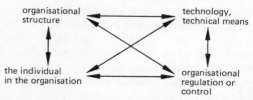

Fig. 5.1. FRAMEWORK FOR A SOCIOLOGICAL APPROACH TO
ORGANISATIONAL FUNCTIONING

(i) *Organisational structure*

Structure is a central concept in the analysis of all types of social systems, and the discussion of organisational structures allows us to draw attention again to the continuities of social action across the boundaries of such entities, as family, community, and organisation, which have been identified as the figural elements within the social field. Analysis of the social structure of *societies* is the special province of students of social stratification, who investigate in particular the distribution and configurations of power, economic class, and status. Distinctions have thus been made between primitive, feudal, industrial and post-industrial societies, between capitalist and communist developed and underdeveloped societies. The investigation of *family* structures on the other hand has required the finer tools of psychology and social psychology in identifying patterns of sexual, affective, and authority relationships that together with economic and legal criteria go into such distinctions as those between extended and nuclear, matri- and patri-focal, matri- and patri-linear families. Our knowledge of the structure of *communities* finally, probably owes most to the contributions of political scientists and social ecologists.

As we have suggested earlier, in the case of organisations, purposefulness exercises the critical determinative influence over their forms and functions, and we find consequently that organisational structures are analysed primarily in terms of work-flow and the division and co-ordination of tasks, patterns of communication, and the distribution of authority. While this is an appropriate emphasis, accurately reflecting the differences between organisations and the other kinds of social systems, the discussion of organisational structures has too often ignored altogether some of the other ingredients of social structure, in concentrating on the criteria or principles of structuring relevant to increasing the 'rationality' and efficiency of organisational performance. It ought to be more readily acknowledged by social scientists that passions and power struggles, elitism and discrimination, wealth and status also have consequences for organisational structures however 'irrational' or unconstitutional such influences may be in terms of the formal system. In fact it has been increasingly forced upon the attention of social scientists that organisations are seldom as rationally structured as textbooks on management and administration have assumed, and that the pursuit of optimally efficient structure is a chimerical goal, as likely to lead to serious dysfunctioning as to higher efficiency.

Social structures are not directly observable but have to be inferred from the observation of other phenomena, in particular patterns of interaction. Because of the limited capacity of our minds to come to terms with images of complex dynamic phenomena, we tend to think of structure two-dimensionally as the morphology or 'shape' of an entity, and use metaphors such as the pyramid, the wheel, and the network. Those simple, static conceptions of the structure of something as complex as an organisation have some usefulness, but must not be allowed to obscure the fact that structure in this sense is always an abstraction—a static aspect of a continuous process. Social structure arises out of the regularity of the interactions within a given social aggregate and the reciprocity or closure of these interactions. Without interactions amongst people, or when interactions are entirely random or capricious, there is no structure.

In most kinds of organisations the interactions that take place amongst people arise from their collaborative efforts to produce certain outcomes. They become members of the same social system not by reason of an instinctive predisposition such as the mating urge or because of spontaneous good feelings between one another, but as a consequence of contributing a particular skill or unit of labour-power towards the accomplishment of an organisational end. In other words members are first related through a division of labour, whereby the function of the whole system is differentiated into subtasks and those integrated into a working organisation. These are the relationships that are specified on formal organisation charts or 'blueprints' of the organisation, and that are traditionally thought of as constituting the 'formal' structure.

Because man does not cease to be a social animal when he belongs to an organisation, but continues to need and to seek social support, self-esteem, a favourable position in the patterns of power and status, and so on, he enters and experiences all sorts of other relationships which are only incidental, or even irrelevant, to the performance of organisational tasks. This residue of organisational relationships that are not task-orientated has traditionally been referred to as the informal structure. As we shall discuss below, this conceptual duality of formal and informal structure has increasingly been abandoned in favour of the view that *all* behaviours and relationships that provide for the integration of the individual into the social system are of intrinsic importance as a precondition for successful organisational performance, and the 'informal system' cannot realistically be separated out from the more obviously task-related behaviours.

A small shop or a garage, having just a few staff, usually operates successfully as a simple unstructured unit, the boss or owner working alongside his staff except while performing the essential administrative tasks. The evolution towards structural complexity that inevitably accompanies the expansion of such enterprises has two basic dimensions—hierarchy and differentiation. As the breadth of a simple unit's concerns are extended by increasing output, the incorporation of new functions, the acquisition of new premises or new technology, it differentiates into subunits assuming responsibility for parts of the total organisational task. In so far as the activities of such subunits have to be co-ordinated, some higher-level units become necessary to carry out such co-ordination. We may focus on the character and consequences of structural differentiation by considering the specific contributions of two social scientists to this problem.

(ii) *Territory, technology, and time*

The principles of differentiation of operating units within complex production systems have been explored in some detail by E. J. Miller, who asserts that,

> '. . . there are three possible bases for clustering of role relationships and thus for the internal differentiation of a production system. These are technology, territory, and time. Whenever forces towards differentiation operate upon a simple production system, it is one or more of these dimensions that will form the boundaries of the emergent subsystems and will provide the basis for internal solidarity of the groups associated with them.'[12]

While a particular organisational structure is partly the outcome of historical developments and reactions to the changing environment, it is also invariably influenced by the internal structure of the tasks performed. Tasks are differentiated according to 'the material means, techniques and skills required to perform them' (i.e. technology), and their location in the temporal and geographic spreads of organisational activities. In the structural differentiation of the whole enterprise, different principles of differentiation may be used at different levels, while they may also reinforce or cross-cut one another on the same level. Thus for example a workshop producing a single auto part may expand by the setting up of two further workshops and the introduction of three-shift working. In co-ordinating the nine 'workshop shifts' resulting from this, management can choose between having a foreman responsible for the total production of each workshop (first-order differentiation by territory, second-order differentiation by time), or putting a foreman in charge of each shift (first-order differentiation by time, second-order differentiation by territory). When heterogeneity in technology is introduced, the number of possible alternatives for structuring begins to get quite large.

Differentiation by *technology* includes the separation of procurement, conversion, and disposal systems (purchasing, manufacturing, and sales

12 E. J. Miller, 'Territory, Technology and Time. The Internal Differentiation of Complex Production Systems', *Human Relations* (1966), 13, p. 246.

in the case of an industrial enterprise), and the differentiation of phrases in the conversion process. One of the conditions encouraging technological differentiation is the occurrence of such a degree of technical heterogeneity that specialists manning various parts of the process can no longer encompass each other's skills, or interchange rules. The development of 'distinctive competence' typically enhances the distinctions among operating units which are based on specialised skills and equipment, and it is rare to find subunits differentiated by technology alone. In industry it is most common to find territorial separations coinciding with technological ones.

Differentiation by *territory* refers simply to the geography of task performance. An enterprise may be differentiated simply by territory, when for instance it is constituted of a number of factories, geographically dispersed, making the same product. More typically it coincides with technological boundaries such as those around successive phases of manufacturing operations or around different product lines. When differentiation is *primarily* by territory however, this is usually because subunit activities are specific to particular areas, as in the case of sales organisation and the location of canning factories close to sources of supply.

Miller suggests that forces towards differentiation by *time* arise when the requirements of task performance are such that the length of the working day or working week of the group is longer than the working period of any individual member. The level at which it is appropriate to differentiate structures by time is a function of the time it takes from commencement to completion of the process—the 'throughput time'—mainly because the head of a shift cannot be held fully accountable for his shift's performance if the relevant operation exceeds the duration of the shift. He contrasts a composite spinning and weaving mill, in which it takes three weeks to transform raw cotton to woven cloth, with a power station, in which coal is transformed to steam, and steam to electricity almost instantaneously. In such cases:

'Short throughput time calls for a high level of differentiation along the time dimension because any disturbance in a part of the system has almost immediate repercussions in the rest of it, and swift corrective action is therefore required.'[13]

Miller's article offers many insights into the ways in which the activities of complex organisations may be subdivided and reintegrated, but is less specifically concerned with the structural dimension of hierarchy. Hierarchy is intrinsic to the problem of organisational regu-

[13] ibid., p. 256.

lation, discussed below, but we can usefully consider here some insights into this 'vertical' dimension that have been put forward by Parsons.

(iii) *Institutional, managerial and technical levels*

The traditional and still popular conception of the organisation sees it as a pyramid in which relations of authority and subordination extend from the apex to the base with unbroken transitivity. This is certainly implied in Weber's ideal type conception of bureaucracy. Parsons suggests that in fact one typically finds *qualitative breaks* in line structures, which make it possible to distinguish three distinct organisational levels: the technical, the managerial, and the institutional.

1. The technical system is that which is responsible for the main work of the organisation: the production of goods, teaching of classes, processing of tax returns, and so on. A major distinction is made between the processing of people and the processing of objects, but in each case the technical system has the function that it contributes more or less directly to the needs of the consuming unit (e.g. customers, clients, patients). Technology is one of the major constraints upon the functioning of this level:

'The primary exigencies to which this suborganisation is orientated are those imposed by the nature of the technical task, such as the "materials"—physical, cultural, or human—which must be processed, the kinds of co-operation of different people required to get the job done effectively.'[14]

2. As Miller too discusses, there comes a point in the division of labour at which the performance of co-ordinating functions demands creation of a separate subsystem. The teaching of classes comes to depend upon the determination of curricula and allocation of classrooms and teachers; the administration of taxes presupposes an authority that determines who is to be taxed and the rate of taxation. These are functions of the managerial system. In general it is responsible for administering the internal affairs of the organisation, for procuring the products required by the technical system, and for mediating between the technical system and the users or beneficiaries of its products. While the personnel of the technical system are predominantly operatives (blue-collar and white-collar), foremen and supervisors, at this level they are manager, administrators, and executives. In contrast to the technical system, the managerial level contributes to the 'generalised capacity of the society to perform that category of action'—the pro-

[14] T. Parsons, *Structure and Process in Modern Societies* (Free Press, 1960), p. 60.

duction enterprise for example, produces wealth as well as commodities.

3. However, the procurement of necessary resources and disposal of products and services to other agencies does not exhaust the critical external foci of the organisation. A formal organisation performs functions somehow important to society as a whole and needs to be related to the wider social system that is the source of 'meaning', legitimation, and power which makes implementation of the organisation's goals feasible. This is the function of the institutional level: 'As a technical organisation . . . is controlled and "serviced" by a managerial organisation, so, in turn, is the managerial organisation controlled by the "institutional" structure and agencies of the community.'[15] This institutional level is represented for example by boards of governors of schools, boards of directors of companies, political and governmental bodies.

According to Parsons, the institutional system mediates between the managerial and technical organisations, and the higher order community interests which on some level the organisation is supposed to serve. Its special function is to contribute to the integration of the higher order system within which the generalised capacity of the managerial level is placed. Its procurement problems tend to be the attraction of finance for investments and the negotiation of power and legitimacy within the wider social field. For such purposes the bulk of the personnel at this level are typically drawn from the community and other institutional spheres, and are not necessarily expected to be professionally qualified in the sphere of activity in which the organisation is engaged.

The managerial and technical levels are the larger and more complex, typically having a number of separate levels within them, and they have been more studied than the institutional level. The discontinuities between them are of course relative, the higher level typically possessing veto power that can be used to settle disputes between them. Executives must take the advice of the technical heads on specialised matters, but the technical experts operate within guidelines framed by the managerial system. Differences between the levels are frequently emphasised by the use of separate recruitment channels and patterns of institutionalisation. In the latter regard unionisation and the professionalisation of management have had decisive effects. The lower levels are not simply 'lower-order spellings-out' of the levels above, because their articulation depends on a two-way interaction whereby adjacent levels are able to interfere with the functioning of the other and the organisation as a whole.

[15] ibid., p. 64.

The frameworks employed by Miller and Parsons together provide a way of interpreting the structural differentiation of organisations. The concept of organisational structure will be further developed in considering now the ways in which structure interacts with technology, with prevailing assumptions about man and his motivation, and with modes of organisational control.

(iv) Technology and structure

The pervasiveness of organisations and the results of their activities, the tendencies towards greater size, efficiency, and often, impersonality, are intimately related to progress in science and its applications in technology. If we use the term 'technology' to refer to the techniques and human and material resources that are used by organisations in transforming the objects or people that constitute their inputs, it is clear that it is not simply the accomplishments or industrial organisations that are dependent upon and shaped by existing technology.

It is equally the case that the performance of administrative, therapeutic, and educational tasks, as exemplified for example in government bureaux, hospitals, and schools is to an extent determined by the technologies available in these fields. The structure and the functioning of the administrative bureaucracy reflects the presently available technical means of communication and calculation (telephone, telex, typewriter, duplicator, Xerox, calculator, computer, etc.) just as the structures and performances of enterprises producing cars or cloth are ultimately dependent upon the given technologies in textiles and mechanical engineering. Equally the changing technology of education, in the development of programmed learning, closed circuit television, language laboratories and so on, alters the possibilities for the structure of schools.

Galbraith defines technology even more generally as: 'the systematic application of scientific or other organised knowledge to practical tasks', and continues with the observation that 'its most important consequence, at least for purposes of economics, is in forcing the division and subdivision of any such task into its component parts'.[16] The increasing sophistication of available technology has he says a number of important consequences: (a) an increasing span of time separates the beginning from the completion of any task; (b) increasing amounts of capital are committed to the enterprise; (c) the commitment of time and money tends to be made even more inflexibly to the performance of a particular task; (d) enterprises require more and more specialised manpower; advanced technology requires massive and complex organisa-

[16] J. K. Galbraith, The New Industrial State (Hamish Hamilton, 1967), p. 12.

tions; (e) due to the time and capital that must be committed, the inflexibility of this commitment, and the needs of large organisations, it becomes more and more essential to engage in planning. The more sophisticated the technology, the greater in general will be each of these requirements.

A great many writers about organisations have given particular attention to the way in which organisational structures are influenced by the type of technology that the organisation makes use of. We discuss elsewhere distinctions that have been made between types of technology, in particular those suggested by Woodward (small batch and unit, large batch and mass, and process production), Blauner (craft, machine-minding, assembly-line, and continuous process technology), and Thompson (long-linked, mediating, and intensive technology). While there is little dispute about the fact that, as Blauner observes, the historical progression from craft towards process technology has resulted in greater and greater structural complexity of organisations, the extent to which technology determines structure has been disputed by organisation theorists for some years.

The survey of more than 200 Essex manufacturing firms first reported by Woodward in 1958 tended to support the view of those who maintained that technology exerted a determining influence.

> 'When the firms were grouped according to similarity of objectives and techniques of production, and classified in order of the technical complexity of their production systems, each production system was found to be associated with a characteristic pattern of organisation.'[17]

Ranking these firms and placing them into groups according to the extent to which their production processes were controllable and its results predictable (technical complexity) produced the three types referred to above. A positive linear relation was found between technical complexity and the number of levels of management (i.e. length of line of command), the span of control of the chief executive, and the ratio of managers and supervisors to non-supervisory staff. A negative relation was found when increasing technical complexity was correlated with the span of control of middle management. These findings lead to the following sort of conclusion:

> 'The small spans of control and the long lines of command characteristic of process industry meant that in this type of industry management structure could be represented by a long and narrowly based

17 J. Woodward, *Management and Technology* (HMSO, 1958), p. 4.

pyramid. In unit production the pyramid was short and broadly based.'[18]

The proposition that the technological system selected by an organisation to make possible the performance of its primary task exercises a determinative influence over the social structure of the enterprise leaves unanswered the question as to whether the resulting system of organisation as a whole is as effective as it might be. The testing of Weber's ideal type construct of bureaucracy by Blau, Merton, Gouldner and others, and studies of mass production and assembly-line organisations seem to suggest that even when the organisation to perform a particular function is optimally designed according to criteria of technical and economic rationality, the socio-psychological consequences for employees may be such as to bring into question the appropriateness of the organisation.[19]

The work of Trist and his colleagues at the Tavistock Institute has been of fundamental significance in demonstrating that there is no simple one-to-one relation between the requirements of the technical system and the structure of the social system, and that there is on the other hand considerable scope for choice in the design of a social system to operate a particular technology.

In a series of coal-mining studies it was shown that two very different forms of organisation could operate economically within the same seam and with identical technology. The conventional longwall system combined a complex formal structure with simple work roles, while the composite system combined a simple formal structure with complex work roles. The question that has to be asked in choosing between alternative work organisations is whether the benefits of structuring work according to criteria of technical and economic rationality are undermined by the social and psychological consequences for employees.[20] Schein comments as follows on the socio-technical system concept:

'The idea of a socio-technical system . . . implies that any productive organisation or part thereof is a combination of technology (task requirements, physical layout, equipment available) and a social

[18] J. Woodward, *Industrial Organization: Theory and Practice* (OUP, 1965), p. 53.

[19] P. M. Blau, *The Dynamics of Bureaucracy* (University of Chicago Press, 1955); R. K. Merton, 'Bureaucratic Structure and Personality', Ch. 6, *Social Theory and Social Structure* (Free Press, 1957); A. W. Gouldner, *Patterns of Industrial Bureaucracy* (Free Press, 1954).

[20] E. L. Trist, G. Higgin, H. Murray and A. Pollock, *Organisational Choice* (Tavistock, 1963).

system (a system of relationships among those who must perform the job). The technology and the social system are in mutual interaction with each other and each determines the other. In keeping with this concept, it would make just as little sense to say that the nature of the work will *determine* the nature of the organisation which develops among workers as it would to say that the sociopsychological characteristics of the workers will *determine* the manner in which a given job will be performed.'[21]

The Tavistock work has been important in demonstrating that the technical systems used by enterprises invariably offer *some* choice in the structure of work relationships, and that the resulting social system are just as 'objective' and as important in determing effectiveness as the structure of the technical system itself.

(v) *Individuals in organisations*

Once it has acquired the technical means essential to the carrying out of its mission, the most basic requirement of the organisation is that it engages individuals to perform those tasks which are dictated by the technological requirements. To become activated, to produce results, the technical system has to be manned. At the simplest level, tasks and persons have to be so matched that the demands made upon the individual fall within the range of what is physically possible in terms of such characteristics as his strength, intelligence, stature, sensory capabilities, and so on. It is no longer acceptable however, as it may have been in slave-manned enterprises such as the construction of fortifications and the propulsion of galley boats, to match men and tasks solely in terms of their physical capabilities, so that they become expendable tools as long as further manpower is available. The direction of development of dominant values concerning the worth of the life of the individual in society, has made it increasingly necessary for men and tasks to be interrelated in ways that take account of the psychological characteristics and requirements of the individual, in addition to satisfying the technical requirements of the organisation.

It is the case therefore that what an organisation can accomplish and the manner in which its work can be done is limited not only by the currently available technology, but also by the nature of the human beings that are available to man this technology. That this is self-evident to us now should not obscure the fact that it was not always so, and that the relative importance given to satisfying the needs of these human elements has been steadily increasing.

21 E. H. Schein, op. cit., p. 107.

Assumptions about human beings The individual member is an important link between organisational space and the environing social field, being able by virtue of the occupancy of roles in each realm to convey meanings, experiences, and skills acquired in one, to the other. The integral human is only partially included in the organisation, his life-space typically encompassing his involvement in other spheres such as family, community, leisure, and so on. While the manning of the organisation is usually discussed from the point of view of the organisation as the agent, and consideration given to the problems of selecting, socialising and motivating individuals who have decided or been compelled to belong to it, it is as well to give explicit recognition to the fact that an organisational role is a unit in a career, the unfolding of an individual life, as much as it is a unit in an organisation, and to consider the individual-organisation relation from the individual's point of view as well.

The difficulties faced by the organisation as a recruiter are mitigated in industrial societies by what Thompson has called the 'homogenising influences of culture'—the tendency within such societies to socialise all individuals in the direction of certain dominant standards, beliefs, values, and expectations. The requirements of production enterprises have powerfully influenced the socialising effects of home, school, and media in such matters as ways of perceiving and categorising reality, beliefs about cause-effect relationships, definitions of legitimacy and attitudes towards authority, orientations towards times, conceptions of the worthwhile life and methods of assessing success.[22] The provision to all members of society of a minimal level of skills in use of the native tongue and mathematical calculation by means of compulsory universal education is but the basic platform of this 'homogenisation'.

In spite of such tendencies however, it is still the case that one of the only characteristics of organisation man that writers agree on is his complexity. Throughout this century differing sets of assumptions about individual needs and motivations have been fashionable and have influenced, often in very subtle ways, the design of organisations, and philosophies of management.

The 'scientific management' school inspired by Frederick Taylor, which was the dominating influence of the early decades, founded its recommendations to managers on a concept of man as a rational-economic animal, guided in his actions by a pleasure-pain calculus that would lead him to exert effort in proportion to the rewards offered and sanctions applied. His feelings were irrational, and his activities had to be carefully circumscribed and controlled to ensure that they would

[22] J. D. Thompson, *Organisations in Action* (McGraw-Hill, 1967), p. 102.

not interfere with the effective performance of organisational tasks.[23]

The famous Hawthorne Studies, conducted by Elton Mayo and others, propounded a new conception of organisation man as a social animal, motivated essentially by social needs for friendship and recognition, and responsive primarily to the social forces of the peer group rather than the economic incentives and controls of management. Mayo's pioneering work influenced a generation of further studies of the importance of social relationships in the work place that are now subsumed under the rubric of the Human Relations Movement. Employees were no longer to be regarded as appendages to machinery, and managers were exhorted to treat their subordinates as 'whole men', engendering satisfactions for them by showing an interest in their personal accomplishments and welfare. The objective was to make the organisational member feel a useful and important part of the overall effort.[24]

While the 'scientific management' school, economic theorists of the firm, and traditional management theory, have all tended to operate with a mechanistic conception of the organisation and to treat the individual participant as an automaton, or a perfectly rational creature, responding to economic incentives and to formal rules in a calculating and therefore predictable way, in some respects the revelations of Hawthorne induced an over-reaction from this simplistic or rationalistic point of view. The human relations school made a fetish of the importance of the work group in propounding the argument that human behaviour is to be understood predominantly in terms of sentiments, motivations, and personal values, which typically arise within and find expression through the informal group.

Each side has tended to neglect if not to ignore the other. The rationalistic theories on the one hand, inclined to treat the factor of labour as 'given', advocated the pursuit of maximum efficiency through controlling the physical environment, designing the perfect organisation structure, and by searching for the 'one best way' in making decisions. Managerial philosophies leaning on these assumptions espoused the belief that co-ordination, conformity to orders, and the will to produce, could be brought about by the multiplication of formal regulations and the use of financial incentives. The human relations approach relegated the formal structure to the status of an external variable in the informal system, and has consequently neglected the problems of

[23] F. W. Taylor, *Scientific Management* (Harper & Row, 1947).
[24] F. J. Roethlisberger and W. J. Dickson, *Management and the Worker* (Harvard University Press, 1939). See also H. A. Landsberger, *Hawthorne Revisited* (Cornell University Press, 1958).

planning and co-ordination, and the purposive, goal-orientated activities which are characteristically the *raison d'être* of the organisation. Managerial philosophies issuing from this background have proclaimed the importance of permissive supervision, of group rather than individual incentives, and of employee participation in decision-making as the necessary conditions for the attainment of efficiency. While the classic rationalists considered the participants as cogs in the organisational machine, the human relations approach made it possible to consider the members also as creatures of feeling.

Two further models of man have sought to overcome the limitations of these conceptions. The first has been advanced mainly by psychologists interested in the effects of organisations upon individuals, and has been called by Schein 'self-actualising man'.[25] In contrast to the assumptions made by the Human Relations School concerning people's values and abilities, this conception of organisation man focuses attention on all organisation members as reservoirs of untapped resources, of physical skills and energy, of creative ability and capacity for responsible, self-directed, self-controlled behaviour. The most influential contributors to this perspective have been writers such as Maslow, McGregor, Argyris, and Likert, and we may think of them as belonging to the 'Human Resources' Movement.[26]

In Maslow's influential interpretation of human motivation, self-actualisation represents a higher-order need of the individual to be his 'self', and to strengthen and amplify this self by developing new and more adequate channels for its expression. This need is assumed to become particularly salient when more fundamental needs for food, warmth and shelter, for physical and emotional safety and security, for belongingness and love, and for esteem have been adequately met.[27]

Like the social man model it espouses the goal of membership participation in organisational affairs, but for rather different reasons. In the human relations model, the manager is exhorted to share information, discuss departmental decisions, to encourage self-direction and self-control in order to improve subordinate satisfaction and morale. Improved satisfaction is regarded as an intervening variable ultimately responsible for improved performances. The human resources model on the other hand proposes the more open and democratic style of

[25] E. H. Schein, op. cit., p. 65.
[26] A. Maslow, *Motivation and Personality* (Harper & Row, 1954); D. McGregor, *The Human Side of the Enterprise* (McGraw-Hill, 1960); C. Argyris, *Personality and Organisation* (Harper & Row, 1957); R. Likert, *New Patterns of Management* (McGraw-Hill, 1961).
[27] Maslow, op. cit.

management as a *direct* means to the improvement of decision-making and overall efficiency.[28]

There is finally a newly emerging model of man, variously designated as 'complex' or 'neo-rational' man which is characterised in particular by its insistence that organisational members are implicated in a complex and dynamic socio-political system in which human and social satisfactions, and the performance of organisational purposes have to be achieved in the context of a system of power relationships, which are a distinct dimension of the socio-technical system itself. It may be that this emphasis is most usefully considered as complementary to, rather than as an alternative for, the human resources model.

The importance of power relationships in understanding organisational life and the behavioural accommodations of individual members to them has been emphasised by Michael Crozier in his analysis of interindividual and intergroup relations in a large clerical agency and the French Government's tobacco industry. Crozier, without disputing the significance of the conceptual distinction between the 'rational' and the 'social', the formal and the informal aspects of the organisational structure, proposes that the really important matter is to go beyond this 'lip-service integration' and to attempt to discover how each set of determinants establishes the limits of the other sets' possibilities of application. For him, the theoretical nurturing of the hybrid 'socio-political man' is the essential part of the neo-rationalist orientation, because it provides a model of man which allows action to issue from sentiments as well as from formal commands, and which can accommodate the enduring features of both 'rational-economic' and 'social' man, without giving primacy to either. In a remark of epigrammatic quality, Crozier transcends the traditionalists: 'A human being does not only have a hand and a heart. He also has a head, which means that he is free to decide and to play his own game.'[29]

(vi) *Organisational roles and structural principles*

The effective co-operation of large numbers of individuals in the rational accomplishment of specified ends is dependent upon some means for specifying the nature of the contributions that particular individuals or groups of individuals are required to provide, and subsequently, some means for continuously ensuring that these specified contributions are made. We are concerned at the moment with the first requirement. In the vernacular the terms 'job', 'occupation', and 'profession' designate

[28] See R. E. Miles, 'Human Relations or Human Resources', *Harvard Business Review* (1965), 43, 4, pp. 148–54.

[29] M. Crozier, *The Bureaucratic Phenomenon* (Tavistock, 1964), p. 149.

clusterings of knowledge and skills by means of which individual contributions or organisational ends are specified. They refer to the way in which the world of work as distinct from the world of leisure, is channelled to individuals, with 'jobs' being the domain of blue-collar, and 'occupations' and 'professions' the domain of white-collar workers. Sociologists have in many instances taken over these terms, but in general it has been found more useful to employ the concept of role, which is both more general and of greater theoretical significance.

The concept of role may be regarded as a point of theoretical articulation between psychology and sociology—a socio-psychological construct by means of which the interdependence of the individual and society may be explored. In the context of the study of organisations, role designates the performance that is required by the organisation of the occupant of a particular position within it. An organisational role designates the tasks, duties and responsibilities that are expected of the occupants of particular positions, and usually includes some specification of relations with the product, the technology, and other roles that are entailed. (This formulation if the role concept has been designated as prescribed role, and distinguished from subjective and enacted role, which refer respectively to behaviour thought appropriate by the actor, and what the actor actually does, in occupying a particular social position.) The organisational prescription of roles is at the same time the means of subdividing the total task of the organisation (the division of labour) and the means for reducing the variety of individual's behaviour.

Roles are ubiquitous in social life. In even the least structured of situations people respond to one another in terms of expectations associated with sex and age roles, and the collective definitions of kinship roles such as son or wife. Organisational roles are characterised by a much higher degree of specificity, and by the fact that they are usually formally or legally established in documents that can be used in the case of conflicts or disagreements in judgements concerning whether, or to what extent, an individual has met the requirements of the role that he occupies. The degree of specificity with which particular roles are, or can be defined, is naturally subject to considerable variation, but is in general inversely related to the status and responsibility that adhere to the performance of particular functions. The school-teacher has a wider area of discretion in the carrying out of his duties than the assembly-line worker, or practically any shop-floor worker, but his role is typically defined to him in more detail than that of the university lecturer or a company director.

As we have indicated, a role in an organisation carries with it not only responsibility for the performance of a particular function, but also certain expected ways of behaving towards other members of the organisation and non-members that the incumbent may come in contact with as an organisational member. His formal role relates the individual to other individuals with regard to the carrying out of tasks by defining his position in the system of work relationships, and also relates him to others in terms of the structure of command by specifying those to whom he is accountable and those over whom he has responsibility. One way of conceptualising the relations between the individual member and the organisation therefore is to view the latter as a role system of which each constituent role is occupied by a particular individual. In fact things are seldom so simple. Some roles may be unoccupied, and some individuals may occupy more than one role. It is important to appreciate also the existence of informal roles that come into being alongside the formal system.[30]

The decomposition of the aims of the organisation as a whole into large numbers of relatively specialised tasks and sub-processes has the effect of making more likely continuity, reliability and predictability of performance by reducing dependence upon particular individuals or rare skills. The costs of this increasing functional specialisation are located in part in the need to amplify communication and co-ordination systems, but also in the reduced possibilities for members of acting autonomously, taking responsibility, self-expression, changing tasks, and so on. Costs of the latter sort have to be measured in the less tangible terms of job satisfaction, commitment, morale, etc., and they have not been so readily taken into account.[31]

The life-spaces of organisation members are conditioned in particular by the degree of role specificity that operates, defining their 'zone of free movement' or area of discretion. We are accustomed to the view that members of senior echelons customarily enjoy a much greater variability in the tasks confronting them and much greater freedom to develop initiatives. It is also the case nowadays that they tend to spend much greater amounts of their time on organisational tasks than do lower echelons. Members of those technical or operative grades typically have roles which are far more circumscribed allowing less opportunity for self-direction and self-expression. It is as though we have thought it appropriate for managers, executives, directors and so on to be able to satisfy their need for self-actualisation but have found it more convenient to persevere with the economic man or social man images in relation to rank and file members.

[30] See for example the various change agent roles identified by Donald Schon, *Beyond the Stable State* (Templeton Smith, 1971), p. 58.
[31] See Merton, op. cit.

Emery has suggested that in seeking accommodation between the properties of individuals and the requirements of organisations we are confronted with a choice between two basic 'design principles'. Complex adaptive systems of every kind—computers, ant and bee colonies, and formal organisations, need to have built into them some redundant (or 'spare') capacities in order to be able to respond appropriately to the variable demands from their environments.

'The redundancy may be achieved by having redundant parts but then there must be a special control mechanism (specialised parts) that determine which parts are active or redundant for any particular adaptive response. If the control is to be reliable it must also have redundant parts and the question of a further control emerges. In this type of system, reliability is bought at the cost of providing or maintaining the redundant parts, hence the tendency is towards continual reduction of the functions and hence cost of the individual part. The social system of an ant colony relies more upon this principle than does a human system, and a computer more than does an ant colony. The alternative principle is to increase the redundancy of functions of the individual parts. This does not entail a pressure towards higher and higher orders of special control mechanisms, but it does entail effective mechanisms within the part for setting and resetting its functions—for human beings, shared values are the most significant of these self-regulatory devices. Installing these values of course increases the costs of the parts.'[32]

Organisations operating relatively simple technologies in stable environments are more likely to be structured in terms of the redundancy of parts, pushing the level of skills required down to the lowest possible level. Gains thus achieved in the substitutability of labour and the relative simplicity of structures of control tend to be offset by the alienative involvement of individuals deprived of discretion and variety in their tasks. As Burns and Stalker have shown, organisations operating complex technologies, in uncertain environments experience pressures to structure themselves more in terms of redundancy of functions, coming to depend more on individuals who have multiple skills who can be shifted amongst various production tasks. Burns and Stalker characterised the management systems of such organisations as 'organic' in contrast to the 'mechanic' systems of the former type of organisation.[33]

[32] F. E. Emery, 'The Next Thirty Years. Concepts, Methods and Anticipations', *Human Relations* (1967), 20, 3, p. 230.
[33] T. Burns and G. M. Stalker, *The Management of Innovation* (Tavistock, 1961).

(vii) *Organisational regulation and human purposefulness*

The distinctiveness or individuality of an organisation—the organisational culture—arises from the exercise of choice by organisational members, especially those in senior positions. Choices are generally available in the use of technology, in the organisational structure, the definition and allocation of roles, and so forth. Individuality is developed in the day-to-day interpretation and operation of structure and policy. We have tried to sketch some of the alternatives that are available with regard to the character and interrelations of technology, structure, and role systems, recognising the high degree of interdependence amongst feasible alternatives in each domain.

We must now acknowledge that choice may also be exercised over the way in which organisational activities are controlled or regulated, and that, furthermore, there are reasons for believing that choices made in this area are becoming more strategic and contributing more to organisational character formation that has historically been the case. Growing awareness of the need to subordinate once more our technological means to societal needs and values, to weigh 'growthmania' against the nascent 'survival' ideology which equates progress with stability and more equitable distribution rather than simply growth, and changing conceptions of the relative importance of individual and organisational goals, are indicative of cultural shifts which have important implications for the way in which control may be exercised.[34]

As we have seen, conceptualising organisations as open systems existing in changing environments has made possible the identification of two rather different regulatory functions. One is the control of the 'boundary conditions' affecting the organisation and the management of organisation-environment relations. This, we suggested in the previous chapter, is the function of the institutional leader or dominant coalition. The other is the internal regulation, management, or control of the system itself, and this is our present concern. Leaders of course need to be sensitive to the changing internal conditions of the organisation as a whole to be able to relate it effectively to its environment, but internal regulation is not their primary function. Parson's distinction between institutional and managerial systems seems to have implications of this sort.

This subject matter is perhaps most commonly referred to as organisational *control*. Tannenbaum, in a book devoted to this topic, describes it as follows:

[34] On 'growthmania' see E. J. Mishan, *The Costs of Economic Growth* (Penguin, 1969). On individual-organisational interrelations see C. Argyris, *Integrating the Individual and the Organisation* (Wiley, 1964).

'Characterising an organisation in terms of its pattern of control is to describe an essential and universal aspect of organisation which every member must face and to which he must adjust. Organisation implies control. A social organisation is an ordered arrangement of individual human interactions. . . . It is the function of control to bring about conformance to organisational requirements and achievement of the ultimate purposes of the organisation.'[35]

A recent article identifies five distinct types of control in organisation and examines why organisations use the kind of controls they do, and the conditions under which they are effective. Distinctions are made between *structural controls* (conditions surrounding appointment, dismissal, promotions, etc.) *rewards and sanctions* (coercive, utilitarian, or normative), *institutional control* (control over movements, activity, possessions, privacy, free time), *control by orientation* (processes of induction, assimilation, resocialisation, to direct and maintain attitudes and aspiration), and *informal control* (the informal system of status, rewards, sanctions, etc.). The main factors influencing the effectiveness of different types of control in particular situations are identified as the nature and level of members' presocialisation, the norms prevailing in the informal social system and in the outside society, and the extent to which members are dependent upon the organisation.[36]

However, the ability to exercise control within an organisation is frequently confused with the holding of formal positions of power, and organisational control viewed as the exclusive domain of management. It is they after all who set goals and standards and determine the rules and rewards. While it is of course beyond dispute that the distribution of formal power and authority determines some of the limits and possibilities of organisational behaviour, overemphasis on the formal system has in the past resulted in a lack of understanding of the extent to which organisational control is in the hands of or can be commandeered by the rank-and-file participants. The concept of organisational control implies a somewhat determinative relation, between those who control, and that which is controlled, a conception that seems to accord more with the states of affairs described on organisation charts than with the realities of organisational life.

Some of these realities for example are reported by Roy in his study of quota restriction and the more general characteristics of 'institutionalised underworking' that resulted from a year's participant observation

[35] A. S. Tannenbaum, *Control in Organisations* (McGraw-Hill, 1968), p. 3.
[36] S. Millham, R. Bullock and P. Cherrett, 'Social Control in Organisations', *British Journal of Sociology* (1972), 23, 4, pp. 406–21.

as a worker in a machine shop. Norms of the informal system restricted output in order to protect existing piece-work rates, while several groups within the shop co-operated with the machine operators in the illegal facilitation of 'making out' the necessary quotas of work.[37] Gouldner's study of a gypsum plant led him to the conclusion that one of the functions of bureaucratic rules is the 'preservation of apathy': 'The rules served as a specification of a minimum level of acceptable performance. It was therefore possible for the worker to remain apathetic, for he now knew just how little he could do and still remain secure.'[38] Working to rule is just one mode of 'bureaucratic sabotage' whereby lower participants may exert a controlling influence upwards, by threatening organisational effectiveness, with strike action as the ultimate weapon. Crozier describes how, because of their unique capacity to rectify machine breakdowns, maintenance workers in the French tobacco industry occupied a position of power *vis à vis* production workers and supervisors not at all in accord with the official position. He suggests the general principle that power is acquired within the organisation by those groups which are able to control the sources of strategic uncertainty: '. . . new power relationships develop around the loopholes in the regulatory system. Groups fight for control of the ultimate strategic sources of uncertainties, and their fates in the group struggles depend on their ability to control these'.[39]

The evidence is that for even the most bureaucratic and rigid organisation, capacity to influence the effectiveness of the enterprise as a whole does not necessarily correlate closely with formal position, but may be generated or acquired in any part of the organisation under certain circumstances. While certain veto powers and ultimate sanctions are likely always to reside with leadership, many sources of influence over running operations can never be accounted for in organisational blueprints or action programmes because they depend on the exploitation of contingencies and the personal qualities of particular members. Mechanic has put forward the hypothesis that:

'The most effective way for lower participants to achieve power is to obtain, maintain, and control access to persons, information, and instrumentalities. To the extent that this can be accomplished, lower participants make higher-ranking participants dependent upon

---

[37] D. Roy, 'Quota Restriction and Gold-bricketing in a Machine Shop', *American Journal of Sociology* (1952), 57, pp. 427–42; and 'Efficiency and "The Fix": Informal Intergroup Relations in a Piece-work Machine Shop', *American Journal of Sociology* (1954), 60, pp. 255–66.

[38] Gouldner, op. cit., p. 174.

[39] Crozier, op. cit., p. 111.

them. Thus dependence together with the manipulation of the dependency relationship is the key to the power of lower participants.'[40]

Factors affecting the acquisition of personal power include possession of expertise, amount of effort and interest, personal attractiveness, and location in organisational space.

Another factor making it necessary to modify the traditional conception of organisational control is the progressive abandonment of the view propounded by Taylor, Urwick, Fayol and others that in the performance of organisational tasks there is generally to be found 'one best way'—a single most 'rational' course of action from the alternatives available. Simon has suggested as an alternative to this 'optimising' model that most organisations most of the time are in fact engaged in 'satisficing'—doing well enough given limited resources and the multiple demands on them. Satisficing as a criterion of performance means that chosen courses of action may fall within a range of alternatives, so that control can no longer be a binary function.[41]

For these reasons the concept of regulation seems more appropriate than the concept of control in trying to understand the manner in which the relationships amongst the parts and processes of a dynamic open system are maintained while the system as a whole does work. Organisational survival and effectiveness depends upon these inter-relationships being kept within certain tolerance limits, and this cannot be ensured by formal power holders alone. In so far as there is some leeway in the combination of organisational resources and capabilities for the accomplishment of its ends, and people in all parts and at all levels are potentially able to take an active role in determining what combinations are feasible, the problems of integration for the organisation are more like those of the biological organism than the mechanical system or machine. (They remain distinctive, however, in the important respect that for social systems the parts as well as the whole itself are purposeful.) In the body, the nervous system dominated by the brain, and the endocrine system dominated by the pituitary gland, regulate such matters as body temperature, the volume of bodily fluids, osmotic pressure, pH levels, and so on, keeping these within limits that allow the whole system to adapt to its environment and to grow. The adaptability of organisations is similarly dependent upon mechanisms for the regulation of information flows, work flows, morale ('social climate'),

[40] D. Mechanic, 'Sources of Power of Lower Participants in Complex Organisations', *Administrative Science Quarterly* (1962), 7, p. 356.

[41] On the 'satisficing' model see H. A. Simon, 'A Behavioural Model of Rational Choice', *Quarterly Journal of Economics* (1955), 69, pp. 99–118, and H. A. Simon and J. G. March, *Organisations* (Wiley, 1958).

output quality and quantity, budgets, and so on, which keep these within certain limits. 'Control' has more determinative connotations that seem to negate the real variability in the manner in which living systems achieve integration. There is an important and basic sense in which every organisation is an *instrument*—a tool more or less consciously fashioned by man himself to make possible the production of outcomes that are beyond the capabilities of single individuals. Since groups of cave-dwellers combined and took special roles in the hunting of animals our organisational instruments have so expanded in size and power, and the outcomes they produce become so remote from the goals and contributions of individual members, that it requires an effort of imagination to regard them still as tools for the furtheration of societal ends. One typifying problem remains more or less constant however, and that is the reconciliation of individual and organisational objectives. This we suggest, is the key problem of organisational regulation.

Human beings are purposeful—they display will, and enjoy a high degree of independence from the environments that they exist in. As independent causal agents in the social field, capable of meaningful learning and problem-solving, they are able to formulate and modify their own goals, acquire more effective ways of proceeding towards them, and take actions that change the character of their environments so as to make new adaptive behaviours possible (e.g. building a canoe for travel and fishing; lighting a fire for cooking, or for warmth). While all human beings have these properties, they are also all fundamentally unique, a uniqueness which we express as their personality. One of the central needs of human beings is for the expression and development of this individuality—for 'self-actualisation'. The growth of the personality is bi-polar, requiring development in the direction of *autonomy* or independence on the one hand, and towards *homonomy*—interdependence, or inclusion in supra-individual entities on the other. Becoming fully human in other words, requires both a capacity for self-reliance and a capacity for becoming integrated in a group.

The problems we are concerned with arise from the fact that organisations in modern society have increasingly required of their members specialisation in their tasks, dependency and impersonality in their relations with the collectivity, rationality and predictability in their behaviours. Inclusion in any formal, rationally organised social structure requires of the individual a certain effort in the subordination of private troubles and aspirations so that these do not interfere with organisational functioning. Formal organisations differ therefore from 'natural' social groups based on kinship, friendship, community, and so forth, which, although demanding a certain conformity to group norms, values, beliefs and customs, have other characteristics which serve to expand the choices of ends and means available to members.

Problems of the reconciliation of individual and collective ends arise from the fact that organisations themselves behave purposefully, and it is an essential precondition of effectiveness in accomplishing organisational objectives that they are able to regulate the behaviours of their constituent individuals and groups, making it possible for them, with appropriate technical means, to jointly produce the organisation's chosen outcomes. The continuing problem has been to find ways of curtailing the spontaneity of members' behaviour and to persuade them to behave and go on behaving in accordance with organisational requirements, even when the *intrinsic* rewards for doing so are reduced to insignificance. Any solution has to take into account that the mental and physical energies of human beings do not stay at a constant level, and that they do not perform well in the long run in situations which are threatening, or when the activities required of them are too boring or meaningless. The problems of designing and maintaining complex machinery seem fairly simple by comparison.

Failures of organisational structure and ways of operating to provide for human beings to meet their needs in the process of achieving organisational objectives are manifest in such behaviour patterns as ritualism, retreatism, and rebellion. Merton's famous essay on 'bureaucratic structure and personality' shows how overconformity, ritualism, and 'trained incapacity' can be unintended consequences of bureaucratic systems of organisation:

> 'Discipline, readily interpreted as conformity with regulations, whatever the situation, is seen not as a measure designed for specific purposes but becomes an immediate value in the life-organisation of the bureaucrat. This emphasis, resulting from the displacement of the original goals, develops into rigidities and an inability to adjust readily. . . . This may be exaggerated to the point where primary concern with conformity to the rules interferes with the achievement of the purposes of the organization.'[42]

Retreatism, or withdrawal of commitment is a common symptom of alienation, and amounts to 'cutting one's losses', contributing the bare minimum to the organisation. The malady in this case is not 'red tape', but a chronic under-utilisation of human resources. Rebellion is a more active response to a dissatisfactory situation, issuing from resent-

[42] Merton, op. cit., p. 199.

ment, and is manifest in such behaviours as sabotage of operations, theft and other crime, wild-cat strikes, and so on.

As Etzioni has suggested solutions to the problem of the relations between the organisation and the human beings who belong to it have been much influenced by changing historical circumstances.[43] In the early years of industrialisation, especially with the invention of the factory, compliance was obtained by coercion—workers produced according to organisation specifications or risked starvation—or by the exercise of traditional authority in the type of organisation that Weber called patrimonial bureaucracy (see below pp. 145–46). The advance of industrialisation and the maturation of capitalist society brought a shift towards contractual relations between organisations and their members with wages exchanged for work done under mutually agreed conditions. Growing state responsibility for the 'casualties' of industrialisation, strengthening and amplification of the principle of equality before the law, and the growth of the trade union movement were correlates of the increased independence of individuals from the organisations they served, and the evolution within these organisations of new forms of rational-legal authority, exemplified in the growth of bureaucracies. For work organisations (leaving aside for the moment the many kinds of voluntary organisations and total institutions in which the basic nature of individual-organisation relations inheres in the organisational function, irrespective of cultural transformations) such changes encouraged the *calculative* involvement of members, such that regulation of their behaviours become dependent upon the manipulation by managers by primarily financial, but also symbolic and psychological rewards and sanctions.

During the past few decades it has become more and more apparent that systems of organisational regulation, based on the remunerative power of the organisation and the calculative involvement of members, are not appropriate under the conditions of advanced industrial society for getting the most out of increasingly scarce human and material resources. This is in part because the societal trends referred to above have continued, and, augmented by the arrival of mass affluence and mass education up to tertiary level, have begun to erode the dependency relation between organisations and their members.

The basic design choice   As we have already indicated, the designer of complex adaptive systems confronts a basic choice in the design of controls. He may make use of more parts than will ever be in operation

[43] A. Etzioni, *A Comparative Analysis of Complex Organisations* (Free Press, 1961).

at one time and overlay these with a hierarchy of decision-makers to determine which parts will be active when, or he may use a smaller number of multifunctional parts and design into them mechanisms for setting and resetting their functions in response to what needs to be done. In organisations, where the parts are human beings, the former strategy leads towards centralised, hierarchical structures in which reduction of the probabilities of human error is sought through the amplification of authority relations and decomposition of the total activity to simplified repetitive tasks. While there are today strong reasons for rejecting this mode of organisational regulation, Weber's conclusion that it contributes positively to the speedy and efficient accomplishment of tasks cannot be automatically dismissed. Crozier, furthermore, has presented the challenging thesis that the centralised, bureaucratic type of organisation is in fact a condition of the individual members' freedom. Crozier contends that in the bureaucratic type of organization that he describes, the individual members enjoy a fairly good combination of independence and security. Impersonal rules and centralisation order their behaviour and deprive them of initiative, but at the same time are the condition of their freedom from any arbitrary interference.[44]

The second strategy on the other hand is in some respects more risky, and demands more of the human parts. It leads towards decentralised, organic forms of organisation, in which hierarchy and authority are far less salient. Individuals, being multiskilled and more autonomous, become more capable of self-regulation within the framework of organisation purposes and values, especially when they belong to groups enjoying functional autonomy. With the first strategy, regulation is relatively more dependent upon shared understanding of rules and respect for authority; with the second it is relatively more dependent upon a shared appreciation of the organisational mission and the acceptance of common values.

[44] Crozier, op. cit., p. 203 ff.

6

Organisations and Society: Legacies of Sociological Thought

(a) HERBERT SPENCER: ORGANISATION AS FRIEND AND ENEMY

Central to Spencer's sociology is the presentation of society as a social organism. Constant attention is paid to the structure, function and growth of the social organism and one discovers frequent reference to the biological analogy of the individual organism in order to illustrate the point. Spencer's fondness for the analogy should not obscure his intention:

> 'Though, in foregoing chapters, sundry comparisons of social structures and functions to structures and functions in the human body have been made, they have been made only because structures and functions in the human body furnish familiar illustrations of structures and functions in general. The social organism, discrete instead of concrete, asymmetrical instead of symmetrical, sensitive in all its units instead of having a single sensitive centre, is not comparable to any particular types of individual organism, animal or vegetal.'[1]

[1] H. Spencer, *Principles of Sociology* (Williams & Norgate, 1893), Vol. 1, p. 580.

What he is interested in is the extent to which organisation promotes and the extent to which it hinders co-operation. On this we may offer a number of observations:

1. There is first his discussion of the way in which society as an organised entity comes to be differentiated into mutually dependent elements—the sustaining, the distributing and the regulating systems. The sustaining system refers to industrial and agricultural production; the distributing system relates to forms of communication and, the agencies for facilitating exchange; the regulating system has to do with the governmental-military sphere. Spencer seeks to tease out the ways in which these parts of the total system may be interrelated. For example, as the division of labour develops to the point where co-operation between individuals and groups who are geographically separated is involved, then the growth of channels of communications and appropriate distributive agencies becomes necessary. Again the regulative system is seen as affected by the scale and complexity of society and, in particular, the centralisation of political authority is judged to accompany the increasing size of society. The distributive system in its turn comes to be affected by the demands of the regulative system, as well as those of the sustaining system. The point Spencer makes here in his treatment of the growth of the social organism is this:

'The general result . . . is that in societies, as in living bodies, the increasing mutual dependence of parts, implying an increasingly efficient regulating system, therefore implies not only developed regulating centres, but also means by which the influence of such centres may be propagated.'[2]

However in complex industrial societies Spencer adds to this three-fold differentiation of sustaining, distributive and regulative systems the idea that the sustaining and distributive elements develop their own autonomous regulating systems (separate that is to say from the State and its administrative apparatus). He portrays the industrial regulating system as being carried out through the mechanism of the market—both local and national. He is actually describing a *laissez-faire* arrangement:

'There is now no fixing of prices by the State; nor is there prescribing of methods. Subject to but slight hindrances from a few licences, citizens adopt what occupations they please; buy and sell where they please. The amounts grown and manufactured, imported and exported, are regulated by laws; improvements are not enforced

[2] ibid., p. 526.

nor bad processes legislatively interdicted; but men carrying on their businesses as they think best, are simply required by law to fulfil their contracts and commanded not to aggress upon their neighbours.'[3]

This relationship between the State and an industrial organisation spelled out here is one which Spencer embraced as desirable and coloured his judgement of certain collectivist developments, as we note below.

The regulating system of the distributive apparatus is, for Spencer, the banking and allied financial institutions which promote and facilitate the movement of capital. Although the general point is clear enough, the separation of this from the industrial regulating system is somewhat artificial since this also is part of the market mechanism and impinges directly upon the operation of the industrial system.

What Spencer is attempting, however, is a functionalist analysis of society in which, as social structures change and become differentiated, the interrelationships between the aggregate and the organisations which go to make up each part—sustaining, distributive and regulative —may be explored. Furthermore, in principle, the functional significance of the differentiation within one or other of these systems may be considered. And, as we shall see, the evaluative position which Spencer adopts, is to see how far co-operation is maintained and coercion checked and in particular, how far the State becomes the focus for centralised power at the expense of the autonomy of other parts of society.

2. The problem of co-operation versus coercion and the role of organisations in promoting one or the other is approached by Spencer in his type formulations of militant and industrial societies. This is a contrast conception which cuts across Spencer's classification of societies in terms of scale and complexity, that is to say both militant and industrial societies may be found at various levels of social development. The militant society is marked by coercion (or compulsory co-operation) as the major organising principle and exists to promote offensive and defensive actions against antagonistic societies: 'The militant type is one in which the army is the nation mobilised while the nation is the quiescent army, and which therefore, acquires a structure common to army and nation.'[4] This embodies a system of centralised control with a hierarchical chain of superordination and subordination. In discussing simple societies of a militant character Spencer emphasises how political and religious authority may be fused and how industrial systems are subordinated to the needs of govern-

[3] ibid., pp. 532–3.

[4] ibid., p. 545.

mental-military structures. It is a system in which state control over the activities of individuals permeates all spheres of life with an accompanying system of discipline which is based on the threat that the members exist for the benefit of society as a whole rather than the converse. Although many of Spencer's examples are drawn from ancient societies—Peru, Mexico, Sparta, Egypt—he also cites contemporary examples:

> 'Even now when the military organisation has been kept in vigour by military activities as in France, we are shown by the peremptory control of journals and suppression of meetings, by the regimental uniformity of education, by the official administration of the fine arts, the way in which its characteristic regulating system ramifies everywhere.'[5]

So the concept of militant society purports to delineate the characteristic organising principle of society as a whole and the relationships between the regulating system and other organisations in society. The hierarchical principle has double application: the subordination of all organisations to the State and the hierarchy of rank within particular organisations, with its accompanying imposed discipline on individuals.

The industrial society is characterised by a decentralised organisational arrangement in which the sustaining system is separate from and not dominated by the regulating system. It is peaceful in relation to other societies and is based upon the principle of voluntary co-operation. Spencer cites examples of simple societies, like the Arafuras and the Mishinis but is more interested in the industrialised European nations. He stresses, for example, the differentiation of political, economic and ecclesiastical institutions, the relative autonomy of these spheres; together with the accompanying growth of diverse beliefs and the possibility of dissent and resistance to authority. The sovereignty of the citizen is asserted and is reflected in contractual relationships freely entered into which are mutually beneficial; it is further reflected in a system of representative government which could be observed in a whole range of organisations, political groupings, trade unions, joint-stock companies and various voluntary associations. The representatives are voted in, and accountable to others who elect them and can in principle be removed from office if they fail to satisfy the membership.

The militant/industrial dichotomy is a contrast conception—an ideal type polarisation which Spencer acknowledges will rarely if at all be found in its purity.

> 'Excluding a few simple groups . . . all societies, simple and com-

[5] ibid., p. 551.

pound, are occasionally or habitually in antagonism with other societies; and . . . tend to evolve structures for carrying on offensive and defensive actions. At the same time, sustenation is necessary; and there is always an organisation, slight or decided, for achieving it. But while the two systems in social organisms, as in individual organisms, co-exist in all but the rudimentary forms, they vary immensely in the ratios they bear to one another.'[6]

What is clearly important in Spencer is a treatment of organisations which sees them as interrelated in a number of possible ways and which is crystallised for purposes of analysis into the militant/industrial contrast; and further which sees these organisational arrangements and interrelationships as a response to the environment—hostile or non-threatening.

We should note that although Spencer tends to the view that simple societies probably have to go through a militant stage of development, complex societies may or may not be industrial in his special sense of the term.

'How, since the establishment of a stronger centralised power in Germany by war, a more coercive regime has shown itself, we see in the dealings of Bismarck with the ecclesiastical powers; in the laying down by Moltke of the doctrine that both for safety from foreign attack and guardianship of order at home, it is needful that the supplies for the army should not be dependent on a parliamentary vote; and again in the measures taken lately for centralising the State-control of the German railways. In France we have as usual the chief soldier becoming the chief ruler. . . .'[7]

But Britain's fall from grace is also discerned and serves to remind us that, while at one level Spencer is portrayed as an optimistic evolutionary theorist, it is far from the whole story. In his view developments in Britain give cause for pessimism. Spencer refers explicitly to the military character of imperialist activity and the growth of expenditure on armaments. This is reflected in the re-emergence of a militant organisation in British social institutions generally. The individual is consequently threatened by encroaching state control and even the Liberal Party now encouraged the growth of state administration at the expense of individual liberty (he is thinking of the post-1850 period).

It should be added that the militant/industrial contrast with its implication that the industrial was much to be preferred to the militant is itself seen against a third possibility—the basis, we might say, for an alternative society.

[6] ibid., p. 544.   [7] ibid., p. 568.

'. . . a type which, having a sustaining system more fully developed than any we have at present, will use the products of industry neither for maintaining a militant organisation nor exclusively for material aggrandisement; but will devote them to the carrying on of higher activities. As the contrast between the militant and the industrial types is indicated by inversion of the belief that individuals exist for the benefit of the State into the belief that the State exists for the benefit of individuals; so the contrast between the industrial type and the type likely to be evolved from it is indicated by inversion of the belief that life is for work into the belief that work is for life.'[8]

Why should Spencer have thought it necessary to transcend the industrial type given all the qualities of individual freedom he ascribes to it? Perhaps, as Peel has suggested, because his direct knowledge and experience of the division of labour in industry made him well aware of the monotonous, degrading and imprisoning character of work. To connect ideas of liberty with those who might just have a little choice as to the way they will spend their working hours, was highly extravagant.[9]

3. Whatever one may think of the type distinction outlined above, it is clear the reflections on militant organisation—and especially its hierarchial and coercive character—prompts Spencer to reflect on the problem of bureaucratic rigidity. He points to the possibility of repressive organisation which can hinder rather than help that which it purports to serve. This may be because vested interests are at stake and become entrenched once organisations reach a certain size. An example from the educational field in nineteenth-century England is instructive:

'The struggle going on between secularism and denominationalism in teaching, might alone show to anyone who looks for the wider meanings of facts, that a structure which has ramified throughout a society, acquired an army of officials looking for personal welfare and promotion, backed by classes, ecclesiastical and political, whose ideas and interests they further, is a structure which, if not unalterable, is difficult to alter in proportion as it is highly developed.'[10]

However, it is the political sphere to which Spencer most frequently turns. Given his preoccupation with the danger of state regulation to the freedom of the individual this should not surprise us. At the beginning of the twentieth century he is looking with great distaste at the

[8] ibid., p. 563.
[9] J. D. Y. Peel, *Herbert Spencer. The Evolution of a Sociologist* (Heinemann, 1971), p. 216.
[10] Herbert Spencer, *The Study of Sociology* (Ann Arbor, 1960), p. 62.

growth of government by administrative order in Britain. This he believes to be represented by the growth of executive power *vis-à-vis* Parliament and the individual private member; together with the concentration of executive power in fewer hands. This is accompanied by the growth of government departments which strengthen the effective power of the executive. Thus at the same time as the franchise is being extended, the real liberty of the citizen is diminishing because the spheres of action of elected representatives are restricted. It is the administrative class that Spencer sees as becoming increasingly powerful in the modern state. This he sees as an ironic, because unintended, consequence of socialist thinking:

> 'Instead of the rule of powerful political classes, men are elaborating for themselves a rule of official classes, which will become equally powerful or probably more powerful—classes eventually differing from those which socialist theories contemplate, as much as the rich and proud ecclesiastical hierarchy of the Middle Ages differed from the group of poor and humble missionaries out of which it grew.'[11]

There is in Spencer a populist suspicion of government and administration with the accompanying cry, now again in vogue in discussions on participation, of power to the people. This point, in *Social Statics*, he turns against socialists who advocated increased state regulation as the solution to class oppression: 'If, therefore, class legislation is the *inevitable* consequence of class power, there is no escape from the conclusion that the interests of the *whole* society can be secured, only by giving power to the hands of the *whole* people.'[12] It is a position which, now, perhaps, would be sympathetically appreciated by socialist humanists, who have come to see the state apparatus in the hands of ruling parties as an instrument of oppression rather than liberation.

(b) EMILE DURKHEIM: ORGANISATIONAL BREAKDOWN AND RECONSTRUCTION

The central place of the *anomie* concept in Durkheim's sociology is a constant reminder of his preoccupation with the problem of social order. It was a problem which posed questions concerning the relationship of the individual to society and concerning the relationship between the 'parts' of society which go to make up the whole. In a small scale, undifferentiated society, the question of the relationship of the parts to whole scarcely arose and individuals were bound to

[11] *Principles of Sociology*, Vol. 3, p. 597.
[12] Cited in S. Andreski (ed.), *Herbert Spencer* (Nelson, 1972), p. 183.

society by the operation of a collective conscience—which promoted and maintained social solidarity. The process of social differentiation is discussed by Durkheim in *The Division of Labour*.[13] The growth in population is postulated as intensifying competition between individuals and at the same time increasing the scale of society. The division of labour is regarded by Durkheim as the peaceful solution to the growing competition which population growth and increased social interaction tended to produce. But at the same time the process of differentiation is seen as diminishing the effectiveness of the collective conscience of society. This entailed the need for new forms of moral regulation if society was to hold together. These collective forces in preindustrial societies could, Durkheim argued, be manifested in and through the main organs of society: the family, religion, the polity and trade. Stable patterns of interaction in these spheres could produce stable moral codes, together with accompanying rewards and sanctions which could be applied to individual members.

It is the Industrial Revolution and its concomitants which create for Durkheim the problem of social order in an acute form and is analysed both in terms of the inadequacy of old organisational forms (in so far as they have survived) to serve as moral regulators and the need to create new organisational forms if man as a social animal is to survive. Analytically, the treatment of *anomie* reflects Durkheim's sensitivity to the disjunctions encountered in the developmental trend from mechanical to organic solidarity (which is embedded in his work). It also reflects his moral concern that the social condition of individual freedom be realised. Mechanical solidarity did not do this; indeed only in conditions of a small scale group with a homogeneous population could its uniform control system flourish. Differentiation was both the prerequisite of individuality for Durkheim and the death knell of mechanical solidarity. At the same time, the collective forces which Durkheim observed operating in preindustrial differentiated societies, while they could be regarded as promoting social solidarity in relatively stable conditions, were forces which exercised moral power that could also be coercive and tyrannical in relation to the individual. The organisational breakdown of industrial societies had therefore to be viewed in terms not only of the threat which this posed to social survival, but also of the possibility which co-existed for constructing an organisational base within which individual freedom could develop as never before in human history.

When Durkheim writes of the political and social malaise of industrial societies, it is with the dominant thought in mind that between

[13] E. Durkheim, *The Division of Labour in Society* (Free Press, 1964).

the State and the individual there should be secondary associations which would both check against the dominance of the state over the individual and, in the framework of the rule of law, would themselves be checked from exercising absolute power over their members. It is instructive to see how Durkheim treats organisations as social constructions in and through which individual selfishness can be transcended and yet which are the product of individual interactions. This is particularly demonstrated in periods of social disintegration where organisational vacuums exist:

'. . . in the final analysis, it is from the actions and reactions through direct exchanges amongst individuals that the whole system of social and political organisation has been evolved. Therefore when it occurs that system is carried away by time without any other taking its place as it disintegrates, it is inevitable that social life must go back in some degree to its primary source, that is, to the individuals, to be elaborated afresh. Since they stand alone, it is through them direct that the society has to operate. . . . They themselves have to make good the organisation that is lacking. That is our situation at present, and although there is a remedy, and one may see in it a necessary phase of evolution, we cannot disguise the critical element in it. A society made of a substance so unstable is liable to disintegrate if it suffers the least shock. There is nothing to protect it against things from without or within.'[14]

It is as though Durkheim is claiming that a philosophy and practice of individualism is not enough to preserve democracy and the social individual. The elaboration of organisations, although it is initiated by individuals, must proceed so that what is constructed takes the weight off the shoulders of the individual architects. He is very explicit about this, with particular reference to French society:

'It is on the mass of individuals that the whole weight of the society rests. It has no other support. . . . Instead of offering this absence of organisation, wrongly called democracy, as an ideal, a limit should be set to that condition. . . . The primary duty is to work out something that can relieve us by degrees of a role for which the individual is not cast. To do this, our political action must be to establish these secondary organs which, as they take shape, will release the individual from the State and vice versa, and release the individual, too, from a task for which he is not fitted.'[15]

[14] E. Durkheim, *Professional Ethics and Civic Morals* (Routledge & Kegan Paul, 1957), pp. 106–7. [15] ibid., pp. 108–9.

If we inquire as to the character of these secondary organisations which are to be constructed, it is the professional model which is set before us. What Durkheim was impressed by in societies where the division of labour was at all advanced, was the moral pluralism reflected in particular rules having binding power over specific groups—doctors, scientists, teachers and so on. These were strong where stable organisation was in evidence and within the framework of society were comparatively autonomous, self-regulating groups. As such (over and against mechanical forms of solidarity) they represented a decentralisation of the moral life for Durkheim. It is the absence of such organisational arrangements making for professional consciousness in trade and industry that concerns him. The expansion of economic life has not been accompanied by appropriate organisational arrangements so that anarchic competition becomes the hallmark of industrial society. Conflict is not regulated in any moral sense but is a matter of the spoils going to the strongest.

'But since this subjection is only a *de facto* condition sanctioned by no kind of morals, it is accepted only under duress until the longed for day of revenge. Peace treaties signed in this fashion are always provisional forms of truce that do not mean peace to men's minds. This is how ever-recurring conflicts arise between the different factions of the economic structure.'[16]

The development of professional consciousness within the industrial order is then, for Durkheim, a priority to deal with the moral vacuum.

In both *Professional Ethics* and *The Division of Labour* (the Preface to the second edition) Durkheim does appear to make something of a jump in the argument. What he terms occupational associations are analogous to, but not synonymous with, professional associations. The latter relate to particular occupational groups such as doctors or lawyers. The former relate to corporate groupings which include employers and employees. Groups of employers and unions he accepts as legitimate and necessary But, in his view, there exists no common organisation which brings them together, where they can develop common forms of regulation which will determine the relationship between them in an authoritative fashion, without either of them losing their own autonomy.'[17] It is then the creation of a new organised group to which Durkheim looks to fill the moral vacuum—not putting the clock back to localised guild organisations, which could not effectively regulate national and international market relations, nor accepting the individualistic doctrine of survival of the fittest through unfettered competition.

16 ibid., p. 11.   17 Durkheim, *Division of Labour*, pp. 4–10.

One should not interpret Durkheim's corporate solution as shoring up the capitalist system. Always it is related to a concern with an equitable distribution of social goods, which he does not think possible in a system characterised by inherited wealth and, consequently, contractual relations based on power inequalities between the parties. This brings him close to a socialist position in terms of his actual assumptions and this is further suggested in his treatment of the forced division of labour, which dwells upon the reality of class exploitation given actual power disparities in capitalist society.[18] There are one or two speculative points made by Durkheim which are also worth noting. The first is that, while he tends to view the growth of economic organisational forms as a secondary association intervening between the state and the individual, at times he suggests that the state as traditionally understood may be replaced ultimately by his new organisational form.

'Professional life . . . takes on increasing importance as labour goes on splitting up into divisions. There is therefore reason to believe that it this professional life that is destined to form the basis of our political structure. . . . The corporative body . . . and its organs are always in action and therefore the governmental assemblies that would issue from them would never lose touch with the councils of a society: they would, too, never run the risk of being isolated within themselves, or of not feeling quickly and vividly enough the changes that happen to occur in the deep lying strata of the population. . . . The councils of the government would then be genuinely what the brain is to the human organism a reflexion of the social body. All the living forces, all the vital organs would be represented there according to their relative importance. In the groups thus formed, the society would truly gain consciousness of itself and of its unity; this unity would follow naturally from the relations that would develop amongst those representing the different professions thus placed in close contract.'[19]

The second point is that, by and large, Durkheim's moral basis for organisational reconstruction is rooted in the concept of the just contract. This does not, however, erode inequalities of merit. Yet he suggests that the moral sentiment of sympathy takes one beyond the strict measure of justice to challenge these remaining inequalities:

[18] See J. E. T. Eldridge, *Sociology and Industrial Life* (Nelson, 1973) for a fuller discussion of this theme. See also A. Giddens (ed.), *Emile Durkheim. Selected Writings* (CUP, 1972), where this point is taken up in his introductory essay.

[19] *Professional Ethics*, pp. 104–5.

'Charity ignores and denies any special merits in gifts or mental capacity acquired by heredity. This, then, is the very acme of justice. It is society, we find, that is coming to exercise complete dominion over nature, to lay down the law for it and to set this moral equality over physical inequality which in fact is inherent in things.'[20] The organisational programme for the corporate groupings in such a still hypothetical society would consequently shift its basis. In any event the tone of Durkheim's approach here is that of socialist humanism and suggests a sceptical attitude towards those who regard him as an arch-conservative.

(c) KARL MARX: THE ORGANISATIONAL WEAPON

It is a little curious that books on the sociology of organisations pay scarcely any attention to the Marxist tradition of organisational analysis.[21] This relative neglect is to be regretted although, as we shall hope to indicate, the nature of the legacy is somewhat problematical.

Given Marx's preoccupation with the nature of class antagonisms in capitalist society, it is not surprising that permeating his writing is an elucidation of the way in which various organisational forms may be used by the ruling class to exploit the working class; conversely attention is given to the nature and aims of proletarian organisations.

Central to an understanding of Marx's perspective is his treatment of the state and bureaucracy. This can be deduced from his theoretical, historical and, for that matter, journalistic writings. For example, in his *Critique of Hegel's Philosophy of Right*, Marx takes issue with a view of the modern State that would see it above sectional conflicts, representing the public good and embodied in constitutional monarchy, which therefore was the generator of individual freedom. For him, on the contrary, the State is the arena in which the conflicts of interests in civil society are fought out; society as a whole does not benefit. The State in reality is an instrument of the ruling class, a fact which is masked by its claims to representativeness and democracy (the affinity with Spencer's view discussed above is noteworthy). The State is, of course, served by a bureaucratic apparatus, staffed, and rightly so according to Hegel, by a middle class with a developed intelligence and consciousness of right. This same bureaucracy, in Hegel's view, is to serve as a bridge between the State and civil society. But take away the assumption of the State as representing the common good and the

[20] ibid., p. 220.
[21] See, however, N. P. Mouzelis, *Organisation and Bureaucracy* (Routledge & Kegan Paul, 1967), pp. 8–15.

bureaucracy its servant is redefined in terms of special interests (albeit interests which mask themselves in the language and rhetoric of the common good). Hence the Hegelian vision of the State is for Marx a mystification, an expression of alienation, because in reality state, property and ruling class interests are interlocked. To accept the claims of the State that this is not the case is simply to accept a rationalisation and to ignore the material reality. It may be noted here that Hegel's claims for the state and its bureaucracy to be a 'universal class' that is genuinely representative of society as a whole is to be countered by Marx's claim that the working class is the universal class, because in revolutionary activity private property and classes will be abolished. Upon such a premise is predicated a more problematic concern with the conditions promoting and organisational forms expressing proletarian consciousness, which are juxtaposed necessarily against the ultimate withering away of the State.

The power of the State as something over and above society is something Marx spells out in his historical study of France, *The Eighteenth Brumaire of Louis Napoleon*:

'This executive power with its enormous bureaucratic and military organisation, with its ingenious state machinery embracing wide strata, with a host of officials numbering half a million, besides an army of another half million, this appalling parasitic body, which enmeshes the body of French society like a net and chokes all its pores, sprang up in the days of the absolute monarchy, with the decay of the feudal system which it helped to hasten. The signorial privileges of the landowners and towns became transformed into so many attributes of the state power, the feudal dignitaries into paid officials and the motley pattern of conflicting medieval plenary powers into the regulated plan of a state authority whose work is divided and centralised as in a factory . . . Napoleon perfected this state machinery. The legitimist government and the July monarchy added nothing but a greater division of labour, growing in the same measure as the division of labour within bourgeois society created new groups of interests, and, therefore, new material for state administration. Every *common* interest was straightaway severed from society counterposed to it as a higher, *general* interest, snatched from the activity of society's members themselves and made an object of government activity, from bridge and schoolhouse and the communal property of a village community to the railways, the national wealth and the national university of France. . . . All revolutions perfected this machine instead of smashing it. The parties that contended in turn for domination regarded the possession of this huge state edifice as the principal spoils of the victor.'[22]

The implication is that revolutionary activity should go beyond yet another takeover bid for the State and bureaucratic apparatus. However, it would seem that such a takeover would be an essential prelude to the withering away of the State in communist society. In the Communist Manifesto the call to the working class is to take over the State, which hitherto has been the organisational weapon of the ruling class, a weapon which could perpetrate violence and repression in defence of capitalism, whilst at the same time seeming to stand above class conflict. And the dictatorship of the proletariat entails centralising all the instruments of production in the hands of the State. This is clearly seen as a necessary but transitional stage in the abolition of the State:

'Political power, properly so called, is merely the organised power of one class for oppressing another. If the proletariat during its contest with the bourgeoisie is compelled by the force of circumstances to organise itself as a class, if, by means of a revolution, it makes itself the ruling class, and, as such, sweeps away by force the old conditions of production, then it will, along with these conditions, have swept away the conditions for the existence of class antagonisms and of classes generally, and will thereby have abolished its own supremacy as a class. In place of the old bourgeois society, with its classes and class antagonisms, we shall have an association in which the free development of each is the condition for the free development of all.'[23]

But how in organisational terms is the proletariat to proceed ? Further, how can one be sure that what is done in the name of the proletariat leads to a dictatorship which is truly proletarian (and hence transitional) ? In Marx's own writings it is evident that conditions in different countries might lead to a variety of answers to the first question. Lefebvre has suggested, for example, that at least three revolutionary strategies are to be located in Marx's writings. First, there was the situation in England and the United States at the time he was writing, in which he thought the workers could secure their ends by peaceful means, through political organisation and the advent of universal suffrage. Secondly, there was the situation in Germany where the movement, with the support of the majority of the working class, would have to fight the ruling class in order to control the State. Bismarck's Germany supported by a wealthy, numerous and powerful bourgeois class would not hand

[22] Marx/Engels, *Selected Works* (Lawrence & Wishart, 1968), pp. 170–1.
[23] ibid., p. 53.

over its dominant position without a fight. Thirdly, as in France, the revolutionary path was held to be in terms of an active minority, which is sufficiently energetic and well organised to do battle with the ruling class on behalf of the working class. The forging of the organisational weapon and its use in practice against the ruling class could be different although the ultimate end was the same.[24]

As least the preceding interpretation may help to explain why different socialist treatments of the organisation weapon could draw upon some aspects of Marx's writings for legitimation in sectarian debates. One crucial issue is the relation of the party as an organisation to the working class. This was at the core of the controversy between Lenin and Rosa Luxemburg to which we may briefly refer.

Lenin lay great stress on the Communist Party as an organised vanguard of the proletariat, the membership being totally committed in a disciplined way, first to the overthrow of the bourgeois State and then to the maintenance of the proletariat State against the threats of counter-revolution. This organisation he distinguished from trade union organisations, which he argued not only quarrelled with each other on a sectional interest basis at the expense of the working class as a whole, but also tended to concentrate on short-term gains at the expense of transforming the social order. 'Mere' trade union consciousness (as Lenin saw it) needed the stimulus of revolutionary political organisation and action to raise it to the level of working-class consciousness, so that it would become aware of the irreconcilability of its interests to those of the bourgeois State instead of trying to accommodate to them. In *What Is to Be Done?* Lenin sets out a number of propositions which he clearly believes to be sociologically and ideologically correct:

'I assert: (1) that no revolutionary movement can endure without a stable organisation of leaders maintaining continuity; (2) that the broader the popular mass spontaneously drawn into the struggle, forming the basis of the movement and participating in it, the more urgent the need of such an organisation, and the more solid this organisation must be (for it is much easier for demagogues to sidetrack the more backward sections of the masses); (3) that such an organisation must consist chiefly of people professionally engaged in revolutionary activity; (4) that in an autocratic State, the more we *confine* the membership of such an organisation to people who are professionally engaged in revolutionary activity and who have been professionally trained in the art of combating the political police, the more difficult will it be to unearth the organisation and (5) the *greater* will be the

[24] See H. Lefebvre, *The Sociology of Karl Marx* (Allen Lane, 1968), pp. 168 ff.

number of people of the working class and of the other classes of society who will be able to join the movement and perform active work in it.'[25]

It is the party which forms the spearhead of revolution and it is the party which rules when victory is achieved, basing itself on the doctrine of democratic centralism. The organisation of the party is deliberately monolithic in structure. This was not only necessary but desirable, since it was the only efficient way to combat counter-revolution and to educate the masses into a true socialist consciousness, as a prerequisite of the classless society. It was against the principle of centralism, as interpreted by Lenin, that Luxemburg wrote and campaigned, arguing that it could not be democratic and that in reality it created a gulf between the party and the proletariat which could not be justified. The party is created out of working class struggle, rather than working class consciousness being implanted from above by the party. One cogent expression of this viewpoint is the following:

'Social Democratic activity arises historically out of the elementary class struggle. It spreads and develops in accordance with the following dialectical contradiction. The proletarian army is recruited and becomes aware of its objectives in the course of the struggle itself. The activity of the party organisation, the growth of the pro-letarian's awareness of the objectives of the struggle and the struggle itself, are not different things, separated chronologically and mechanically. They are only different aspects of the same process. Except for the general principles of the struggle, there do not exist for the Social Democracy detailed sets of tactics which a Central Committee can teach the party membership in the same way as troops are instructed in their training camps. Furthermore, the range of influence of the Socialist Party is constantly fluctuating with the ups and downs of the struggle in the course of which the organisation is created and grows.'[26]

Where Lenin decried the spontaneous activity of the masses as an amateur misguided basis for revolutionary action and paraded as a virtue the professional approach of the vanguard party of workers and intellectuals, Luxemburg sees this spontaneity in the struggle as the safeguard against replacing one form of domination (the bourgeois

[25] V. I. Lenin, *What Is to Be Done?*, in *Collected Works* (Moscow, 1961), Vol. 5, p. 464.

[26] Rosa Luxemburg, 'The Role of the Organisation in Revolutionary Activity', in R. Looker (ed.), *Rosa Luxemburg, Selected Political Writings* (Jonathan Cape, 1972), p. 98.

State) by another (the Central Committee). In particular she criticises Lenin's view of socialist organisation as mechanistic because the discipline of the members is imposed from above and reproduces the habits of obedience and servility which already characterise the capitalist state. Against this she postulates the need for self-discipline and 'self-centralism' which implies the spontaneous co-ordination of the conscious political acts of a body of men. 'What is there in common between the regulated docility of an oppressed class and the self-discipline and organisation of a class struggling for its emancipation?'[27] Hence her emphasis on the general strike and spontaneous street demonstrations as a means of awakening and symbolising working-class consciousness. In a sense Luxemburg is protesting against the over-organisation of revolutionary activity because it can lead to an undesirable separation between leaders and followers. Let the organisation be sensitive and adjust to movement from below. 'Policy must not be formulated in such a way that the masses are always confronted with *faits accomplis.* . . . The masses must make themselves heard in order to propel the party ship forward.'[28] Indeed, in this respect, organisation becomes a product rather than a cause of revolutionary action and the ensuing socialist organisation is predicated upon new principles.

The difference between Lenin and Luxemburg on organisation was sufficient to stimulate the Marxist scholar Georg Lukacs to explore the questions raised.[29] Lukacs maintains that Luxemburg wrongly plays down the role of party organisation in revolutionary activity, because she overestimates the role of spontaneity in accomplishing revolution. In particular, it is to place too much faith in the masses who can fight on the side of the bourgeoisie as well as for revolution. Indeed Lukacs takes the Menshevik workers' party as a paradigm of the way in which the proletariat may be subject to the process of bourgeoisification:

'These organisations [political—trade union] now consciously labour to ensure that the merely spontaneous movements of the proletariat . . . should remain on the level of pure spontaneity. They strive to prevent them from turning their attention to the totality. . . . In this the unions tend to take on the task of atomising and depoliticising the movement and concealing its mention to the totality. Whereas the Menshevik parties perform the task of establishing the reification in

[27] ibid., p. 100.
[28] 'The Political Mass Strike' in Looker (ed.), op. cit., p. 185.
[29] See 'Critical Observations on Rosa Luxemburg's "Critique of the Russian Revolution" ' and 'Towards a Methodology of the Problem of Organisation', in George Lukacs, *History and Class Consciousness* (Merlin Press, 1968), pp. 272–342.

consciousness of the proletariat both ideologically and on the level of organisation. They thus ensure that the consciousness of the proletariat will remain at a certain stage of relative bourgeoisification.'[30]

Consequently, in Lukacs's judgement, Luxemburg underestimated the need for conscious revolutionary organisation that he held to be embodied in the Communist Party and which represents a higher level of consciousness than that of an ideologically divided proletariat. Where there is disunity between different individuals, groups and strata of the proletariat then the organisational separation of the party from the class is inevitable: but it is in the Communist Party that class consciousness has been objectivised. Hence he is able to assert:

'The party as a whole transcends the reified divisions according to nation, profession, etc., and according to modes of life . . . by virtue of its actions. For this is oriented towards revolutionary unity and collaboration and aims to establish the true unity of the proletarian class. And what it does as a whole it performs likewise for its individual members. Its closely knit organisation with its resulting iron discipline and its demand for total commitment tears away the reified veils that closed the consciousness of the individual in capitalist society. . . . Precisely because the rise of the Communist Party can only be the conscious achievement of the class-conscious workers every step in the direction of true knowledge is at the same time a step towards converting that knowledge into practical reality.'[31]

It could be argued that the party organisation Lukacs is depicting with its call to total commitment of the members is in part a visionary picture against which the party could criticise itself and its feelings; alternatively it could be suggested that Lukacs's sophistry is simply a form of apologetics for the party in which party actions are justified with reference to the high level of consciousness of the party. Those who disagree are by definition in a state of false consciousness.

Another issue of great importance is the role of the bureaucracy in the proletarian state. This was a matter to which Trotsky addressed himself in his strictures upon Lenin and Stalin. In *The Revolution Betrayed* Trotsky argues that the bureaucracy in Russia has become a ruling class:

'The bureaucracy is in the full sense of the word the sole privileged, and commanding stratum in the Soviet society. . . . The Soviet bureaucracy has expropriated the proletariat politically in order by

[30] 'Towards a Methodology of the Problem of Organisation', op. cit., p. 310.
[31] ibid., p. 339.

methods of its own to defend the social conquests. But the very fact of its appropriation of political power in a country where the principal means of production are in the hands of the State, creates a new hitherto unknown relation between the bureaucracy and the riches of the nation. The means of production belong to the State. But the State so to speak "belongs" to the bureaucracy.'[32]

Whereas Lukacs emphasised that the proletariat contained within it revolutionary and counter-revolutionary potentialities, Trotsky says the same for the bureaucracy. Indeed for him it is the bureaucracy which has betrayed the revolution and has a vested interest in maintaining privileges and hierarchies. He portrays the Soviet Union as a contradictory society half way between capitalism and socialism. A backslide to capitalism he sees as wholly possible; the movement to socialism would necessitate the overthrow of the bureaucracy which would set in motion social and economic changes of an egalitarian nature. Precisely because one is dealing with a society permeated with contradictions, the problem of predicting the outsome is tinged with uncertainty—an uncertainty with which he realises the doctrinaire ideologist will not be satisfied.

'Sociological problems would certainly be simpler if social phenomena had always a finished character. There is nothing more dangerous, however, than to throw out of reality, for the sake of logical completeness, elements which today violate your scheme and tomorrow may wholly overthrow it.'[33]

Perhaps this cautionary note still has relevance for sociologists today, not least in the study of organisations.

(d) MAX WEBER: STABLE AND UNSTABLE ORGANISATIONS

Whenever Weber discusses his ideal-type mode of analysis—types of action, types of authority, types of organisation, types of bureaucracy—he is invariably at pains to point out that, while he regards them as indispensable for analysis, they are not to be confused with historical realities which are more 'mixed' or 'fluid' than his pure formal types. Despite the disclaimers, Weber is commonly attacked on the grounds that his types do not fit this or that historical circumstance. Methodologically the question to be asked of them is: are they useful? If for the problem in hand they are not, it then becomes necessary to invent new

[32] L. Trotsky, *The Revolution Betrayed* (New Park Publications, 1967), p. 249.
[33] ibid., p. 255.

types and concepts. We would suggest that while comments on Weber's contribution to the sociology of organisations focuses with some justification on his analysis of bureaucracy, this is too often done in a static, formalistic manner which takes the ideal type out of context and consequently distorts the intention of the author.

In his depiction of the purely buraucratic type of administration, which he terms monocratic, Weber in fact concerns himself with the nature of the organisation and the official. This may be set out for convenience in a parallel manner as follows:

<table>
<tr><td align="center">Ideal type of
rational-legal
bureaucracy</td><td align="center">Ideal type of
official in rational-legal
bureaucracy</td></tr>
<tr><td valign="top">1. Continuous organisation of official functions bound by rules.</td><td valign="top">1. He is personally free and subject to authority only with respect to impersonal official obligations.</td></tr>
<tr><td valign="top">2. Specified sphere of competence involving: (a) sphere of obligations to perform functions which have been marked off as part of a systematic division of labour; (b) incumbent with necessary authority to carry out functions; (c) necessary means of compulsion clearly defined and used subject to definite conditions. This constitutes an administrative unit.</td><td valign="top">2. He occupies a position in a clearly defined hierarchy of offices.
3. As an official he has a clearly defined sphere of competence.
4. The office is filled by a free contractual relationship so that, in principle, there is free selection.
5. Selection is dependent on technical qualifications. Officials are appointed not elected.</td></tr>
<tr><td valign="top">3. Offices are organised on a hierarchical principle—the lower offices controlled and supervised by the higher.</td><td valign="top">6. Remuneration for office is in the form of a salary, usually with pension rights attached.
7. The office constitutes a full-time occupation.</td></tr>
<tr><td valign="top">4. Technical rules or norms regulate concept of an office.
Technical training is necessary to qualify a person to be a member of an administrative staff.</td><td valign="top">8. Promotion is dependent on the judgement of seniors. Advancement from one office to another constitutes a career.</td></tr>
<tr><td valign="top">5. The administrative staff are separated as a matter of principle from ownership of the means of administration. The official is accountable for the resources he uses.</td><td valign="top">9. He is separated from ownership of the means of administration and cannot appropriate his position.</td></tr>
<tr><td valign="top">6. Incumbents cannot appropriate their offices, although they may be able to claim certain rights by virtue of their office.</td><td valign="top">10. He is subject to strict systematic discipline and control in the conduct of his office.[34]</td></tr>
</table>

[34] See M. Weber, *The Theory of Social and Economic Organisation* (Free Press, 1964), pp. 330–4.

7. Administrative business is
formulated, recorded and
conducted on the basis of
written documents.

Concerning these formulations we would make the following comments:

1. Weber is much preoccupied in his sociology with the ways in which domination of the leaders over the led is secured, maintained and changed. One form of authority expressed in ideal-type form was rational-legal. The claim to the legitimacy of this form of domination rests on a belief that the rules through which leadership is exercised are lawful. Authority is established and exercised by law. Monocratic bureaucracy is located within the rational-legal system of authority and as such is a mechanism promoting the everyday routine control of action. But in this respect it may be contrasted with the ideal type of traditional authority. Here routine control of actions may be established with reference to precedents from the past and the acceptance by the led of those in positions of authority (usually hereditary) to interpret those precedents, and govern with reference to them. The chief in a traditional system of authority is himself bound by the tradition which sanctions his personal authority.

When Weber pursues the question of traditional authority he observes that the leader may operate with or without an administrative staff. This distinction allows of further differentiation as suggested in Fig. 6.1.

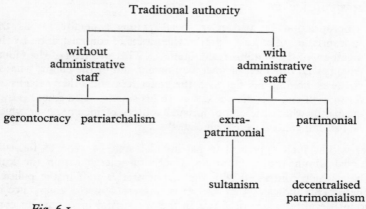

Fig. 6.1

In the simplest example of traditional authority the leadership is dependent on the willingness of the group to accept authority, since there is no machinery to enforce it. This may involve accepting the personal rule of the elders (gerontocracy) and/or the rule of an individual based upon a principle of inheritance (patriarchalism). Where an administrative staff does emerge it is established on the basis of personal loyalty to the chief rather than the impersonal obligations of office. Administrative posts are filled on the basis of ties of kinship, household and the selection of 'favourites'. This personalised form of administration (patrimonial bureaucracy) is explicitly contrasted by Weber with rational-legal bureaucracy, an impersonal mode of office bearing. It does not have an impersonal system of rules and defined spheres of competence, a rational hierarchy, a regular system of appointment and promotion, fixed salaries, nor the requirement of technical training. Within the generic patrimonial form, however, an important contrast emerges. Where the chief has the administrative staff centralised under his personal control he is able to exercise more arbitrary power (sultanism). This becomes a borderline case of traditional authority, since arbitrary rule tends to break out of traditional limitations. Against this form of absolute authority may be set decentralised patrimonialism in which the administrative staff appropriates particular powers and economic rights and can institute at least formally a separation of powers between the chief and the administration. The decisive point for Weber is that the members of the administration have independent rights. Although he acknowledges that no patrimonial state has existed in pure form he argues that medieval political organisation in Western Europe approximated to it:

> 'Appropriation by particular social groups generally means the appropriation of at least a part of the means of administration by the members of the administrative staff. . . . This was true of the feudal knight, who provided his own equipment and of the count, who by virtue of holding his fief took the court fees and other perquisites for himself and met his obligations to his superior lord from his own means, in which these appropriated sources of income, over which he had full control were included.'[35]

Yet within such approximate patrimonial states a type of formally rational administrative grouping is seen to emerge within the legal sphere which contrasted with the administrative staff in the political sphere. This indicates that Weber is interested in the emergence of rational-legal bureaucratic forms in the West. And his argument concerning the technical advantages of monocratic bureaucracy must be seen in this comparative perspective not in absolute terms.

[35] Weber, op. cit., pp. 349–50.

2. In one important respect traditional and rational-legal systems of authority are contrasted against a third form of authority, namely the charismatic. This is the leader who obtains obedience from his followers by virtue of specific qualities of character such as heroism or sanctity. Concerning this Weber writes:

'The genuine prophet, like the genuine military leader and every true leader in this sense, preaches, creates or demands, *new* obligations. In the purer type of charisma, these are imposed on the authority of revelation by oracles or of the leader's own will, and are recognised by the members of the religious, military or party group, because they come from such a source. Recognition is a duty. . . . Both restraint and traditional authority are specifically forms of everyday routine control of action; while the charismatic type is the direct antithesis of this. Bureaucratic authority is specifically rational in the sense of being bound to intellectually analysable rules: while charismatic authority is specifically irrational in the sense of being foreign to all rules. Traditional authority is bound to the precedents handed down from the past and to this extent is also orientated to rules. Within the sphere of its claims, charismatic authority repudiates the past, and is in this sense a specifically revolutionary force. It recognises no appropriation of positions of power by virtue of the possession of property, either on the part of the chief or of socially privileged groups.'[36]

Charismatic authority not only creates instability by challenging existing and alternative forms of authority: it is also an unstable basis of organisation. The charismatic leader gathers round him a group of people who have obeyed his call. He may lose his authority in his own lifetime if the followers come to believe that his powers have deserted him; certainly after his lifetime there is the question: what will happen to the leaderless group? Weber is interested in how routine control structures re-emerge and this is worked through in a schematic way in his discussion of the routinisation of charisma. This process refers both to the ways in which charismatic leadership may be transformed and to what happens to the administrative staff if it does not disband or disintegrate. On the first aspect, Weber indicates the various modes in which the succession problem is handled: these may include the leader choosing his successor, or the leader's staff choosing a successor and can result in the establishment of hereditary charismatic leaders, in whom the qualities of the original leader may be altogether absent— although of course claims or attributions may be made. So far as the

[36] ibid., pp. 361–2.

administrative staff of the leader is concerned, Weber argues that its members have strong material and ideal interests which involve them in the quest for stable routines and secure status. The charismatic movement may become traditionalised or legalised and notably is crystallised.

3. Weber is impressed in practice with the complex mixture of claims to authority which exist in historical reality, and the potential for changes in emphasis. So one may discover traditional and legal forms of authority with leadership based on the charisma of office; or charismatic leaders like Napoleon developing bureaucratic organisations in the state. The function of the ideal types is to identify the complexion of particular organised groups. Always there is the sense that even the most stable organisational structures cannot be so indefinitely. This is at least in part because of the problematical relationship between the chief and his administrative staff:

'It is most important . . . to realise that historical reality involves a continuous, though for the most part latent, conflict between chiefs and their administrative staffs for appropriation and expropriation in relation to one another. For the development of culture as a whole it has been crucial in what way this struggle has worked out and what has been the character of the class of officials dependent upon him which has helped the chief win out in his struggle against the feudal classes or other groups enjoying appropriated powers.'[37]

When, therefore, Weber writes of the victory of monocratic bureaucracy in modern industrial society over other forms of administrative organisation the victory is not to be regarded as an absolute one. Here we would make three points:

(a) The ways in which the elective principle may modify monocratic administration:

'Once the elective principle has been applied to the chief by a process of reinterpretation of charisma, it may be extended to the administrative staff. Elective officials whose legitimacy is derived from the confidence of those subject to their authority and to recall if confidence ceases to exist, are typical of certain types of democracies, for instance, the United States. They are not "bureaucratic" types. Because they have an independent source of legitimacy, they are not strongly integrated into a hierarchical order.'[38]

(b) The collegial principle can weaken the strict application of the bureaucratic principle. Instead of a decision being taken by the chief and simply transmitted through the ranks of the bureaucratic hierarchy

[37] ibid., p. 384.   [38] ibid., p. 387.

for implementation, other forms of co-ordination and co-operation may be entailed, involving a plurality of people who reach some kind of majority decision. This may be the level of supreme authority as in Parliament or Cabinet; at the level of the bureaucracy itself which may still have some elements of collegiality built in; or in agencies outside of the bureaucracy which serve to check, question or obstruct decisions.

(c) Even the existence of an unalloyed type monocratic bureaucracy would not eliminate conflict. This would obviously include conflict over who is to control the administration, notably in periods of succession to the leadership. Again Weber emphasises that bureaucracy is to be seen as a system of domination. Thus to see its speed and precision in achieving ends as of decisive importance for its emergence in capitalist society is not to ignore the fact that 'the bureaucratic apparatus may, and actually does, produce definite obstacles to the discharge of business in a manner suitable for the single case'.[39] Nor is it to ignore that to discharge its business on the basis of calculable rules in an 'objective' way might invite resistance from persons who find themselves in the way of the action. This point is strongly pursued by Weber when he notes that, while a bureaucratic administration may offer reasons for its actions in terms of a weighing up of ends and means and offering a rational outcome, this does not and cannot eradicate conflicts of interests. For example 'propertyless masses especially are not served by a formal 'equality before the law' and a 'calculable' adjudication and administration as demanded by 'bourgeois' interests. Naturally in their eyes justice and administration should serve to compensate for their economic and social life opportunities in the face of the propertied classes.'[40]

[39] M. Weber, 'Bureaucracy', in H. Gerth and C. W. Mills (eds), *From Max Weber* (Routledge & Kegan Paul, 1948), p. 221.
[40] ibid., p. 221.

7

Organisations and Society: Thematic Continuities and Cross-currents

(a) TOTALITARIAN ORGANISATIONS

A totalitarian society implies certain organisational arrangements. The precise nature of these arrangements and more particularly the factors and events which produce them remain matters for debate. Nevertheless certain ideal-typical delineations have been suggested. The following examples may be paralleled to indicate how various authors try to fix the phenomenon in their sights:

Aron	Friedrich and Brzezinski	Kornhauser
1. One party monopolises political activity.	1. An official ideology covering all vital aspects of man's existence. It is characteristically focused and projected towards a perfect final state of mankind.	1. Dictatorship based on mass support.
2. The party confers absolute authority on to its ideology. This becomes the official truth of the state.	2. Single mass party led typically by one man, the dictator. The party has a hard core of members committed to and prepared to spread the party ideology.	2. Elite domination of centralised organisation.

The party is hierarchically oligarchically organised and typically either superior to or completely intertwined with the bureaucratic government organisation.

3. The official truth is imposed by the double state monopoly of the means of coercion and the means of persuasion. The means of communication are directed and commanded by the state and its representatives.

3. Terroristic police control supports but also supervises the party and its leaders. It is directed against the 'enemies' of the regime and also arbitrarily selected classes of the population.

3. A permanently mobilised mass movement which seeks to control all aspects of life.

4. Economic and professional activities are subject to the state and are coloured by the 'official truth'.

4. The near-monopoly control of the means of communication are in the hands of the party and its subservient cadres.

4. Dictatorship involves total domination. It is not limited by received laws or codes nor by boundaries of governmental functions since the distinction between state and society is obliterated.

5. Errors in economic and professional activity are defined as ideological faults. At most there is a politicisation of all individual crimes accompanied by police and ideological terrorism.

5. The near-monopoly control of effective armed combat in the hands of the party and its subservient cadres.

6. Central control and direction of the economy through the bureaucratic co-ordination of formerly independent corporate entities.

7. Administrative
control of justice
and the courts.[1]

These depictions clearly have much in common, although curiously perhaps Aron leaves out the concept of the dictator in his formulation. It is possible to suggest, as Lane has done, that one may portray this in terms of a general model.

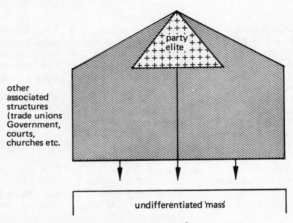

other
associated
structures
(trade unions
Government,
courts,
churches etc.

undifferentiated 'mass'

Fig. 7.1. TOTALITARIAN ELITE MODEL[2]

Lane takes the view that in fact the thinking behind such a model had important political usages during the Cold War period because it was a label which served to focus on the illiberal aspects of the Soviet Union. He further argues that such a model is undiscriminating because it does not adequately distinguish between the Soviet Union and Nazi Germany as organisational entities. Finally, he suggests that the model is unsatisfactory because it is 'static'. 'It does not pay sufficient attention to the end pursued by the Soviet political leaders. Emphasising that the population is kept in a state of constant activity and that the elite pursues a chiliastic claim tends to ignore the momentous social change accomplished by the Stalin regime. A more dynamic model is

---

[1] See R. Aron, *Democracy and Totalitarianism* (Weidenfeld & Nicolson, 1965); C. J. Friedrich and Z. K. Brzezinski, *Totalitarian Dictatorship and Autocracy* (Praeger, 1966); W. Kornhauser, *The Politics of Mass Society* (Routledge & Kegan Paul, 1960).

[2] See D. Lane, *Politics and Society in the USSR* (Weidenfeld & Nicolson, 1970), p. 192.

necessary to evaluate properly this era.'[3] We should note that whatever political usage is made out of concepts like totalitarianism it is logically separate from the validity of what they purport to describe. Further, to make typical delineations is not to describe empirical reality as such but to offer guide lines for analysis, drawn, it is true, from historical experience in order to examine particular societies. Certainly there is no reason to dispute that different societies do not become identical simply by labelling them totalitarian; but if they do have certain characteristics in common then we may assume some affinity which may be reflected in organisational arrangements. Again it is not clear why in principle the totalitarian model is too static. It might be incorrectly applied but it is not difficult to incorporate social change into the concept and in terms of labour mobilisation purges within and outside the ranks of the party and, of course, the conduct of war. However, it should be acknowledged, and this perhaps is what Lane means, that even in a totalitarian regime social conflict cannot be abolished or dissent eradicated, however much it may be desired by the rulers. This has been commented upon by Dahrendorf. For him the organised ruling class in a totalitarian society is juxtaposed against the unorganised subject class. Yet latent or undercover conflict can be expressed paradoxically through 'official' political channels. Here Dahrendorf makes reference to an aspect of totalitarian organisation not touched on in the three typologies noted above, namely the role of 'discussion'.

'... "discussion" is one of the crucial features of totalitarian government. Nowhere is there as much "discussion" as in the one-party countries of the modern world: meetings in one's factory or office, street or house, trade union, co-operative society, choir or football club, school etc., serve the one purpose of "discussing" things. These "discussions" are not, to be sure, opportunities for a free exchange of ideas. They are above all attempts at indoctrination and at soliciting that brand of "voluntary co-operation" so peculiar to modern totalitarian states. But *inter alia* and in a minor way, the meetings and "discussions" which loom so heavy in the life of every subject of totalitarian government provide a chance to voice, cautiously and in the accepted language, criticisms of individuals and policies, suggestions, and demands. . . . It is no accident that the revolts in communist countries originated among those who meet most often in large numbers: building workers, steel workers, students.'[4]

[3] Lane, op. cit., p. 190.
[4] R. Dahrendorf, *Class and Class Conflict in an Industrial Society* (Routledge & Kegan Paul, 1959), pp. 312–13.

In the passage cited, Dahrendorf emphasises the way in which opinion from below may modify action from above. While this may be seen as gnawing away at the totalitarian features, it can also be seen as an adaptive mechanism whereby the monolithic social structure is maintained. But there is a further consideration: it is that in so far as a totalitarian regime emphasises as part of its ideology the need to suppress conflict that it contributes an element of precariousness into he social structure:

> 'Due to the lack of the conditions of organisation, there is a permanent, and often growing, quantity of unreleased pressure in totalitarian states which imbues their latent political conflicts with an intensity unknown in free societies, where pressure in released almost as soon as it is created. There can be little doubt that repression of conflict by force raises the cost of victory or defeat.'[5]

The portrayal of social antagonisms in totalitarian societies is also to be located in Neumann's *Behemoth*.[6] For example, he describes the ways in which labour was controlled and mobilised. Every employee had to possess a work book with details of his occupation and work experience. This was used as a method for terrorising the worker, who no longer had the support of independent trade unions. But it is not easy to coerce a whole labour force into higher productivity, and conflict was expressed in the relatively concealed mode of go-slows and works-to-rule. Neumann notes the slow-down of miners in the Ruhr in 1938–9. This was reflected in a decline in coal production and of average productivity per man and resulted in increases in piece-rates and overtime pay being granted. Again, more generally, war legislation attempted to implement wage freezes and remove the protective legislation surrounding the conditions of work together with stopping employment insurance. This resulted in very widespread passive resistance and the regime was forced to reintroduce new legislation, broadly restoring what it had taken away and reintroducing various forms of payments for overtime and holidays. In other words, all the organised power of the State and party could not eliminate conflict, although it could affect the form of its expression. It could not obtain universal support for official policy even through coercion.

Neumann also argues that the elite groups were not homogeneous and that the army, the party, industry and the bureaucracy represented different interests and were held together by fear: fear engendered by

[5] ibid., p. 315.
[6] F. Neumann, *Behemoth. The Structure and Practice of National Socialism* (Harper, 1966).

the reign of terror and by the thought that the collapse of the regime
would destroy them all.

'Devoid of any common loyalty, concerned solely with the preservation
of their own interests, the ruling groups will break apart as soon as
the miracle producing leader meets a worthy opponent. At present,
each section needs the others. The army needs the party because the
war is totalitarian. The army cannot organise society "totally": that
is left to the party. The party, on the other hand, needs the army to
win the war and thus to stabilise and even aggrandise its own power.
Both need monopolistic industry to guarantee continuous expansion.
And all three need the bureaucracy to achieve the technical rationality
without which the system could not operate.'[7]

A sociological account of totalitarian organisation must then take into
consideration the realities of conflict and antagonism within and between
its organised constituents. But we may still ask whether any principles
of totalitarian organisations may be observed. In the context of Nazi
Germany, Neumann suggests that five major principles of National
Socialist organisation may be inferred:

1. National Socialism takes all organisations under its wing. They
   become official administrative agencies, hence the 'total' character
   of the organisation.
2. The individual is atomised, thus: 'Even leisure time is completely
   organised down to such minute details as the means of transportation provided by the authoritarian Strength through Joy
   Organisation the less important the individual member and the
   greater the influence of its bureaucracy, National Socialism has
   set about increasing the size of its social organisations to the
   utmost limit. The Labour Front has twenty-five million members.
   Of what account can the individual be? The bureaucracy is
   everything.'[8]
3. Differentiation and elite formation are deliberately designed to
   strengthen the hold of the leadership over the masses.
4. The masses must be kept in a constant state of tension through
   propaganda. This demands many transient slogans and the
   transformation of culture into propaganda.
5. Propaganda is supplemented by terror. Hence violence is a
   fundamental organisational principle.

The concept of totalitarian organisation has been impressively and

[7] ibid., pp. 397–8.   [8] ibid., pp. 401–2.

fully discussed by Hannah Arendt.[9] Although aware of the different historical configurations leading to the emergence of Hitler's Germany and Stalin's Soviet Union, she argues that there are important organisational similarities. These include, for example, in the prepower stage, the creation of front organisations. Hitler, for example, distinguished between party members and sympathisers. Whilst the former were a relatively small hard core, the latter group was constantly expanding and being enrolled into front organisations. Such organisations perform a double function:

> 'The fellow traveller organisations surround the totalitarian movements with a mist of normality and respectability that fools the membership about the true character of the outside world as much as it does the outside world about the true character of the movement. The front organisation functions both ways: as a facade of the totalitarian movement to the non-totalitarian world, and as the facade of this world to the inner hierarchy of the movement.'[10]

The front organisation is thus a recruiting agent by its presentation of ordinariness and respectability; it gives the sympathiser a positive role to play and thus encourages his further commitment to the movement. In addition it helps to resolve cognitive dissonance for the party member, in his perception of the outside world. If the fellow traveller is a 'normal' person who yet shares his beliefs then the gap between fictitious beliefs and the stock of knowledge available in the outside world can be imagined away.

A second organisation factor is the existence of a fluctuating hierarchy. This is done in order to maintain tension and the appropriate level of militancy in the movement and for the continuing effort that had to be made to control the controllers. So the stormtroopers (SA) were founded in 1922 within the party as a counter to the supposed loss of radicalness in the party as a whole. This new elite was subsequantly replaced by the SS in 1926. At first the SS constituted a core elite within the SA. In 1929, however, it was organisationally separated from it and directed by Himmler. Further elite formations within the SS were later to be spawned, each making claims to a high degree of militancy—the Shock Troops, the Death Head unity, the Security Service and the Office for Questions of Race and Resettlement. Arendt points out that the para-military formations were organised after the model of criminal gangs and used for organised murder:

> 'In this respect the practice of elite formations is the very opposite

[9] Hannah Arendt, *The Origins of Totalitarianism* (Allen & Unwin, 1967).
[10] ibid., p. 367.

of that of the front organisations: while the latter lend the movement an air of respectability and inspire confidence, the former by extending complicity make every party member aware that he has left for good the normal world which outlaws murder and· that he will be held accountable for all crimes committed by the elite. . . . For the movement, organised violence is the most efficient of the many protective walls which surround its fictitious world, whose 'reality' is proved when a member fears leaving the movement more than he fears the consequences of his complicity in illegal actions, and feels more secure as a member than as an opponent.'[11]

A third organisational feature relates to the creation of duplicate organisations. Arendt argues that in the prepower stage such fake organisations convey the impression that the party contains within its ranks all elements of society. Its practical value upon the seizure of power was clear enough. In Nazi Germany all manner of professional and voluntary associations could be swiftly transformed in character as the duplicate organisations replaced the originals.

A fourth characteristic to be observed is the organisational similarity of totalitarian movements to secret societies. Hierarchies within the organisation are accompanied by initiation ceremonies regarded as appropriate for a particular stratum; members who are expected to lie to non-members, to be obedient to the organisation in an unquestioning way, and more particularly to swear allegiance to a leader who is seen as the possessor of mysterious qualities. And there is the emphasis on ritual, the marches and the celebrations, to emphasise in a symbolic way the bonds that hold the members together. The paradox was, as Arendt points out, that totalitarian organisations adopted so many of the devices of the secret societies without attempting to keep their own intention secret. Arendt suggests that in the case of Nazi Germany, the Nazis modelled themselves more or less consciously on the secret society of the Elders of Zion practically from the outset: in the Soviet Union, the sequence of movement from one-party dictatorship to politbureau dictatorship to the dictatorship of one man, Stalin, created for him the need to enforce the conditions of a secret society within mass organisation. Hence the emphasis on enemies within the without, the search for and punishing of conspiracies, the utilisation of scapegoats who are seen as representing a threat to the movement. The need for a secret police to confront and reveal these ever-present threats follows from this and the method of terrorisation is again seen to be an essential part of the totalitarian structure. Essential too to the portrayal is the

[11] ibid., pp. 372–5.

concept of a society of conspirators set against a world-wide conspiracy that can penetrate even the inner sanctum of the party (whose most respected members, therefore, are never entirely safe).

'The obvious contradiction between a mass organisation and an exclusive society, which alone can be entrusted to keep a secret, is of no importance compared with the fact that the very fact of secret and conspiratory societies could translate the totalitarian ideological dichotomy—the blind hostility of the masses against the existing world regardless of its divergences and differences—into an organisational principle. From the viewpoint of an organisation, which functions according to the principle that whosoever is not included is excluded, whoever is not with me is against me. The world at large loses all the nuances, differentiations and pluralistic aspects which had in any event become confusing and unbearable to the masses who had lost their place and their orientation in it. What inspired them with the unwavering loyalty of members of secret societies was not so much the secret as the dichotomy between Us and all others. This could be kept intact by imitating the secret societies' organisational structure and emptying it of its rational purpose of propagandising a secret.'[12]

One final point which needs emphasis is the role of the leader. Giving the opportunity for the organisational principles already discussed to flourish, the leader emerges as one who is above the law—the will of the Führer becomes the supreme law. In this Stalin was to follow Hitler's example. Arendt maintains that the most important organisational aspect of the leader principle is that every functionary is conveying orders which come from the one source only: the leader, with whom they are identified in a total all-embracing way.

The leader principle was, as we have seen, not emphasised by Aron and is not clearly articulated in Lane's model noted above. There is an important corollary in relation to this omission which has recently been taken up by Schapiro.[13] It is that it may not be wholly satisfactory to describe totalitarian organisations simply in terms of the extension of state power. The leader through his personal role, given the organisational conditions which have thrust him into power, seeks to dominate the State itself and reduce that and the party which spawned him to a mere apparatus of his role. It is this which distinguishes if from other forms of elite domination, ruling oligarchies, military regimes and one-party states, even though these may contain some of the necessary

[12] ibid., pp. 380–1.
[13] See Leonard Schapiro, *Totalitarianism* (Macmillan, 1972).

conditions for totalitarian organisation. It represented a distinctive form of lawlessness and is most unambiguously located in the role of Hitler and Stalin. Hence Schapiro concludes:

'Totalitarianism is a new from of dictatorship which grew up in the conditions of mass democracy after the First World War. It was characterised by the predominance of the leader of the victorious movement, who with the aid of his subordinate elite and a manipulated ideology, aimed total control over state, society and individual. Leaders and elite, by claiming the right to interpret the official ideology, in effect embodies both Church and State: they subverted the law to their own ends and claimed to control private morality. They mobilised mass support and enthusiasm from which they claimed to derive their legitimacy.'[14]

(b) ORGANISATION AND THE 'IRON LAW OF OLIGARCHY'

The statement 'who says organisation, says oligarchy' serves as a challenge to any student of organisations. Michels's development of this theme was prompted by his reflections on the place of political parties and trade unions in industrial societies.[15] He was in some measure anticipated by Ostrogorski's work on political parties[16] and the Webbs' study of trade unions.[17] Both of these sources were cited by him. More generally he was influenced by Weber's treatment of bureaucracy and indeed dedicated the first German edition of *Political Parties* to him. Further he shared with Pareto a sense of the ways in which ideologies can mask political and social realities. In particular he was impressed with the oligarchical tendencies of large organisations even where they proclaimed a democratic ideology. Although he is sometimes depicted as an elitist who through his writings attacked the content and substance of democratic organisations, this was not how he viewed his activity. He spells out the role of the sociologist in a somewhat Weberian way:

'The present study makes no attempt to offer a "new system". It is not the principal aim of science to create systems, but rather to promote understanding. It is not the purpose of sociological science

---

[14] ibid., pp. 118–19.
[15] See R. Michels, *Political Parties. A Sociological Study of the Oligarchical Tendencies of Modern Democracy* (Collier, 1962).
[16] M. I. Ostrogorski, *Democracy and the Organisation of Political Parties* (Anchor, 1964).
[17] S. and B. Webb, *Industrial Democracy* (London, 1911).

to discover, or rediscover, solutions, since numerous problems of the individual life and the life of social groups are not capable of "solutions" at all, but must ever remain "open". The sociologist should aim rather at the dispassionate exposition of tendencies and counter-operating forces, of reasons and opposing reasons, as the display in a word of the warp and woof of social life. Precise diagnosis is the logical and indispensable preliminary to any possible prognosis.'[18]

Michels's arguments concerning the oligarchical tendencies in mass organisations may be expressed in a series of tendency statements:

1. Large organisations find it practically impossible for all members to participate equally in discussion and decision-making.

2. There is a tendency for mass organisation to be divided into a minority of leaders and a majority of led.

3. Such organisations as thus develop exhibit a tendency to differentiate functions and activities. They become progressively bureaucratised with a centralised administration.

4. The bureaucratic administration is interposed between the leaders and the led. It increases the social, psychological and educational differences between them.

5. For administrative, technical and tactical reasons such organisations to be successful need professional leadership. But in fulfilling this need the gap between the leaders and the led is reinforced. Further, as fighting organisations in the political arena they have an elective affinity with military organisations: hence the preoccupation with promptness of decision, unity of command and strictness of discipline.

6. There is a psychological need on the part of the masses for leadership, which need is sometimes accompanied by a leadership cult. Oligarchical tendencies are encouraged by the unwillingness or inability of the masses to interest themselves in the affairs of the party or union, but are happy to leave it to the few who will take the time, trouble and energy.

7. Once in office, leaders of mass organisations tend to stay there to have considerable say as to who shall fill the chief offices and actively seek to control who shall succeed them.

8. There is a tendency for the leader to take the view—'*Le parti c'est Moi*' and to become despotic even when the organisation exists for democratic purposes.

Michels reaches therefore his celebrated conclusion: 'It is organisation which gives birth to the dominion of the elected over the electors, of

18 Michels, op. cit., p. 6.

the mandatories over the mandators, of the delegates over the delegators. Who says organisation, says oligarchy.'[19]

In noting the above propositions, we should add that inasmuch as Michels was focusing on socialist organisations, other propositions which more specifically relate to the fate and conduct of the class struggle are formulated. These include: (a) The growing tendency of the leadership either to be selected from the ranks of the bourgeois or to become embourgeoisified. (b) The tendency of proletariat leaders to sell out to or accommodate to the capitalist system. (c) Increasing status differentiation within the working class leading to a decline in militant class consciousness. Those who for one reason or another raise their standard of living may 'secure a position in which, though they may not completely lose the common human feeling of never being able to get enough, from which millionaires are not altogether exempt, they will become so far personally satisfied as to be gradually estranged from the revolutionary aspirations of the masses towards a social system utterly different from their own—aspirations born of privation'.[20]

It should be carefully noted that Michels in the main is making statements which are in principle subject to further exploration. He presents evidence which he believes substantiates the statements but in any event they are in the market-place of debate. And he is offering a statement of tendencies which in certain circumstances might be open to modification. For example:

1. Leadership struggles. These can be important in their own right. They may be founded in conflicts between old and aspiring leaders, conflicts between bureaucratic functions, or between local and national leaders.

2. Ideology. If there are illusions about democracy and its operation Michels does not conclude that the democratic ideal be abandoned nor that it makes no difference:

'It is in fact a general characteristic of democracy, and hence also of the labour movements, to stimulate and to strengthen in the individual the intellectual aptitudes for criticism and control. We have seen how the progressive bureaucratisation of the democratic organism tends to neutralise the beneficial effects of such criticism and such control. None the less it is true that the labour movement, in virtue of the theoretical postulates it proclaims, is apt to bring into existence (in opposition to the will of the leaders) a certain number of free-spirits, who, moved by principle, by instinct, or by both

[19] ibid., p. 365.   [20] ibid., p. 276.

desire to revise the base on which authority is established. . . . They are never weary of asking an eternal "Why?" about every human institution.'[21]

3. Education of the masses. It is this which may diminish the gap between leaders and led and by the same token, increase the capacity for criticism and control of the leadership.

A number of studies have found theoretical stimulus from Michels's work. There is, for example, R. T. McKenzie's *British Political Parties*, which concerns itself with the distribution of power in the Conservative and Labour Parties of the UK.[22] In concluding his impressive and detailed study McKenzie takes the view that the technical and psychological factors which Michels claimed prompted the emergence of oligarchical leadership operated in the case of both parties. However, in the British context, he is less persuaded of the overall strength of oligarchical tendencies. The qualifications he puts forward are two-fold. First, the relationship between party leaders and the membership of the mass organisation cannot be taken for granted by the leadership as one which always entails obedience: 'Blind appeals to loyalty (either to the person of the leader or to the party itself) are frequently resorted to, and often they achieve their purpose. But, they are rarely successful in bridging a real gulf when one does develop between leaders and followers.'[23] Since McKenzie made this point, further experience would appear to substantiate it. The disaffection of the Labour Party membership with the Labour Government by the end of its term of office in 1969 was widely observed and commented upon and the party machine for the election was undermanned and often half-heartedly operated. McKenzie further maintains that Michels's version of democratic practice extended the control of the party leaders by the members of the organisation and that this contrasts with democratic theory in the British parliamentary system, which holds that MPs and political parties are responsible to the electorate:

'. . . a crude application of Michels's theories would ignore what might be termed the division of labour within British political parties. It would ignore the fact that the primary function of the mass organisations is to sustain competing teams of potential leaders in the House of Commons in order that the electorate as a whole may choose between them. All other functions (involving attempts by the mass organisations to influence the formulation of policy and

21 ibid., p. 369.
22 R. T. McKenzie, *British Political Parties* (Mercury, 2nd edn, 1964).
23 ibid., p. 644.

the emergence of leaders within the parliamentary party) are and must remain subsidiary. The mass organisations may be permitted to play some part in these respects; but if they attempted to arrogate to themselves a determining influence with respect of policy or leadership they would be cutting across the chain of responsibility from Cabinet, to Parliament, to electorate which is fundamental to the theory of the British parliamentary system.'[24]

The thrust of the second point is not altogether clear. Certainly Michels was preoccupied with the relationship of leader to led in mass organisations as part of the problem of realising democratic organisation. But this problem was part of and couched in the context of the general problem (following Rousseau) of whether representative democracy was democracy at all. One question is whether the electoral system impinges upon the iron law by modifying or reinforcing party oligarchy. Or is one saying that the theory of parliamentary democracy simply serves to settle the question which oligarchy will govern for the next period of office?

Another political sociologist to pay great attention to Michels's work is S. M. Lipset.[25] He is broadly in sympathy with Michels's thesis. In discussing trade union organisations, for example, he argues that the tendency towards bureaucratisation which they exhibit characteristically puts effective control in the hands of an administrative oligarchy over and against the rank and file or opposing factions. Control relates to such matters as financial resources, internal communications, and the political machine of the union, all of which may be used to claim and sustain the legitimacy of the oligarchy. An important counteracting tendency is however noted by Lipset, namely where the membership becomes actively involved in the organisation. In their study of the International Typographical Union, Lipset and his colleagues explore in great detail the internal political organisation of that union and highlight a number of factors which work against the oligarchical tendencies which they concede to be widespread in large scale organisations. It is suggested, for example the membership involvement in trade union organisation is encouraged by the existence of an occupational community, opportunities for on-the-job informal social contacts, sense of occupational identification and interest in the work

[24] ibid., p. 645.
[25] See S. M. Lipset: 'The Political Process in Trade Unions', *Political Man* (Mercury, 1963); *Agrarian Socialism* (Anchor, 1968); with M. A. Trow and J. S. Coleman, *Union Democracy. The Internal Politics of the International Typographical Union* (Free Press, 1956); and introductory essay to the Collier edition of Michels's *Political Parties*.

tasks. Again where unions are federally organised with branch autonomy built into the arrangement the conditions for democratic unions are partly met. This touches on the issues of decentralisation of decision-making which Michels tends to gloss over by saying that this is simply a struggle between the local and the national oligarchy. This is to make light of an important organisational difference concerning the distribution of power and decision-making.

Lipset et al. further suggest that where there is little internal occupational stratification in a union and where the gap between the status of union leaders and occupational status is very small, the chances for union democracy are enhanced; and when the occupational status of the union grouping is high then the tendency to want to participate in the decision-making processes of the union will be strong. Such factors reduce the hierarchical nature of the organisation. Moreover they underline the importance of education in minimising oligarchical tendencies, which Michels had himself stressed. To all this Lipset et al. add the importance of an institutionalised party system existing in the trade union such that, the incumbent leadership can, according to established rules of the game, be removed from office by an opposing faction.

Although Lipset's study of the ITU was primarily a case study in depth of a particular union, it may fairly be said to have elaborated the point (as McKenzie likewise did for political parties) that there is more variation in the internal organisation of trade unions than a simple-minded application of the iron law of oligarchy would seem to imply.

(c) ORGANISATIONS AND THE CONCEPT OF PLURALISM

Pluralism as a sociological term is perhaps beyond redemption, simply because of the wide-ranging, sometimes ambiguous and sometimes inconsistent connotations which are attached to it. This presents a very considerable problem for the sociology of organisations. What we can attempt to do in an indicative and illustrative way is to disentangle some of the usages and their import. We shall make a broad distinction between usages of the term as applied to an organisation and as applied to relations between organisations.

(i) *Pluralism within an organisation*
One seemingly obvious point of departure here is to operate the contrast between unitary and pluralist concepts of organisational structure. Although ultimately unsatisfactory it may identify some important issues.

In classical management theory the simplest prescription for achieving organisational objectives was to operate a hierarchical line of command. Unity of command was to be ensured by not missing any links in the single hierarchical structure and by proceeding on the basis that the flow of instructions and information went one way—downwards. The nearest approximation to this model was probably to be found in the army—although even there it would be foolish to suppose that the prescription was identical with the reality—alternative sources of power might manifest themselves within the ranks to provide a check on or resistance to the power of the commander. Nonetheless, if one attempts to implement a prescription then it will affect the formal organisation structure and those who oppose the laid down pattern of authority could become victims of very stringent sanctions, including the loss of life itself for refusing to obey an order.

As organisations grow in size, however, the single line of command proves an impossible prescription. At the very least, a differentiation of functions can emerge. In the industrial context, for example, the entrepreneur may increasingly feel himself under pressure to use and co-ordinate particular forms of expertise relating, say, to production, finance and marketing. At that point, even regarding the situation purely in formal terms, the possibility of different functional groups competing with one another for such things as rescources, policies, and personnel is written in. It is in essence group differentiation and competition between them for objects, values or goals that they hold important which provides a basis for incipient pluralism. One may seek to impose a unitary ideology on top of this in terms of the unity of command—the chief will decide what is good for the organisation. The importance of holding such an ideology is not to be denied in terms of decision-making implications but, at the same time, the structural reality has to be noted.

When one moves to other modifications of the line principle of unity of command, the point already made is strongly reinforced. The major adjustment in managerial prescriptions was of course the advocacy of line and staff organisation. Basically it is an attempt to graft on advisory functions which in theory will influence, but not determine, line decisions and also to make use of general administrators whose task is to co-ordinate functions and report back to their chief. In other words, the concept of staff suggests the further distinction between specialists and co-ordinators—the first offering advice and the second having delegated executive authority. It is, for example, in the second sense that one may speak of staff linking line and specialist groups vertically, laterally and diagonally (in relation to a formal hierarchical organisation chart). Gulick and Urwick do this in discussing military organisations.[26] This can lead to quite complex models of formal organisation, which in the classical tradition of scientific management might be applied to other large scale organisations, notably in industry and government administration. What is perhaps instructive is that in trying to operationalise the units of command principle some form of unitary ideology is built in almost unconsciously. That is to say, even when functional differentiations are acknowledged as necessary these are seen as subordinate to the command function and as contributing to the work of the team with its image of working towards defined and agreed objective—defeating the enemy, increasing efficiency and so on. Behaviour which does not conform to the unitary ideology is likely to be interpreted as disloyal or irresponsible. A system of rewards and punishments is likely to be formally instituted on this basis. This does not mean that deviations cannot occur but these are treated as organisational pathologies. Take for example this comment from Sargant Florence on military organisation:

'The danger is also inherent in staff and line organisation of creating back-room boys or a superior high-brow set who may further increase the "idle" overhead. Certainly the staff have been pictured as sitting at headquarters devising paper forms and questionnaires to annoy the executive line officers and the men doing the "donkey work" at the actual front. In both first and second world wars some still remember, even if they cannot print, what the infantry-men in the trenches thought of the "red-tabs" or "brass" segregated at the base.'[27]

What is dangerous is that which detracts from the achievement of the overall organisational objective and this is defined by the authorised leadership which seeks to implement the personnel and resources of the organisation towards that end. When Sargant Florence discusses industrial organisation it is in terms of what arrangement is best suited to promote efficiency and this in turn is related to the type of production system:

'The staff and line system coupled with co-ordinating committees is probably that best adapted for the efficient large-scale production of a few articles within one firm, i.e. for large-scale operation. If with lateral or vertical integration many processes are performed or

[26] See L. Gulick and L. F. Urwick, *Papers on the Science of Administration* (Institute of Public Administration, 1937).

[27] P. Sargant Florence, *The Logic of British and American Industry* (Routledge & Kegan Paul, 1953), p. 161.

many products made each on a small scale, many separate departments must be created each with an executive officer in charge and
the organisation logically tends to the hierarchical or functional
pattern. But . . . it will pay, if there are only a few processes or
products each on a large scale, to do more specialised but co-ordinated
planning and checking of the specific problems of each, and to
discuss in committee the closely related work of those thinking and
acting upon a single process or product.'[28]

If one accepts Sargant Florence's assumptions, it then becomes possible
to detect organisational pathologies and to suggest prescriptions whereby
the ideology and the reality of the unitary system of authority come more
closely together in practice.

At a more explicitly analytical level the question of the nature of
pluralism in organisations has also been sociologically discussed. There
is for example Gouldner's treatment of functional autonomy within
organisations.[29] By way of critique he attacks 'rational' models of
organisation because of what one might now term a unitary perspective.
This views the organisation as a structure of manipulable parts which
may be modified to achieve organisational efficiency by careful planning
and decision-making. In essence it assumes a view as to what constitutes
efficiency and desirable long-term objectives and conviction that the
parts of the organisation can be brought into conformity with the plan.
Such a model, we may note, may be constructed by social scientists
and may obviously provide hope to those in organisations who are in
positions of authority and are looking for a theoretical base for their
prescriptive activities. Gouldner is, however, also dissatisfied with
what he terms the natural system model of organisations. This is a
model based on the assumption of the organisation striving to survive
and maintain its equilibrium. This focus on the organisation as the
unit of analysis can, in Gouldner's view, emphasise homeostatic
mechanisms and the emergent normative structures with an accompanying view of shared organisational values. Independent action and
the possibility of a plurality of values within the organisation is consequently minimised.

Part of Gouldner's argument is that both of these models are inadequate as total approaches to organisational analysis and that more
conceptual subtlety is called for. The notion of functional autonomy
for example 'directs attention to the fact that *some* parts may survive

---

[28] ibid., p.162.
[29] See A. Gouldner, 'Organisational Analysis', in R. K. Merton *et al.* (eds),
Sociology Today (Harper Torchbooks, 1965), pp. 400–28.

separation from others, that parts vary in their dependence upon one another, and that their interdependence is not necessarily symmetrical'.[30] This is a modifying statement about natural systems which does not take for granted the mutual interdependence of the parts of an organisation. Asymmetry as well as symmetry may be detected. Thus one may examine what parts of an organisation may survive in times of crises and what parts may be pared down or disappear. In a business organisation, in times of cut-back, research and development or welfare functions may prove to be more vulnerable than production functions. But conceptually the unitary/pluralism polarity becomes a matter of centripetal versus centrifugal forces:

> 'Assuming that the organisation's parts, no less than the organisation as a whole, operate to maintain their boundaries and to remain in equilibrium, then the parts should be expected to defend their functional autonomy, or at least some measure of it from encroachment. This suggests that a basic source of organisational tension may derive, on the one hand, from the tendency of the parts to resist encroachment on their functional autonomy and, on the other, from contrary tendencies of the organisation's controlling centre to limit or reduce the functional autonomy of the parts. The widely noted tensions between field officers and main officers, as well as the common organisational oscillation between centralisation and decentralisation seem to support this assumption, as do the frequently observed rejection of 'close supervision' and the pressure which almost all role players exert to maintain some social distance from and freedom from control by those most crucially concerned with their work.'[31]

The importance of this kind of presentation is that conflict is built into the analysis, based upon competition between the parts and between the whole and the parts, and upon the postulate of asymmetrical relationships within the system. Hence assumptions about agreed organisational goals, or about strains towards organisational equilibrium cannot remain unexamined. The empirical question becomes how much functional autonomy may be observed in particular organisations and how is this to be explained. Thus high functional autonomy suggests a form of pluralist organisation and low functional autonomy a more unitary one. Another important example at this level of our exposition is Burns's significantly titled paper 'On the Plurality of Social Systems'.[32] Burns shares with Gouldner doubts about the adequacy

[30] ibid., p. 419.   [31] ibid., pp. 420–1.
[32] T. Burns, 'On the Plurality of Social Systems', in M. Gilbert (ed.), *The Modern Business Enterprise* (Penguin, 1972), pp. 105–21.

of rationality models of the organisation. Yet a resurgent interest in formal organisations has, in his opinion, tended to bring back into focus classical management theory conceptions of unitary structures and his critical comments are on similar lines to those of Gouldner. However, his analytical response is not in terms of functional autonomy of sub-systems in relation to the overall organisational system: rather he postulates the existence of distinct social systems which are interrelated in an organisational milieu. In a business enterprise, for example, he differentiates three such systems: the working organisation, the career system and the political system. Each of these supposes individuals and groups in competition with each other, in an arena where ground rules exist but are themselves challenged from time to time. A plurality of means-ends systems for achieving certain posts may co-exist for the individual. This will be reflected and represented in the social relationships and conduct of the individual organisation members. Over and against the unitary view, which would treat the working organisation as central and other relationships as deviant, Burns argues for the necessary pluralism of the organisation and consequently contends that the political system and career structure necessarily influence the character of the working organisation. This is so whether or not the ideology of the organisation is based upon unitary or pluralist premises. The methodological question becomes, in Burns's analysis, to discern the patterns of individual commitments in order to account for the particular mixture of co-operation and conflict in the organisation. The general point about the relationship between the individual and the organisation in this pluralist conceptual analysis is well brought out in the following comment:

'The interaction of all these systems rests on the fact that an individual may invoke any of them as the dominant reference system for this or that action, decision or plan, even though an outside observer, or the individual himself, for that matter, may see other manifest relevance of what he is doing to all or any of the other systems. What I have called systems exist for the individual as social *Gestalten*, without which acts cannot be seen as items in means-end or cause-effect change, and decisions cannot be given any preference ordering.'[33]

The co-existence of plural and interacting social systems was, of course, impressively delineated in the Western Electric studies which took place in the 1920s and 1930s at the Hawthorn Plant, Chicago.[34]

[33] ibid., pp. 119–20.
[34] See F. T. Roethlisberger and W. T. Dickson, *Management and the Worker* (Wiley, 1964).

This was much more than contrasting formal organisational demands with informal group behaviour. Major distinctions are drawn between:

1. The technical organisation of an enterprise, that is the organisation of raw materials, tools and machines for accomplishing the productive task.

2. The human organisation. This is interpreted at the level of the individual members who come to their jobs with varying needs and expectations, which are viewed as a product of personal biography and social conditioning together with social relationships within and outside the plant.

3. The social organisation. This refers to the occupational and group categories which may be discerned in an enterprise and the patterned relationships emerging from interaction. The relationships, although they may become standardised and even depend on stereotyped conceptions of 'the other', can also be complex and allow of fine gradations. For example, the relationship between a foreman and his subordinate may vary depending on whether or not the manager is present. Roethlisberger and Dickson might be ethnomethodologists before the term was coined when they write:

> 'These subtle nuances of relationships are so much a part of everyday life that they are commonplace. They are taken for granted. The vast amount of social conditioning that has taken place by means of which a person manoeuvres himself gracefully through the intricacies of these finely shaded social distinctions is seldom explicitly realised. Attention is paid only when a new social situation arises where the past social training of the person prevents him from making the necessary delicate interpretations of a given social signal and hence brings forth the "socially wrong" response.'[35]

4. The formal organisation. This is a prescriptive set of rules, policies and procedures which purport to lay down what the goals of the enterprise are and how the members are to relate to one another in order to realise the defined objectives. These rules will be of a prescriptive nature and will seek to provide the grounds for a control system to secure the co-operation of the organisation's members.

5. The informal organisation. Behaviour in organisations cannot be captured in formal statements about the ways in which functional groups are supposed to relate for technical and production purposes. There are other bases upon which individuals and groups are differentiated and evaluated. The various work groups studies at Hawthorn

[35] ibid., p. 555.

unearthed important examples of just such informal organisations and provided the impetus to many other such studies subsequently.

6. The ideological organisation. The concern here is with the system of beliefs and values which may be located in an organisation. These may be general throughout an organisation, or they may be connected with particular segments of the organisation, formal or informal. Examples of the kinds of value systems Roethlisberger and Dickson have in mind are: the logic of cost—the set of ideas concerning the evaluation of the economic purposes of the organisation; the logic of efficiency—ideas as to how to maximise the collaborative efforts of organisations members to achieve efficiency; and the logic of sentiments—the values placed on human relationships within and between particular groups. What is interesting here is the sense of a plurality of belief systems co-existing within the organisation, different in range, intensity and content and certainly not always complementary. One tries to discuss what their beliefs are, how and why they are appropriated and what connection they have with reality (this last on the assumption that the investigator can check out on what constitutes reality).

Some of these ideas and beliefs represent more closely the actual situation than others. In all cases, however, they are abstractions from the concrete situation. In this respect they are to the concrete situation as maps are to the territories they represent, and like maps these abstractions may be either misleading or useful. They may be misleading because sometimes the person using them fails to realise they are representing only one part of the total organisation. Sometimes in the minds of certain individuals these abstractions tend to become divorced from the social reality and in effect, lead an independent existence.'[36]

What is of interest about the kind of differentiation of organisational elements noted above is, first, the strong sense of the need to appreciate the interconnectedness of the parts of the organisation. Although the matter need not detain us in this context, we may briefly observe that the starting points for charting changes in relationships between the parts are two-fold. Outside the organisation is the economic problem—how does it adjust to meet changing market situations? Inside the organisation is the matter of changes in the technical system. The investigators note, for example, the possibility of disparities in the rates of change in technical systems and social organisations. Since the ideological organisation of the plant is interlaced with the technical,

[36] ibid., pp. 562–3.

human and social organisation, the ramifications in terms of conflict and co-operation in the enterprise are extensive and complex.

The second point of interest is that the implications of this kind of analysis were spelled out with reference to managerial control. If management wished to control the direction of organisational activity then, the argument ran, it must first understand the pluralistic nature of the enterprise. Roethlisberger and Dickson essentially posed the question, how can organisational effectiveness be achieved? This question is directed at management and an answer along the following lines is suggested:

1. Do not have an over-simple view of how to control an organisation. 'Scientific controls have been introduced to further the economic purpose of the concern and of the individuals within it. Much of this advance has gone on in the name of efficiency or rationalisation. Nothing comparable to this advance has gone on in the development of skills and techniques for securing co-operation, that is for getting individuals and groups of individuals working together effectively and with satisfaction to themselves.'[37]

2. Do not have an unrealistic or faulty ideology. Recognise, for example, the reality of informal organisation both at worker and management level. Do not condemn this as 'bad' or attempt to eradicate such organisation since this is impossible; rather consider how it may facilitate purposive co-operation and communication. Sectional interests can be transcended in this way: 'What the Relay Assembly Test Room experiment showed was that when innovations are introduced carefully and with regard to the natural sentiments of the workers, the workers are likely to develop a spontaneous type of informal organisation which will not only express more adequately their own values and significance but is also more likely to be in harmony with the aims of management.'[38]

Consequently the pluralist analysis of the enterprise moves to a prescriptive statement about how the organisation as a whole might more effectively be controlled by management through the operation of a human relations ideology. This is done on the grounds of realism. The authenticity of management is thus legitimated on the grounds that, through collaboration with all groups, management is acting in the interests of all organisation members. The true interests of management, based on a realistic appraisal of the pluralistic character of the enterprise are identical with the true interests of the constituent groups.

[37] ibid., pp. 552–3.   [38] ibid., pp. 561–2.

This emphasis on the need for managerial ideologies to be realistic has also more recently been explicitly articulated by Fox.[39] In his discussion of industrial organisation he poses this question:

'What is the closest analogy to the enterprise—is it, or ought it to be, analogous to a team, unified by a common purpose, or is it more plausibly viewed as a coalition of interests, a miniature democratic State composed of sectional groups with divergent interests over which the Government tries to maintain some kind of dynamic equilibrium?'[40]

He suggests that the way we answer the question affects the way we expect people to behave or ought to behave, how we respond to their actual behaviour in the organisation. Further it will also affect our prescriptions as to how to change behaviour we regard as inappropriate. It is perhaps as well to note that 'we' in the above sentence, primarily refers to managers, as does the term Government in the quotation.

Fox then contrasts the unitary and pluralist conceptions of the industrial enterprise and suggests that many managers hold a unitary view which is, he argues, demonstrably at variance with the facts. In pursuing his analysis Fox is concerned to demonstrate the reality of conflicts of interests in the enterprise and the existence of competing sources of authority for employees' allegiances both within and without the enterprise. Against this he sets unitary managerial ideologies which interpret conflict in terms of personalities, or failure in communication, or agitators who are 'rocking the boat' and which treat co-operation in the enterprise as axiomatic and consequently do not examine the assumption it contains.

Yet the analysis of pluralism is addressed to managers who through understanding the pluralist nature of the enterprise may be able more effectively to control and change it: 'A management which fully accepts the reality of work-group interests which conflict quite legitimately with their own will seek honestly and patiently to understand the causes of particular group practices and policies, in the full awareness that imaginative understanding is a precondition of success in modifying behaviour.'[41] And again in commenting on restrictive practices and workers' resistance to change he says: 'Only a pluralistic view can see them for what they are: rational responses by sectional interests to protect employment, stabilise earnings, maintain job status, defend group bargaining power or preserve craft boundaries. The unitary view can condemn them as morally indefensible: the pluralistic view can understand them, and by understanding is in a position to

[39] See Alan Fox, *Industrial Sociology and Industrial Relations* (HMSO, 1966).
[40] ibid., p. 2.   [41] ibid., p. 10.

change them.'[42] The discussion then centres around the idea of transcending conflicts of interest by moving to a higher level of mutual advantage. Yet such advantages, while mutual, need not be evenly distributed nor for that matter need they be total. What is under discussion is how the government (established management) can continue to govern, given competing sources of authority. And the pluralistic analysis is put forward as a more realistic way of proceeding. Within that context 'the managerial method in future must increasingly be that of winning consent of work-groups through the medium of ordered relationships with those groups; relationships which recognise their independence and their right to express it through their own leaders.'[43] It is important to add that Fox's general analysis of pluralism has significantly shifted since that paper was written.[44]

(ii) *Pluralism and the relationship between organisations*

In labelling relationships between organisations as pluralistic one encounters the fact that this sometimes has reference to particular kinds of organisations, say religious, and sometimes to a whole complex of organisations in society, say religious, political, military, economic and legal. We will use this basic distinction as a point of departure for this section and will hope to elucidate a range of issues and problems which are thereby thrown up to serve at least as an exercise in clarification. However, there is one general point which may be made at the outset. It is that there is an implied contrast between a monopolistic organisation and organisations that are in competition with each other. The nature and degree of that competition invites much more specific examination. The extreme contrast, drawing upon economic terminology, is between a total monopoly on the one hand and an organisation operating in conditions of perfect competition in a designated market situation.

It may be recalled that when Joseph Schumpeter, himself a distinguished economist, wrote *Capitalism, Socialism and Democracy*, he constructed a theory of political competition which was derived from the economic concept of competition. He did not, however, imagine that a situation of perfect competition could be realised, but he does make the following comment: 'Between this ideal case which does not exist and the cases in which all competition with the established leader is prevented by force, there is a continuous range of variations within which the democratic method of government shades off into the auto-

---

[42] ibid., p. 12.   [43] ibid., p. 14.
[44] See A. Fox, 'Industrial Relations: A Social Critique of Pluralist Ideology', in John Child (ed.), *Man and Organisation* (Allen & Unwin, 1973), pp. 185–233.

cratic one by imperceptible steps.'[45] In the political sphere, therefore, the contrast is drawn between autocracy and democracy and the possibility of imperfections and inequalities in the competitive struggle as between groups is built in. This is an important qualification, for without it the pluralist conception of political activity is liable to be presented as an equilibrating process in which organisations of roughly equal strength achieve parity in the distribution and exercise of power. Such an assumption, if permitted, tends to justify whatever outcomes occur in the competitive struggle as democratic. But this assumes what has to be proved and, as Miliband has suggested: 'What is wrong with pluralist-democratic theory is not its insistence on the factor of competition but its claim (very often its implicit assumption) that, the major organised "interests" in these societies, and notably capital and labour, compete on more or less equal terms, and that none of them is therefore able to achieve a decisive and permanent advantage in the process of competition. This is where ideology enters and turns observation into myth.'[46] The above quotation touches also on the question of the relationship between the strictly political sphere and other spheres of social life and we shall return to that. For the moment, however, we proceed to reflect on the fact that the pattern of competition between organisations is one thing and the pattern of competition of individuals and groups within organisations another. This is implied in Fig. 7.2.

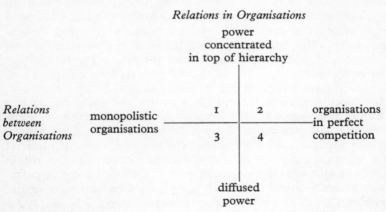

Fig. 7.2

[45] J. Schumpeter, *Capitalism, Socialism and Democracy* (Allen & Unwin, 1943), p. 271.
[46] R. Miliband, *The State in Capitalist Society* (Weidenfeld & Nicolson, 1969), p. 146.

As soon as one cross-cuts the power dimension in organisations with the market situation of organisations the distinction between elitist and participatory forms is suggested. Accordingly, organisational arrangements falling in sections 2 and 4 express pluralistic relationships: the former however are elitist and the latter participatory. Because of his view of the nature of political parties in large-scale societies, Schumpeter's own emphasis was on elitist pluralism as the only effective and realistic way to approximate democracy. By a simple semantic manoeuvre one is able to equate democracy with elitist pluralism. If, however, one applied the scheme to political parties (and allowing that in reality we are dealing with continuous variables) one might label the four sections as follows: (1) one-party dictatorship; (2) multi-party bureaucracies; (3) one-party democracy; (4) multi-party democracy. An underlying theme of this kind of arrangement relates to the question of accountability. This suggests that accountability is maximised where party diversity in a competitive situation is fused with involvement of the party members and adherents in the activities of the party.

We can see then that when a set of relationships is labelled as pluralistic the question 'what kind of pluralism?' needs to be asked. Take, for example, organised religion. There the question of pluralism has been fruitfully pursued by Peter Berger.[47] He points to the monopolistic position which religious establishments have typically enjoyed in society throughout most of human history, in and through which the legitimation of individual and collective life has been obtained. Religious organisations thus constituted regulatory agencies governing thought and action. This might proceed on the basis of absorption of rival definitions of reality, as in the case of Hinduism. Together with a self-encapsulating character which segregated it from rivals, such as Christianity and Islam, which it would not absorb. An alternative case, exemplified in Christianity and Islam was the attempt to maintain or extend a monopolistic position by force—in which inquisition, crusades, holy wars and persecution of Jews, Turks and infidels figure prominently. On this reading, of course, the classic disputes of medieval Europe between Church and State were conflicts taking place within a monopolistic Christian situation, 'more like a fight between two factions within a co-operation than like competition *between* co-operations'.[48] This treatment of religious monopoly serves as an important contrast with religious pluralism, which Berger defines as follows:

'The key characteristic of all pluralistic situations . . . is that religious

[47] Peter L. Berger, *The Social Reality of Religion* (Faber, 1969).
[48] ibid., p. 136.

ex-monopolies can no longer take for granted the allegiance of their client populations. Allegiance is voluntary and thus, by definition, less than certain. As a result, the religious tradition which previously could be authoritatively imposed, now has to be *marketed*. It must be "sold" to a clientele that is no longer constrained to "buy". The pluralistic situation is, above all, a *market situation*. In it, the religious institutions become marketing agencies and the religious traditions become consumer commodities. And at any rate a good deal of religious activity in this situation comes to be dominated by the logic of market economics.'[49]

Berger's own main field of illustration here is the USA. There one has a constitutional separation of Church and State (and in that sense a secular society) but a condition of religious toleration permitted by the State. A diversity of religious world views (until the rise of the Black Muslim movement subsumed under Catholic, Protestant and Jew) could be located and were in a competitive relationship with one another. The main emphasis in Berger's analysis is not the experiences of religious differences expressed in the early settlement and frontier situations, rather it is the significance of the growth of denominationalism. Its significance lies partly in the accompanying growth of bureaucracy. This can lead to certain organisational similarities notwithstanding the theological differences. Even a denomination which, as a matter of doctrine, lays emphasis on local church autonomy may tend to centralise decision-making and co-ordinate its activities through a centralised administration.[50] Now although these denominations may in some sense be in competition with one another for the religious adherence of potential members, and although historically they may earlier have had a sect character and been sharply antagonistic with one another, the bureaucratic pluralism which they now represent has an element of collusion about it. The denominational bureaucrats face common problems of membership recruitment, ministerial selection and training, handling problems of finance, investment and the utilisation of resources, and maintaining satisfactory relationships with a range of agencies in government, industry and the social services. In discussion with other denominations the bureaucrats may work out territorial agreements both at home and in missionary situations. The common concern of the bureaucrats for results and a common administrative mentality does supply an important clue to the ecumenical

---

[49] ibid., p. 137.
[50] See for example, Paul Harrison, *Authority and Power in the Free Church Tradition* (Princeton University Press, 1959).

movement. This, as Berger rightly points out, has much of the character of cartelisation about it. There is a process of guided mergers and an attempt to organise the market by agreement:

> 'Both within and beyond Protestantism there has been increasing consultation and collaboration between the large bodies "surviving" the merger process. It is important to see that this process of cartelisation does *not* tend towards the re-establishment of a monopoly situation—in other words, the notion of an eventual "world church" is unlikely to be realised empirically. Rather, the tendency is oligopolistic with mergers in prospect only to the extent that these are functional in terms of rationalising competition. To go beyond this extent, quite apart from the strain this would put on the theological legitimation, would actually be irrational in terms of the institutional interests of the several religious bureaucracies.'[51]

The bureaucratic pluralism noted here is, then, oligopolistic. It should be added that sectarian groupings can and do exist alongside the denominations. Such groupings may have something of a breakaway character emphasising, say, a doctrinal issue or question of ecclesiastical polity. But numerical success tends to set in motion a bureaucratising process, as the Salvation Army in the nineteenth century and the Pentecostal Movement in the twentieth century illustrate. Even groupings which are able to maintain a hostile attitude towards 'the world' and in that respect remain sectarian, such as the Jehovah's Witnesses, are in organisational terms highly bureaucratised administrations.

There is a tendency for bureaucratic organisations by virtue of their hierarchical arrangements to be elitist. Continual comment on the need to liberalise the structures of the Church of Rome or to democratise the organisation of the Church of England is in itself a response to the perceived reality. It is not intended to imply by contrast that sect-type organisations are necessarily democratic; they may be but they may also be highly authoritarian organisations. The discussion of bureaucratic pluralism in the religious sphere prompts us to note that the elitist organisational form and oligopolistic market situation find their parallels in business and trade union organisations and, of course, in the organisation of political parties in modern industrial societies. There is, however, by no means agreement among commentators as to the general significance of this state of affairs. Let us note some of the variations and critiques which are in play.

Peter Drucker and the new pluralism   In contemplating twentieth-

[51] Berger, op. cit., p. 143.

century industrial societies, Peter Drucker has emphasised that in more than any previous era in history, we have witnessed the emergence of a society of organisations.

'To us, the contemporaries, one of these institutions—government, big business, the university or the labour union—often looks like *the* institution. To the future historian, however, the most impressive fact may be the emergence of a new and distinct pluralism, that is, of a society of institutional diversity and diffusion of power.'[52]

Drucker is impressed with the omnipresence of these organisational arrangements and of their size. The speed and the scale of these changes prompts him to write of the age of discontinuity. This is reflected physically, for example, in the building space required to house government departments. Thus 'even the smallest Japanese prefecture has a brand-new office building that rivals the Tokyo ministry buildings that sufficed imperial Japan when it challenged the West for world leadership twenty-five years ago'.[53] This kind of illustration could in principle be reproduced in any industrial society. In other ways too, Drucker conveys a sense of this change in the scale of organisations: the Standard Oil Trust, which the US Supreme Court cut into fourteen segments in 1911 in an anti-trust gesture, some thirty years later was seen to have produced heirs, each one of which was larger than its parent—as measured for example by employees, sales and capital invested. Yet only three of these constituted major international oil companies. Drucker, however, rejects the contention that big business is the determining power in modern society, a view he once entertained.[54] Nor does he see government as the dominant organisational complex: 'Social theory, to be meaningful at all, must start out with the reality of a pluralism of institutions—a galaxy of suns rather than one big centre surrounded by moons that shine only by reflected light.'[55]

Nevertheless one discerns that the new pluralism is not just a description of the way things are: it is a prescriptive statement of how things ought to be given the growth of a society of organisations. The thrust of the argument is that special-purpose institutions should operate within their appropriate sphere and not interfere with the business of other organisations.

Concentration on the specific task emerges as the key to strength, performance and legitimacy of organisation in the pluralist society.

[52] Peter Drucker, *The Age of Discontinuity* (Heinemann, 1969), p. 213.
[53] ibid., p. 214.
[54] See Peter Drucker, *Big Business* (Heinemann, 1946).
[55] Drucker, *Age of Discontinuity*, p. 218.

Opinion can and should differ as to the specific task of a particular organisation. The definition will change as circumstances, social needs, community values and technologies change. Different institutions of the same kind, e.g. different universities within a country, might define their objectives quite differently, as should different businesses within an industry, or even different hospitals. But each of them will be stronger the more clearly it defines its objectives. It will be more effective the more specific the yardsticks and measurements against which its performance can be appraised. It will be more legitimate the more strictly it bases its authority on justification by performance. 'By their Performance you shall know them—this may well be the fundamental constitutional principle of the new pluralist society.'[56] Yet putting aside logical questions like, 'who precisely does the defining of organisational objectives ?' and 'how are priorities determined when there is conflict ?', and noting Drucker's admission that the evaluation of performance in different organisations is fraught with difficulties (even in business organisations which serve as his most developed case), he is clear that the world of modern organisation leaves much to be desired. In particular he writes of the sickness of government organisation—it is too big and too flabby. This turns out on inspection to be an attack on the administrative functioning of welfare state organisations. And the diagnosis is that although governments (including communist and non-communist) are big, they are not able to co-ordinate their own administrations:

> 'Modern government has become ungovernable. There is no government today that can still claim control of its bureaucracy and of its various agencies. Government agencies are all becoming autonomous, ends in themselves, and directed by their own desire for power, their own rationale, their own narrow vision rather than by national policy and by their own boss, the national government.'[57]

There is then postulated the absence of control and political leadership allied with the sprawl of unco-ordinated government agencies. It is this in Drucker's view which needs to be put right. The Government must take on the role of orchestra conductor—drawing the diverse organisations of society together to produce an effective performance:

> 'Just as we praise a composer for his ability to write "playable" music, which best uses the specific performance characteristics of French horn, violin or flute, we may come to praise the law maker who best structures a particular task so as to make it most congenial

for this or that of the autonomous, self-governing, private institutions of pluralist society.'[58]

There is indeed a strong Platonic flavour in Drucker's analysis, suitably updated. Instead of the public interest and justice being defined simply in terms of what individuals are best fitted to do, it is now organisations which do what they are best equipped to do. But the organic metaphor is retained: Drucker constantly has in mind the question how can a healthy organic diversity in the society of organisations be accomplished? It is important to recognise that this is a normative analysis bearing at least a resemblance to Plato, and indeed Spencer, and is not to be construed as a description of organisational diversity in modern society. As such it typifies much that goes under the name of pluralist analysis (although the pluralists themselves are by no means in agreement on questions of diagnosis let alone cure).

J. K. Galbraith and the pluralism of countervailing power   The pluralism of J. K. Galbraith, as represented in his study of American capitalism, is another instructive example of the mixture of tendency statements for which empirical validity under certain circumstances is claimed and policy recommendations relating to the role of the state in advanced capitalist societies are made.[59]

The focus of his study is on market power. The major analytical distinction drawn is between original power and countervailing power. Original power relates to the oligopolistic or monopolistic position which those who produce, process or distribute products are able to establish. As a consequence of this established position they are able to exert control over the prices they pay and ask for in relation to weak suppliers or customers. The typical picture is of a relatively small group operating as buyers or sellers in a market, dominating a larger group of buyers and sellers in the market relationship. Although the major illustration in Galbraith's work has to do with the industrial enterprise as a participant in original power, he makes it clear that in certain circumstances trade unions or farm producing organisations may also be so categorised in the labour market and agricultural market respectively. The essence of countervailing power is that it checks, invades and seeks to neutralise the operation of original power. Further the growth of countervailing power is seen as linked to the growth of original power:

---

[58] ibid., pp. 290–1.
[59] J. K. Galbraith, *American Capitalism. The Concept of Countervailing Power* (Penguin, 1963).

'To begin with a broad and somewhat too dogmatically stated proposition, private economic power is held in check by the counter-vailing power of those who are subject to it. The first begets the second. . . . The tendency of power to be organised in response to a given position of power is the vital characteristic of the phenomenon I am here identifying . . . power on one side of the market creates both the need for, and the prospect of reward to the exercise of countervailing power from the other side. This means that, as a common rule, we can rely on countervailing power to appear as a curb on economic power.'[60]

In simplest outline what one is offered is a two-stage statement about the organisation of economic power: the first describes the trend towards oligopolistic organisation in the market, the second accounts for the growth of countervailing organisations in terms of motives and oppor-tunity. Galbraith offers two main illustrations of the thesis, one drawn from the labour market and the other from the market formed by pro-ducers and retailers.

Galbraith sees the labour market as the most notable exemplar of countervailing power in action, arguing that in the USA industries which are dominated by large corporations—such as steel, automobiles and farm machinery—have been the breeding ground of strong unions. The theory of countervailing power may not offer a total explanation of union growth and organisation, he concedes, but in his view it is consistent with the 'the broad contours of experience'.

The growth of large retail enterprises—chain stores, mail order firms and co-operative buying organisations—are cited by Galbraith as an important example of the growth of countervailing power invading the original power of industrial corporations. Increasingly such groups are able to challenge the prices of the producers. The threat to cut off supplies to a customer which a producer might make to a small retailer in a relationship of dependence, is gradually balanced by the threat of the large customer to withdraw his custom. The threats and sanctions which a large retailer is able to deploy cuts into the original market power of the producer.

Galbriath's thesis contains an argument directed towards fellow economists, a political argument and a general policy prescription. The challenge to classical economic theory is that competition as an autonomous market regulator, and means of defusing market power, is largely discounted by Galbraith. There are too many contrary examples in modern market situations where this does not happen. It is to countervailing power that one must look for this defusing mechanism. The political argument is that unless one recognises the part actually and potentially to be played by countervailing power in modern industrial societies, then Marxist critiques are very persuasive: '. . . the Marxian attack has not been on capitalism but on monopoly capitalism. The fact that the power of the genus of monopoly is ubiquitous has not been difficult to show. So long as competition remains the conservative's defence, the left is bound to have a near monopoly of the evidence and the logic.'[61] The policy argument stemming from this is that the governments of non-communist industrial societies should restrain original market power where appropriate by the use of anti-trust legislation but, in addition, should support the growth of countervailing power where for any reason it is inhibited. To apply anti-trust legislation against countervailing power is, in Galbraith's view, highly undesirable.

Concerning Galbraith's analysis we would make the following brief observations. First, the extent to which the empirical evidence supports his statement that countervailing power is a self-generating force is very unclear. Certainly in the British context it has been challenged by Hunter in the very areas where Galbraith claims it is most developed— the labour market and the retail/producer market.[62] And the examples that Galbraith cites, notably the case of American agriculture, are, as often as not, attempts to establish countervailing power rather than successful achievements. Secondly, there is the enormous qualification to the whole thesis, conceded by Galbraith, that countervailing power 'does not function at all when there is inflation or inflationary pressure on markets'.[63] Since this has been the common experience of Western industrial societies since the Second World War, this could be said to be a generous interpretation of exceptions to the common rule of countervailing power on Galbraith's part. It does, however, provide him with a justification of state intervention in the management of demand of a selective kind—guided, that is to say, by the distinction between original market power (which should be actively restrained) and countervailing power (which should be supported where it exists and created where it does not exist). Thirdly, we should note that the thesis where applicable is pluralism of a bilateral kind between buyers and sellers in a market. It assumes rather than demonstrates that third parties, such as consumers, benefit rather than suffer. Yet one cannot automatically assume that such power-sharing between two

[61] ibid., pp. 182–3.
[62] A. Hunter, 'Countervailing Power?', in K. W. Rothschild (ed.), *Power in Economics* (Penguin, 1971), pp. 255–74.
[63] ibid., p. 142.

groups does have this beneficial effect. As Hunter has put it: 'One is left with the impression that any form of institution or organisation designed to strengthen weak market positions earns Galbraith's uncritical approval. But it would be fallacious to suppose that comprehensive organisation into economic interest groups is a universal panacea for inequality.'[64]

One has to allow for the possibility that bilateral pluralism may involve a form of collusion which is at the expense rather than for the benefit of any third party. In this respect one may have to reckon with a shift in the burden of exploitation rather than its eradication.

Subdued pluralism: views from the New Left   The natural point of departure for expository purposes here is the work of C. Wright Mills and in particular *The Power Elite*.[65] Mills is manifestly well aware of the significance of constitutional theories of democracy which emphasise the separation of powers as a safeguard against tyranny. This theory centrally makes reference to the separation of power between executive and legislative organisations in the State. It also assumes autonomy of action as between the political and economic spheres (and for that matter the religious sphere although Mills does not explore this). Mills maintains that to take this Jeffersonian ideal as though it were directly applicable to mid-twentieth-century American society is to succumb to a romantic pluralism which does not do justice to the facts. It is not that organised and competing interests cannot be located. But to locate them is not to assume a balance of power or even a separation of power in any total sense. On the semantic point as to what constitutes balance of power, Mills fairly notes that this may convey an image of stalemate between contending parties; or a notion of the competing parties taking turns at winning; or a conception of power sharing in which both sides get something from what are essentially bargaining situations. Yet before one can talk about the balance of power in a society one has to have some overall understanding of the distribution of power. Mills's contention is not that we should ignore the plethora of organised interest groups and their activities but that we should see them in perspective. To do this involves gaining an understanding of secular trends in American society, notably the emergence of a mass society with its bureaucratised economic, political and military organisations as distinct from the semi-rural society of independent farmers, small entrepreneurs and artisans. It is within this framework, the argument runs, that one is sensitised to discovering that below the organised

[64] Hunter, op. cit., p. 271.
[65] C. Wright Mills, *The Power Elite* (OUP, 1959).

interests groups are the unorganised population and above these same groups is a power elite—a reasonably cohesive alliance between economic, political and military leaders.

It is precisely because the multifarious organisations of society are seen as dominated and invaded, neutralised or contained by the power elite that is is appropriate to describe Mills's analysis of American society as subdued pluralism. The whole conception of a power elite effectively challenges the traditional checks and balances theory of constitutional democracy. It suggests, for example, within a particular sphere a concentration of power at the top—notably in the political sphere. Mills emphasises the growing power of the executive over and against the legislature. And it points to the growth of presidential power of an increasingly unchecked kind. At the same time the theory is breached by the existence of collusion. The collusion postulated is between the military, economic and political elites. It is a collusion which has diminished independent political activity over the rest of social life because it has become absorbed into the military-industrial ethos and is consequently geared to the 'crackpot realism' of a war economy. That is why he maintains that quite specific national interests are represented in the top councils of the State, which cannot be effectively restrained by politicians—the people's representatives—acting as honest brokers and mediators of conflicting interests. The existence of competing interest groups may indeed form part of the democratic rhetoric and may be utilised by those in power—but it is rhetoric and not reality to which they point. Superimposed on the pluralism that does exist is a community of interests making the 'big' decisions which determine the destiny of the society—and Mills clearly has foreign policy and military decisions uppermost in his mind. Mills's argument is that the power elite is a form of organised irresponsibility because it is not effectively accountable to the public for what it does. The democratic society of publics in so far as it was ever approximated in American society has been eroded and replaced by a mass society which is open to elite manipulation. The public is neither effectively represented in or protected by the plurality of organised interest groups. The flavour of Mills's analysis is well conveyed in the following passage:

'So far as explicit organisation—conspiratorial or not—is concerned, the power elite, by its very nature, is more likely to use existing organisations, working within and between them, than to set up explicit organisations whose membership is strictly limited to its own members. But if there is no machinery in existence to ensure, for example, that military and political factors will be balanced in decisions made, they will invent such machinery and use it, as with the National Security Council. Moreover, in a formally democratic polity, the aims and the powers of the various elements of this elite are further supported by an aspect of the permanent war economy: the assumption that the security of the nation supposedly rests upon the great secrecy of plan and intent. Many higher events that would reveal the working of the power elite can be withheld from public knowledge under the guise of secrecy. With the wide secrecy covering their operations and decisions, the power elite can mask their intentions, operations and further consolidation.'[66]

The main focus of Mills's analysis is of course on American society, but it is clear that he sees affinities with the USSR, despite ideological differences. This is a point which is more emphatically developed in *The Causes of World War III*.[67] And it is a reminder of the link between his work and that of Herbert Marcuse in *One Dimensional Man*.[68] There both kinds of society are labelled totalitarian to signify elite domination of the population. There may indeed be qualitative differences—domination through political terror or domination through economic-technical co-ordination in and through which the needs of the population are manipulated. In the second of these Marcuse writes of subdued pluralism, which from the individual's point of view is nonetheless to be preferred to a 'total administration': 'One institution might protect him against the other; one organisation might mitigate the impact of the other; possibilities of escape and redress can be calculated. The rule of law, no matter how restricted, is still infinitely safer than rule above or without the law.'[69] The objection raised to a system of subdued pluralism, however, is much the same as Mills's— that the higher vested interests can in irresponsible manner direct and control society and that direction is of an exploitative kind. It is irresponsible power because it is not representative or accountable; it is exploitative because it wastes the resources of nature in the pursuit of private profit and threatens to bring about its own destruction because it is geared to military needs and interests. Subdued pluralism then, in Marcuse's view, is not a sufficient guarantee of human freedom because it cannot effectively check the destructive activities of the dominant elite.

It may be clearly seen that in the case of both Mills and Marcuse the

[66] ibid., pp. 293–4.
[67] C. Wright Mills, *The Causes of World War III* (Secker & Warburg, 1959).
[68] H. Marcuse, *One Dimensional Man* (Routledge & Kegan Paul, 1964).
[69] ibid., pp. 50–1.

contrast we drew earlier between pluralism as the presence of some degree of competition between organisations and monopoly as the domination of one organisation has to be modified in the sense that they are not here mutually exclusive. At the highest levels there is a monopolistic view of organised power. This co-exists with a competitive struggle between interest organisations at an intermediary level. While these struggles may be absorbing for the participants, on this interpretation they do not serve as checks and balances to restrain the exercise of power at the highest levels. Such organisations are either irrelevant to what goes on within the power elite or are incorporated and penetrated by it rather than having a critical function to perform. This view excludes the general possibility of what might be called elite pluralism— that is competition between elites for power. Certainly it would not be typical. Yet this conception was one of the mainsprings of Schumpeter's position, as we have seen. It also characterises the pluralism of sociologists such as Raymond Aron and Ralf Dahrendorf.[70]

One study which restates the power elite thesis on a more comparative basis is Miliband's *The State in Capitalist Society*.[71] If anything, Miliband is more explicitly Marxist than Mills, taking his stand on the assertion that the State in capitalist society is run by and on behalf of the bourgeoisie and is a coercive instrument of the ruling class. His argument is that in many advanced capitalist societies the ruling class does not operate by direct dictatorship but works through the institutions that are labelled democratic—the press, the law, Parliament and the party system. Looking at organisation in the economic sphere for example, Miliband suggests that some elite pluralism may be observed. But 'this "elite pluralism" does not, however, prevent the separate elites in capitalist society from constituting a dominant economic class, possessed of a high degree of cohesion and solidarity, with common interests and common purposes which far transcend their specific differences and disagreements'.[72] At the heart of his anlaysis is the contention that political argument and debate take place within a framework of established property rights and unequal economic power, which even social democratic parties have done little to erode. Movements for social reform, to cope with the social problems of unemployment, inadequate education, housing, and poverty have been constrained by this overall structural fact. In so far as advanced capitalist societies are unable to contain social discontent by reformist measures then the

---

[70] R. Aron, *Eighteen Lectures on Industrial Society* (Weidenfeld & Nicolson, 1968); R. Dahrendorf, *Society and Democracy in Germany* (Weidenfeld & Nicolson, 1968).

[71] op. cit.   [72] ibid., pp. 47–8.

option of turning to authoritarian measures is likely to be taken up. The threat is of a movement from bourgeois democracy to conservative authoritarianism. In keeping with much New Left analysis, Miliband is not expecting a revolutionary solution to be found in social democratic parties because they are too readily incorporated into state capitalist societies. Neither is he especially confident about the Communist Party as the vehicle of liberation, because typically it is lacking in internal democracy and does not encourage the conditions for free discussion. The need nevertheless is for an organisational solution. In the immediate future such a solution seems to him unlikely:

> 'For the foreseeable future at any rate, no formation of the Left will be in a position seriously to place the question of socialism on the agenda of most advanced capitalist societies. Nor certainly is this to be achieved by spontaneous eruption. The events of May–June 1968 in France showed well enough the yearning for fundamental change which simmers beneath a seemingly placid political surface, and to use Regis Debray's phrase, the degree to which the "small motor" of a student movement may activate the "big motor" of the working class. But these events showed equally well that in the absence of appropriate political organisation, what is possible is turmoil and pressure but not revolution.'[73]

In the long term he is more optimistic of a revolutionary solution which will subordinate the State to society and inaugurate 'an authentically democratic social order and truly free society of self-governing men and women'.[74] This is based on the conviction that sooner or later the contradictions of advanced capitalist society must be resolved in this way by a working class which will overcome all obstacles to its unification. Whether that is a prophetic statement or a simple case of whistling in the dark, we have no means of knowing. Those who promulgate such a solution are not the first to walk by faith rather than by sight. In any event it does not in itself detract from their critical analysis of our present discontents.

[73] ibid., pp. 275–6.   [74] ibid., p. 277.

PART V CONCLUSION

8

Sociologists and Organisations: Critiques and Apologias

The hydra-headed debates about sociological work naturally have implications for the sociology of organisations. Indeed what sociologists think they know about organisations is sometimes thrown into the argument. The critiques and apologias referred to in the title of this chapter can best be explained through illustration. It will become evident that some critiques are mutually supportive but others appear to be mutually exclusive.

(a) THE SOCIOLOGIST AS AN ORGANISATION MAN

There is usually an ironical, if not polemical, element in categorising sociologists as organisation men. The critique is advanced in C. Wright Mills's comments on the bureaucratic ethos in the *Sociological Imagination*.[1]

The portrayal is of sociologists in large university departments and research institutes who typically work in teams and whose work is connected to a client rather than written for 'the public', a client with particular interests, concerns and problems. The client it may be added is commonly not a particular individual but a large organisation—a corporation, a state department, the military—which commissions the

[1] C. Wright Mills, *The Sociological Imagination* (OUP, 1959), pp. 100–18.

researcher and finances the operation. The core of the argument is that a bureaucratised social scientist will take too much for granted, his own methods and the bureaucracies for whom he works. The problem of control, for example, is seen in bureaucratic terms. It encourages a manipulative social engineering view of social science from the standpoint of the bureaucracies and is consequently seen by Mills as antidemocratic. Such social scientists, in effect, take certain evaluations of the world for granted and then justify them in the name of their science. Their work may be trivial and routinised but its effect is to legitimate the power-holders who may choose to use or ignore research or policy recommendations as it suits them. Social science is thus utilised to restrict moral choice rather than extend it in the practical affairs of men. In short, the social scientist becomes in this context a servant of power, or possibly, if he moves into positions of real influence and involvement in policy decisions, a mandarin in the power structure. Mills's perception of social scientists as servants of power is taken up by Loren Baritz.[2] The essence of his argument, which was specifically geared to industrial organisation, was that managers controlled the social scientists they employed. Employment here could mean literally employment in the organisation. Here the impression conveyed is of social scientists as technicians harnessed to the achievement of managerial goals. Alternatively, they may be industrial consultants (and Baritz has psychologists and sociologists particularly in mind) who have been hired on managements' terms to solve their problems—whether of high labour turnover, absenteeism, militant unionism, low productivity or low morale. Here the solutions have been offered in terms of improving motivation, changing attitudes, improving communications and developing social skills. Although Baritz castigates much of this work done by social scientists as trivial and suspects that some of the consultancy packages that businessmen have purchased are substandard, he does think that social scientists are beginning to learn how to control conduct. To that extent management by manipulation, through social science activity, could become a reality.

Baritz maintains in the context of the USA that social scientists tend to share managements' assumptions and therefore are willing to work for them. They choose to become servants of power whilst claiming to be apolitical and objective. Still, even maintaining Baritz's imagery, the social scientist *may* choose to serve the powerful in different kinds of organisation—for example the trade unions. The social scientist puts his skills—real or claimed—at the disposal of another master. The trade union organisation may well face administrative problems

2 Loren Baritz, *The Servants of Power* (Wesleyan University, 1960).

similar to that of an industrial enterprise and to that extent the social scientist may be asked to solve similar problems. Nevertheless the interests of the trade union are different and in facilitating the work of the organisation the social scientist is supporting by his presence and activity the organisation's interests. To this extent, just as the technologist may exercise some choice over the sphere in which he allows his skills to be utilised, so may the social scientist. For good or ill he is known by the company he keeps. If indeed he is an organisation man, we may properly ask the question what organisation, since different moral standpoints may be reflected in and different consequences flow from, organisational commitment.

Without forgetting the qualitative differences between organisations, in each case they stand in a client relationship to the sociologist when utilising his skills to 'solve' problems. It could be argued that while some sociologists are organisation men in the way we have described and tend to choose clients whose values they broadly share, others are more entrepreneurial. Gouldner, for example, has suggested:

'It would appear that social theorists who are, or conceive themselves as, entrepreneurs *and* who are directly dependent upon the purchase of their skills by various others—who, in short will sell their services on an open market—will more likely disregard the use to which their clients put their services and, correspondingly, will define their skills as value-free techniques. As a further corollary, the more the theorists define their skills as neutral techniques, the wider and more diversified is the market on which they can sell their skills.'[3]

Against the first criticism of taking sides is set the second accusation of moral indifference as the sociologist enters the market place.

Sociologists who accept the client-relationship concept may see this as a mark of their professional status, making them akin to doctors, lawyers, architects and priests. But they may also rest their case on more tangible grounds. A good example of this is to be found in Gross and Fishman's paper 'The Management of Educational Establishments.'[4] Gross and Fishman consider that sociologists may be of service to decision-makers in education in the following ways:

1. Sensitising administrators to the importance of organisational and interpersonal factors. To recognise explicitly the school as an organisa-

---

[3] A. Gouldner, *Enter Plato* (Routledge & Kegan Paul, 1967), pp. 186–7.
[4] Neal Gross and Joshua A. Fishman, 'The Management of Educational Establishments', in Paul F. Lazarsfeld, William H. Sewell and Harold L. Wilensky (eds), *The Uses of Sociology* (Basic Books, 1967), pp. 304–58.

tional entity with a division of labour and system of authority enables one to appreciate that different individuals and groups may hold different beliefs about the 'goals' of the school which are expressed in conflicts of values and conflicts of interest. Consequently, incumbents of particular roles may be subject to conflicting pressures from different partners in the role set. Again, the school organisation can frequently be described as a bureaucracy, with the implication of hierarchy and control from above, and yet it is staffed by professionals, with ideals of personal autonomy and responsibility. This, it may be suggested, is a source of personal and organisational strain. The argument is that this kind of awareness should lie behind any attempts to plan for change. One would, for example, have to consider the nature of clique formation and the informal system of power in a school in attempting an innovation such as team teaching, on the grounds that informal leaders may be key figures in determining the success or failure of innovating schemes.

2. Providing administrators with a greater sense of reality about schools and the environments in which they operate. A school staffing policy for example will be more realistic if it is based on an understanding of teachers' career strategies and the factors affecting their mobility.

3. Providing clues which enable administrators to cope with basic organisational problems. For example, while it is the case that many studies demonstrate a positive relationship between social class and educational administration and that school administrators cannot themselves change the class structure, there may be more specific factors which they can manipulate to improve aspirations. The importance of parental influence is a case in point and suggests the possibility of a counselling programme for parents to make them aware of their child's potentialities, with the end in view of increasing the child's motivation to develop his gifts. Again, ways of improving the achievement of ethnic minorities in slum schools, improving the performance of under-achievers and securing acceptance of innovations may be suggested by sociological findings.

4. Providing administrators with knowledge of research techniques. The use of social survey techniques, for example, may be used by educationalists to ascertain what the public thinks about particular issues. This may indicate matters in which there is confusion or conflict because of lack of information; it may give an idea of the salience of attitudes which might be seen as facilitating or hindering proposed changes in educational organisation. In any event the administrators will be aided in their planning and decision-making activity by this knowledge.

Gross and Fishman maintain that sociologists can look at the assumptions underlying the diagnosis and solutions written into educators' policies and programmes. In particular they suggest:

'A strong case could be developed in support of the proposition that the greatest contribution of sociologists to the educational administrator will derive from their analysis of the validity of the basic assumptions underlying the teaching, learning and social arrangements that presently take place in the schools, their critical appraisal of proposed programmes to improve them, and their sustained research efforts designed to examine the utility of alternative schemes for maximising student learning that are based on sociological as well as on other types of assumptions.'[5]

The servants of power thesis tends to view social scientists as providing information, guidance or advice which is then incorporated into the planning and decision-making activities of the client. The relationship is not always so straightforward, despite Gross and Fishman's comments on the value of the sociologist in providing a reality-orientation to the administrator. Something like a double-take situation can develop as is instructively illustrated in Harvey Wheeler's paper 'The Short and Happy Life of a Research Consultantship.'[6] Wheeler was employed as a consultant to a state reorganisation commission in the USA to provide a report on the office of governor. Both consultant and client were clear that they wanted to be realistic. Realism for the commission proved to be couched in administrative terms—in particular the belief that the Hoover Commission on the Presidency had direct relevance for the role of state governor and that the principles of scientific management could solve the problems of state government. Wheeler argued that this kind of realism masked the political realities and indeed came to suspect that the commission knew this and that the 'administrative solution' was actually a political instrument to prevent anything scandalous emerging. It is one thing to report that the system is not working too well because officials are overworked, it is something quite other to uncover political corruption. If the political scientist accepts the administrative frame of reference Wheeler maintains that this is to participate in the suppression of political analysis: 'The conditions of his employment relationship veto the development of his science when that science touches (as it always must) the mainsprings of power. This means that it is almost impossible in the nature of things

[5] ibid., p. 347.
[6] Harvey Wheeler, 'The Short and Happy Life of a Research Consultantship', in Nelson W. Polsby, Robert A. Dentler, and Paul A. Smith (eds), *Politics and Social Life* (Houghton Mifflin, 1963), pp. 798–802.

for the political scientist truly to ply his art for hire. . . . What the political scientist may ply is formalism and legalism: professional pharisaism. For this commodity there is an exciting market with many long and happy research consultantships.'[7] From this perspective the consultant is more like a licensed jester than a manipulator. The licence certifies that even though he may criticise, he does so within an acceptable format. He is, as the client may sometimes put it, a 'tame' social scientist.

Mills's critique of American sociology was not total but the insidious character of the bureaucratic ethos, as he evaluated it, made him a worried man. A more recent critique of the sociologist as organisation man and which is a root and branch indictment is located in Martin Nicolaus's paper 'The Professional Organisation of Sociology: A View from Below'.[8] Nicolaus does not stand on ceremony. The tenor of his argument is revealed in the opening sentences:

> 'The trunk of political power has many branches. One of these is the professional organisation of sociology, The American Sociological Association. The upper, fatter portion of this branch is grafted seamlessly, with contractual cement, to the civil, economic and military sovereignty which constitutes the trunk. From that source, the organisation spreads outward and downward along the institutional scaffolding, carrying the authoritative views on matters of social reality into the universities, junior colleges and high schools. In addition to the general dissemination of propaganda, professional sociology has the major specific functions of aiding industrial, civil, and military authorities in the solution of manpower control problems of a limited order, and of preparing university candidates for careers in the official bureaucracies. As a source of legitimation for the existing sovereignty, and as a laboratory of refinements in the processes by which a tribute of blood, labour and taxation is extracted from the subject population, the professional organisation of sociology today represents the concrete fulfilment of the charter vision of its founding fathers.'[9]

With that statement as the basic axiom, discussion about the varieties of organisation men (even those who might from some perspectives be regarded as marginal men in the profession) becomes redundant. Even radical sociologists who remain within the profession get caught in a

[7] ibid., p. 802.
[8] Martin Nicolaus, 'The Professional Organisation of Sociology: A View from Below', in Robin Blackburn (ed.), *Ideology in Social Science. Readings in Critical Social Theory* (Fontana, 1972), pp. 45–50.
[9] ibid., pp. 45–6.

Catch-22 trap. This may lead them to inconsistency. In this vein he criticised Richard Flacks, a former officer of the SDS who undertook a study of student revolts. While Flacks promised and ensured the anonymity of the student respondents the net result was that his findings were utilised by the authorities as 'evidence' that the students were spoiled children who 'needed' to be punished. He had not intended that his work should provide ammunition for policies he opposed. But, in Nicolaus's view, whether intentionally or unintentionally, directly or indirectly, this is what happens. The organisation of sociology is such that it is locked into the system and, in effect, becomes an agent of social control. Nicolaus propounds the thesis that in stable situations sociological research is useful to the authorities but in times of social unrest the authorities exchange the subtleties of intellectual weaponry for the more direct agencies of social control exercised by other professions; the police and the army. From this standpoint, therefore, it is clearly not enough to talk about the liberation of sociology: 'Sociology is a branch of the tree of political power, an extension of sovereignty by other means. It has survived many a borer-from-within, a pecker-from-without, and a carver-of-initials-in-the-bark. . . . In the last analysis the only moves towards liberation within sociology are those which contribute to the process of liberation *from* sociology. The point is not to reinterpret sociology but to end it.'[10]

Nicolaus's critique is in tune with views expressed by French students at the time of the 1968 uprisings. The reason for sociology students playing the part that many of them did in these events is attributed not to subversive teachers of sociology but rather because they rejected what they believed their teachers represented. They rejected a sociology which while making scientific pretensions and claiming impartiality for its procedures, was actually a servant of the bourgeoisie. The statement 'Why do we need sociologists?' circulating in Nanterre University says, among other things:

'The practical organisation of capitalism produces a host of contradictions which various branches of sociology are expected to remove. . . . The "theorist" is expected to explain the nature of local conflicts removed from their social context in which alone, their cause can be understood. This allegedly impartial procedure is, in fact, thoroughly partial and biased: phenomena are studied in isolation whereas they are in fact interrelated (e.g. racism, unemployment, delinquency and slums) and the rational nature of the present economic system is taken for granted. Since the word "profit" has

[10] ibid., p. 80.

now lost its respectability, sociologists now speak of "growth". But how does this "growth" arise in the first place, *who* organises it, *whom* does it profit? These questions are apparently too speculative to interest a "pure" science.'[11]

The critique of the sociologist as an organisation man does tend to focus on the supportive part he is said to play in relation to ruling elites. In principle this critique can be applied to capitalist and socialist societies. Thus one may portray social scientists (among other intellectuals) as succumbing to counter-revolutionary subordination in the former or revolutionary subordination in the latter, when, instead of acting as independent critics of ruling organisations, they become agents of powerful governments and their policies. These are the mandarins alluded to in Chomsky's book *American Power and the New Mandarins*.[12] Essentially Chomsky argues in the American case that, as the tradition of social criticism is eroded by the incorporation of intellectuals into an already highly centralised governmental structure, 'the inequities of the society will recede from vision, the status quo will seem less flawed, and the preservation of order will become a matter of transcendent importance'.[13] This issue posed by Chomsky is whether the organisation-orientated social scientist as part of the technical intelligentsia promotes a more efficient system of exploitation or serves to humanise industrial societies. His conclusion is this:

'. . . there are dangerous tendencies in the ideology of the welfare state intelligentsia who claim to possess the techniques and understanding required to manage our "post-industrial society" and to organise an international society dominated by American superpower. Many of these dangers are revealed, at a purely ideological level, in the study of the counter-revolutionary subordination of scholarship. The dangers exist both in so far as the claim to knowledge is real and in so far as it is fraudulent. In so far as the technique of management and control exists, it can be used to consolidate the authority of those who exercise it and to diminish spontaneous and free experimentation with new social forms, as it can limit the possibilities for reconstruction of society in the interests of those who are now, to a greater or lesser extent, dispossessed. Where the techniques fail, they will be supplemented by all the methods of coercion that modern technology provides to preserve order and stability.'[14]

[11] Cited in G. and D. Cohn-Bendit, *Obsolete Communism—The Left-Wing Alternative* (Penguin, 1969), pp. 38–9.
[12] Noam Chomsky, *American Power and the New Mandarins* (Penguin, 1969).
[13] ibid., p. 26.   [14] ibid., p. 104.

A parallel discussion on mandarins in the USSR and cited by Chomsky is Daniel Bell's essay 'Two Roads from Marx: the Themes of Alienation and Exploitation'.[15] To this one might now add Gouldner's comments on this theme in *The Coming Crisis of Western Sociology*.[16]

(b) THE SOCIOLOGIST AS CHANGE AGENT

The above discussion of the sociologist as an organisation man has emphasised the servants of power and mandarin role motifs which are seen as deriving from the client relationship. At times there is disagreement in the literature as to who is using whom and for what purposes. Indeed the assumption of either the researcher or the client as dominant (the one because of his special knowledge, and the other because of his power to act with or against advice) is sometimes relaxed to accommodate the notion of a collaborative relationship. This in fact is the underlying rationale of much action research and concerning which there is now quite a considerable literature.[17] Rapoport for example, argues the practical and intellectual advantages of action research: 'Action research aims to contribute *both* to the practical concerns of people in an immediate problematic situation and to the goals of social science by joint collaboration within a mutually acceptable ethical framework.'[18] He makes the point that the social scientist may see it is necessary to shift the client's perception of his problems, as diagnostic and feasibility studies proceed. The researcher's task is to persuade the client to see that changing an organisation may involve a reformulation of what the problems impeding change really are. On the other hand the client may be intelligent enough to take on the social scientist at his own game, and offer effective logical and methodological critiques of the research activity. To this extent collaboration is seen as a social relationship in which the terms of the contract are continually scrutinised and open to revision. The underlying assumption is that through a process of power equalisation between client and researcher the possibility of manipulation is diminished.

[15] In Daniel Bell, *The End of Ideology* (Free Press, 1962), pp. 355–92.

[16] A. W. Gouldner, *The Coming Crisis of Western Sociology* (Routledge & Kegan Paul, 1971), Ch. 12.

[17] See for example Warren G. Bennis, Kenneth D. Benne and Robert Chin (eds) *The Planning of Change* (Holt Rinehart & Winston, 1969); John M. Thomas and Warren G. Bennis (eds), *Management of Change and Conflict* (Penguin, 1972); Robert N. Rapoport 'Three Dilemmas in Action Research' *Human Relations* (1970), Vol. 23, No. 6; Michael Foster 'An Introduction to the Theory and Practice of Action Research in Work Organisations', *Human Relations* (1972), Vol. 25, No. 6.

[18] Rapoport, op. cit.

Action research literature does have a good deal to say about strategies for change. Foster, in his paper points out that the focus for inducing change has varied. Sometimes change is attempted through changing individuals' behaviour; sometimes it is the interpersonal properties of groups and the attempt to change group norms; sometimes it is the attempt to promote change through appreciating the interaction of organisation structures with their environment. By concentrating on a particular level of action in an organisation the researcher tends to carry with him views about the sources of resistance to change and the problems of implementing innovations (recalcitrant people, groups or organisations responding defensively to their environment). But strategies do not only have to do with the level of action but with assumptions about man and the things which motivate him. This is discussed in Chin and Benne's paper 'General Strategies for Effecting Changes in Human Systems.'[19] Those basic strategies are enumerated:

1. Empirical-rational strategies: 'the rationale underlying most of these is an assumption that men are guided by reason and that they will utilise some rational calculus of self-interest in determining needed changes in behaviour'.[20] Consequently the basic issue is whether the knowledge which is necessary to form a rational judgement is available and disseminated. Action research is directed to that end.

2. Normative-re-educative change strategies. Here the emphasis is on the importance of understanding the normative structure permeating institutions and organisations and shaping the habits, beliefs and practices of man the social animal. The contribution of Kurt Lewin is treated as an important exemplar of this strategy:

'Lewin's contribution to normative re-educative strategies of changing stemmed from his vision of required interrelations between research, training, and action (and for him, this meant collaborative relationships, often now lacking, between researchers, educators, and activists) in the solution of human problems, in the identification of needs for change, and in the working out of improved knowledge, technology, and patterns of action in meeting these needs. Man must participate in his own re-education if he is to be re-educated at all. And re-education is a normative change as well as a cognitive and perceptual change. These convictions lead Lewin to emphasise action research as a strategy of changing, and participation in groups as a medium of re-education.'[21]

[19] Robert Chin and Kennth D. Benne, 'General Strategies for Effecting Changes in Human Systems', in Bennis, Benne and Chin (eds), op. cit., pp. 32–57.   [20] ibid., p. 35.   [21] ibid., pp. 43–4.

3. Power-coercive change strategies. Here the emphasis is on the use of political and economic sanctions to achieve change. Those in legitimated power positions have, by definition, more leverage to achieve their ends. Those without power may or may not realise that this is the case. If they remain in ignorance then they are likely to be manipulated to change in a predetermined direction by the power holders. If they challenge the power holders in an organised way they may be able to negotiate outcomes. Although Chin and Benne point out that a great deal of action research has been of the normative re-educative style, they recognise that the distribution of power in organisations cannot be ignored. But, they conclude, 'this does *not* mean that [action researchers] must develop a commitment to power-coercive strategies to change the distribution of power except when these may be necessary to effect the spread of their own democratically and scientifically orientated methods of changing within society'.[22] This brings out clearly the notion of the ethical and the scientific commitments of the action researcher and the implied fusion. It also perhaps underlines another ambiguity: whereas action researchers are sometimes seen as agents of elitist manipulators (as for example in the Hawthorne counselling programme) they appear at times to espouse the doctrine of power equalisation through patterns of participation. Presumably they can be known by their fruits.

It might be suggested that the differentiation by level of focus, noted by Foster, and the differentiation by assumptions about men, could be cross-classified to delineate a hierarchy of change strategies.

Table 8.1

Level of Change	Assumptions about Change		
	Empirical-rational	Normative-re-educational	Power-coercive
Individual	X		
Group		X	
Organisation and Environment			X

The assumptions about empirical-rational behaviour may have heuristic value at the level of the individual's interests; normative-re-educational assumptions may usefully be applied to group activity: but the organisation/environment level necessitates a power-coercive model. Further the individual and group contexts can only be understood ultimately with

22 ibid., p. 57.

reference to a model which takes account of the phenomena of the distribution of power in the organisation and the wider society.

The politics of change have mainly been discussed so far by assuming the client to be the power holder. Indeed the critique of the client-researcher relationship, as we have seen, mainly stems from the contention that the client can afford to pay and therefore is powerful and that whether intentionally or unintentionally the end result is to support those groups in society that are already privileged in terms of class or status position. But although the material rewards may be less there is no reason why, just as a lawyer may choose to work for under-privileged clients, the social scientist may not deploy his skills on behalf of civil rights organisations, housing pressure groups, prisoners' rights associations and other such oppositional groups. Indeed whereas action research in industrial organisations tends to be labelled in elitist terms as managerial sociology, in community organisations it is more normally seen as reformist and even subversive. It remains the case, however, that such action research is often financed directly or indirectly by funds from government or state agencies. The dilemmas for action research in this respect have been instructively discussed by Herbert Gans.[23] In his paper 'Urban Poverty and Social Planning', Gans describes the emergence of community action and advocate programmes. In the New York action prgramme Mobilisation for Youth, aimed at reducing delinquency, the theoretical assumptions were derived from Cloward and Ohlin's 'opportunity theory' which emphasised lack of opportunity to achieve working-class or middle-class goals as a causal factor in delinquency.[24] Consequently the action programme was aimed at removing obstacles to opportunities. The assumption was not that some segments of the population could be categorised as socially inadequate but that there were political and bureaucratic barriers which impeded individuals' life chances. Advocate programmes involved the use of lawyers to file suits against city officials, landlords and businessmen, neighbourhood service centres where advice on how to process grievances or claim benefits could be obtained, and technical assistance in the organisation of strikes against slum landlords. Activities of this sort on behalf of the powerless aroused the wrath of established group interests including the schools, welfare agencies, the police and the city hall. City hall took action to investigate the programme, instituted

[23] Herbert J. Gans 'Urban Poverty and Social Planning', in Lazarsfeld, Sewell and Wilensky (eds), op. cit., pp. 437–76; Herbert J. Gans, *People and Plans* (Penguin, 1972).

[24] Richard Cloward and Lloyd Ohlin, *Delinquency and Opportunity* (Free Press, 1960).

closer financial control and effectively dampened its militant and politi-cised character. Given the funding problem, the action agencies find themselves in a dilemma; 'Although one can argue that if poverty is to be reduced, the action agencies must . . . side with the clients and develop programmes that will increase their economic and political role, the agencies cannot help but respond first to the sources of present power. Since most power is held by the "Establishment", moral imperatives and programmatic necessities are of lower priority.'[25] Although the problems of evaluating such change programmes in terms of any satisfactory methodology tend to become insuperable the experiences recorded do bear witness to the utility of the power-coercive model of change discussed above. This point is also reflected in Rein and Miller's paper 'The Demonstration as a Strategy of Change'.[26] The central point of the demonstration project is to test alternative ideas whose implementation, it is claimed, would improve the organisational performance of a school, a welfare department, a hospital or whatever. Yet Rein and Miller contend that these relatively small-scale projects do not typically lead to large scale implementation. This may partly be because effective evaluation of change is not always accomplished but it is also suggested that intentionally or not such projects tend to blunt public criticism. If the demonstration project is an instrument of change at all it is only so at the margins: it does not seriously threaten estab-lished organisations and institutions. It is moreover suggested that the blunting effect on significant change may occur because of professional social scientists who seek to control and manage discontent. This may diminish the drama which some social issues contain in their own right. In any event (and parallel to Gans's argument) the professional re-formers typically need to obtain financial support from established agencies. And, as Rein and Miller recognise, the original motif of the demonstration project—its concern to show how pressing problems may be more effectively solved or innovations introduced by organisation reform—is buried under the political accommodations that have to be accepted as part of the bargain for allowing it to proceed at all.

Whatever stance the sociologist does adopt as change agent it is probably fair to say that usually it is within the context of a conception of planned social change. Indeed the sociologist's involvement is seen in its relation to the planning function—whether he be advising on implementing, monitoring or evaluating the plan. This plan itself does

25 ibid., p. 460.
26 Martin Rein and S. M. Miller, 'The Demonstration as a Strategy of Change', in Martin Rein, *Social Policy: Issues of Choice and Change* (Random House, 1970).

not necessarily have to be defined in *a priori* terms as the discussion of the collaborative relationship between client and researcher is meant to illustrate. Whilst allowing for that kind of flexibility the notion of change that is built in is of a gradualist kind rather than suggestive of any radical break with existing structures in a short time span. To that extent certain assumptions about the possibilities of changing organisations and institutions are built in.

Willener in his study of the student movement in France in 1968 has pointed out that the involvement of the younger generation of sociologists in the events of that time was also a form of action research.[27] Willener points out that much of the contemporaneous sociological analysis focused on a critique of the established society—the organisation of science, technology, and the universities in an advanced capitalist society—employing such concepts as compartmentalisation, separation and fragmentation in describing the individual. The passivity of the individual and his spectator role is emphasised and oppositional groups (such as left-wing political parties and trade unions) are seen as being within the established order—an established counter-society. This leads directly to a suspicion and critique of all 'systems' because they squeeze the identity out of an individual. The theme of anti-bureaucracy is central and the focus for reconstruction shifts from the 'system' to the individual in his everyday life. Change on this rendering becomes not the creation of a new system into which men may be absorbed rather 'it is man, who by becoming himself again, will create the system in which he wishes to live'.[28]

But how is such change to be inaugurated? The approaches advocated included the following:

1. 'Unblocking' passivity. This implies the encouragement of action designed to reveal to the actor the repressive character of the system which he has taken for granted hitherto. Willener notes the role of *exemplary action* here in which intervention in a conflict situation concentrates on a few key objectives. An illustrative case is the student occupation of the Senate Council Chamber at Nanterre University in March 1968. This is seen as a testimony to the power of symbols in organisational life: the university authorities are described by the professor of social psychology at Nanterre as 'paralysed by the dispossession of the symbol of their power' and the fragmented student groupings are united in and through the occupation. Such action is seen as lighting a beacon to show to others that impossible changes are in fact

27 Alfred Willener, *The Action-Image of Society* (Tavistock, 1970).
28 ibid., p. 161.

possible and to extend the struggle from one level of organisational life to another, and from one sphere (say the educational) to another (say the industrial). Exemplary action is seen then as a form of apprenticeship in which through participation one learns about the possibilities for change, moving ultimately towards forms of 'self-management' as opposed to bureaucratic control.

2. Festivities. The possibility for change of an anti-authoritarian kind is encompassed here in the rediscovery of a *joie de vivre* over and against a system of organised oppression. This activity is seen as eroding encrusted views of hierarchy and compartmentalisation in social life. Again it is seen as a means of encouraging and stimulating creativity in individuals and the role of organisation is as a vehicle of spontaneity over and against typical 'rational' models. The festival is in some respects an end in itself—a playful, humorous and creative activity. It may also be seen as a means to an end:

> 'The transition from the initial explosion, from the liberating shock, to the permanent festival, and, in short, to the self-management of life and work presents no problem to those who hold the views outlined here. It takes place so quickly that during such a period of improvisation repressed desires rise to the surface and produce, as it were automatically, by simultaneous emergence, a natural reinvention—or rather the *discovery* of what was only latent—of schemas of community life, such as self-management.'[29]

This is one particular vision of how the dichotomy between organisation and community may be resolved—with a value emphasis on creativity, fraternity, equality and spontaneity. All of these values are seen as submerged by the normal organisational structures of industrial societies.

3. The appropriation of power. Here Willener concentrates on the conception of 'dual power' which was advocated by a number of apologists for the movement. Self-managing factories, universities or whatever, which will ignore existing institutionalised sources of power and the bureaucratic administrations which service them. As he points out, in spring 1968 this strategy was given more credence because the political and industrial orders seemed to be unable to exercise real power. But institutionalised power, as the change agents were to discover, cannot disappear simply by being ignored and wished away.

It is not, in the end, the abolition of organisation to which this form of analysis points (which would indeed bring disorder in the most

[29] ibid., pp. 176–7.

literal sense) but rather to a model of organisation created for and by people on the basis of self-management:

'The spread of this type of organisation in small, autonomous social units—the fragmentation of society being the remedy for the present fragmentation of the individual—is seen as the indispensable condition for the re-establishment of communication. The theme of decompartmentalisation . . . is paralleled by the desire to reconstitute the "total" man within these micro-societies. Sociological analyses of France have shown that bureaucratic forms of organisation and the importance of hierarchisation produce a separation of individuals, who do not communicate between groups of different status and even very little within the same group, in view of the division between working life and private life. It is understandable that an anti-bureaucratic and anti-authoritarian tendency should place so much emphasis on the need for dehierarchisation and decompartmentalisation.'[30]

Willener's study draws attention to the fact that action research may stress discontinuity rather than continuity in promoting change. But it also suggests that by concentrating on change from the standpoint of the social participants, the action researchers and the actors tended to proceed as if established structures did not exist. To that extent the society of organisations was treated as a fragile and precarious thing which could be wished away or at least blown away. This did not happen. At the same time, it could be argued, that to proceed as if established structures do not exist can free the imagination. This ability to construct alternative models of organisation and communication can perhaps be learned by sociologists in their analyses of organisations which do exist and exercise very powerful leverage over the lives of men. The sociologist as change agent does not have to operate with a model of man in organisation as puppet or of organisation structures as immutable. A realistic analysis of the possibilities for change in a society of organisations has to take into account the resources and intentions of the powerful. Such constraints are however the penultimate rather than the last word on the matter. They are a gloss on Marx's contention that men make their own history albeit in circumstances not of their own choosing.

[30] ibid., p. 186.

BIBLIOGRAPHY

ABEGLENN, J. C., *The Japanese Factory* (Free Press, 1958).
ACKOFF, R. L., *A Concept of Corporate Planning* (Wiley, 1970).
ACKOFF, R. L. and EMERY, F. E., *On Purposeful Systems* (Aldine Atherton, 1972).
ANDRESKI, S. (ed.), *Herbert Spencer* (Nelson, 1972).
ANGYAL, ANDRAS, *Foundations for a Science of Personality* (The Commonwealth Fund, 1941).
ARENDT, HANNAH, *The Origins of Totalitarianism* (Allen & Unwin, 1967).
ARGYRIS, C., *Integrating the Individual and the Organisation* (Wiley, 1964).
—— *Personality and Organisation* (Harper & Row, 1957).
ARON, R., *Democracy and Totalitarianism* (Weidenfeld & Nicolson, 1965).
—— *Eighteen Lectures on Industrial Society* (Weidenfeld & Nicolson, 1968).
BARKER, R. G. and WRIGHT, H. F., *Midwest and its Children* (Row Peterson, 1955).
BARTIZ, LOREN, *The Servants of Power* (Wesleyan University, 1960).
BELL, D., *The End of Ideology* (Free Press, 1962).
BENNIS, WARREN G., BENNE, KENNETH D. and CHIN, ROBERT (eds), *The Planning of Change* (Holt, Rinehart & Winston, 1969).
BLAU, P., *Dynamics of Bureaucracy* (University of Chicago Press, 1955).
BLAU, P. and SCHOENHERR, R., *The Structure of Organisations* (Basic Books, 1971).
BLAU, P. and SCOTT, W. R., *Formal Organisations* (Routledge & Kegan Paul, 1963).
BLAUNER, R., *Alienation and Freedom* (University of Chicago Press, 1964).
BOULDING, K., *The Impact of the Social Sciences* (Rutgers University Press, 1966).
BROWN, J. F., *Psychology and the Social Order* (McGraw-Hill, 1936).
BUCKELY, W., *Modern Systems Research for the Behavioural Scientist. Source Book* (Aldine, 1968).
BURNS, T., 'The Comparative Study of Organisations', in Vroom, V. (ed.), *Methods of Organisational Research* (Pittsburgh University Press, 1967), pp. 118–70.
—— 'On the Plurality of Social Systems', in Gilbert, M. (ed.), *The Modern Business Enterprise* (Penguin, 1972), pp. 105–21.
BURNS, T. and STALKER, G., *The Management of Innovation* (Tavistock, 1961).
CAPLOW, J., *Principles of Organisation* (Harcourt, Brace & Court, 1964).
CHILD, JOHN, 'Organisational Structure, Environment and Performance—The Role of Strategic Choice', *Sociology* (1972), 6.1, pp. 2–22.
CHIN, ROBERT and BENNE, KENNETH, D., 'General Strategies for Effecting

Changes in Human Systems', in Bennis, Warren G., Benne, Kenneth
D. and Chin, Robert (eds), *The Planning of Change* (Holt, Rinehart &
Winston, 1969), pp. 32–57.
CHOMSKY, NOAM, *American Power and the New Mandarins* (Pelican, 1969).
CHURCHMAN, C. W., *The Systems Approach* (Delacorte Press, 1968).
CLOWARD, RICHARD and OHLIN, LLOYD *Delinquency and Opportunity* (Free
Press, 1960).
COHN-BENDIT, D. and G., *Obsolete Communism—The Left-Wing Alternative*
(Penguin, 1969).
CROMBIE, A. D., *Planning for Turbulent Social Fields* (PhD thesis, Universty
of Canberra, 1972).
CROZIER, M., *The Bureaucratic Phenomenon* (Tavistock, 1964).
DAHRENDROF, R., *Class and Class Conflict in an Industrial Society* (Rout-
ledge & Kegan Paul, 1959).
—— *Society and Democracy in Germany* (Weidenfeld & Nicolson, 1968).
DAWE, ALAN, 'The Two Sociologies', *British Journal of Sociology* (1970),
XXI, 2.
DILL, W. R., 'Environment as an Influence in Managerial Autonomy',
ASQ (1958), 2, pp. 409–43.
DRUCKER, PETER, *The Age of Discontinuity* (Heinemann, 1969).
—— *Big Business* (Heinemann, 1946).
DURKHEIM, E., *The Division of Labour in Society* (Free Press, 1964).
—— *Professional Ethics and Civic Morals* (Routledge & Kegan Paul, 1957).
ELDRIDGE, J. E. T., *Sociology and Industrial Life* (Nelson, 1973).
EMERY, F. E., *Freedom and Justice within Walls* (Tavistock, 1970).
—— 'The Next Thirty Years: Concepts, Methods and Anticipations',
Human Relations (1967), 20.3, pp. 199–237.
EMERY, F. E. and TRIST, E. L., 'The Causal Texture of Organisational
Environments', *Human Relations* (1965), 18.1, pp. 21–31.
—— 'Socio-technical Systems', in Churchman, C. W. and Verhurst, H.
(eds), *Management Sciences Models and Techniques* (Pergamon, 1960).
—— *Towards a Social Ecology* (Plenum Press, 1972).
ETZIONI, A., *A Comparative Analysis of Complex Organisations* (Free Press,
1961).
—— *Modern Organisations* (Prentice Hall, 1964).
—— (ed.), *A Sociological Reader on Complex Organisatians* (Holt, Rine-
hart & Winston, 1970).
EVAN, WILLIAM M., 'The Organisation-set: Towards a Theory of Inter-
organisational Relations', in Thompson, James D. (ed.), *Approaches
to Organisation Design* (University of Pittsburgh, 1966), pp. 173–191.
FEIBLEMAN, J. and FRIEND, J. W., 'The Structure and Function of Organisation', in Emery, F. E. (ed.), *Systems Thinking* (Penguin, 1969), pp.
30–55.
FLORENCE, P. S., *The Logic of British and American Industry* (Routledge &
Kegan Paul, 1953).
FOSTER, MICHAEL, 'An Introduction to the Theory and Practice of Action

Research in Work Organisations', *Human Relations*, Vol. 25, No. 6, pp. 529–56.

FOX, ALAN, 'Industrial Relations: A Social Critique of Pluralist Ideology', in Child, John (ed.), *Man and Organisation* (Allen & Unwin, 1973).

—— *Industrial Sociology and Industrial Relations* (HMSO, 1966).

FRIEDRICH, C. J. and BRZEZINSKI, Z. K., *Totalitarian Dictatorship and Autocracy* (Praeger, 1966).

GALBRAITH, J. K., *American Capitalism. The Concept of Countervailing Power* (Penguin, 1963).

—— *The New Industrial State* (Hamish Hamilton, 1967).

GANS, HERBERT J., *People and Plans* (Penguin, 1972).

—— 'Urban Poverty and Social Planning', in Lazarsfeld, Paul F., Sewell, William H. and Wilensky, Harold L. (eds), *The Uses of Sociology* (Basic Books, 1967), pp. 437–76.

GIDDENS, A. (ed.), *Emile Durkheim—Selected Writings* (CUP, 1972).

GLASER, B., *Organisational Careers: A Sourcebook for Theory* (Aldine Press, 1968).

GLASER, B. and STRAUSS, A. L., *The Discovery of Grounded Theory: Strategies for Qualitative Research* (Aldine Press, 1967).

GOFFMAN, E., *Asylums* (Penguin, 1968).

GOULDNER, A. W., *The Coming Crisis of Western Sociology* (Routledge & Kegan Paul, 1971).

—— *Enter Plato* (Routledge & Kegan Paul, 1967).

—— 'Organisational Analysis', in Merton, R. K. *et al.* (eds), *Sociology Today* (Harper, 1965), pp. 400–28.

—— *Patterns of Industrial Bureaucracy* (Routledge & Kegan Paul, 1954).

GROSS, NEAL, and FISHMAN, JOSHUA A., 'The Management of Educational Establishments', in Lazarsfeld, Paul F., Sewell, William H. and Wilensky, Harold L., *The Uses of Sociology* (Basic Books, 1967).

GUETZKOW, H., 'Reactions among Organisations', in Bowers, R. V. (ed.), *Studies on Behaviour in Organisations* (University of Georgia Press, 1966).

GULICK, L. and URWICK, L. F., *Papers on the Science of Administration* (Institute of Public Administration, 1937).

HARRISON, PAUL, *Authority and Power in the Free Church Tradition* (Princeton University Press, 1959).

HUNTER, A., 'Countervailing Power', in Rothschild, K. W. (ed.), *Power in Economics* (Penguin, 1971), pp. 255–74.

ILLICH, IVAN D., *Deschooling Society* (Calder, 1971).

JORDAN, Z. A., *Karl Marx: Economy Class and Revolution* (Michael Joseph, 1971).

KATZ, D. and KAHN, R. L., *The Social Psychology of Organisations* (Wiley, 1966).

KEPHART, W. H., 'A Quantitative Analysis of Intergroup Relationships', *AJS* (1950), LV, 6.

KINGDOM, D. R., *Matrix Organisations: Managing Information Technologies* (Tavistock, 1973).

KORNHAUSER, W., *The Politics of Mass Society* (Routledge & Kegan Paul, 1960).

LANDIS, BENSON Y., 'Confessions of a Church Statistician', in Schneider, Louis (ed.), *Religion, Culture and Society* (Wiley, 1964).

LANDSBERGER, H. A., *Hawthorne Revisited* (Cornell University Press, 1958).

LANE, D., *Politics and Society in the USSR* (Weidenfeld & Nicolson, 1970).

LAWRENCE, P. and LORSCH, J. W., *Organisation and Environment* (Harvard Business School, 1967).

LEFEBVRE, H., *The Sociology of Karl Marx* (Allen Lane, 1968).

LENIN, V. I., 'What Is to Be Done ?', in *Collected Works* (Moscow Publishing House, 1961), Vol. 5.

LEVINE, S. and WHITE, P. E., 'Exchange as a Conceptual Framework for the Study of Interorganisational Relationships', *ASQ* (1961), 5, pp. 583–601.

LEWIN, K., *Principles of Topological Psychology* (McGraw-Hill, 1936).

LIKERT, R., *New Patterns of Management* (McGraw-Hill, 1961).

LIPSET, S. M., *Agrarian Socialism* (Anchor, 1968).

—— 'The Political Process in Trade Unions', in *Political Man* (Mercury, 1963).

LIPSET, S. M., TROW, M. A. and COLEMAN, J. S., *Union Democracy. The Internal Politics of the International Typographical Union* (Free Press, 1956).

LUKACS, G., 'Critical Observations on Rosa Luxemburg's "Critique of the Russian Revolution" ', in *History and Class Consciousness* (Merlin Press, 1968).

—— 'Towards a Methodology of the Problem of Organisation', in *History and Class Consciousness* (Merlin Press, 1968).

LUXEMBURG, ROSA, 'The Political Mass Strike', in Looker, R. (ed.), *Rosa Luxemburg. Selected Political Writings* (Jonathan Cape, 1972).

—— 'The Role of the Organisation in Revolutionary Activity', in Looker, R. (ed.), *Rosa Luxemburg. Selected Political Writings* (Jonathan Cape, 1972).

MACINTYRE, A., 'Is a Science of Comparative Politics Possible ?', in *Against the Self-Images of the Age* (Duckworth, 1971).

MACIVER, R. M. and PAGE, C. H., *Society* (Macmillan, 1957).

MCGREGOR, D., *The Human Side of Enterprise* (McGraw-Hill, 1960).

MCKENZIE, R. T., *British Political Parties* (Mercury, 2nd edn, 1964).

MCNAMARA, R. S., *The Essence of Security: Reflections in Office* (Harper & Row, 1968).

MCWHINNEY, W. H., 'Organisational Form, Decision Modalities and the Environment', *Human Relations* (1968), 21.3, pp. 269–81.

MARCH, JAMES G. (ed.), *Handbook of Organisations* (Rand McNally, 1965).

MARCUSE, H., *One Dimensional Man* (Routledge & Kegan Paul, 1964).

MARX, K., 'The Eighteenth Brumaire of Louis Napoleon', in Marx, K. and Engels, F., *Selected Works* (Lawrence & Wishart, 1968).

MASLOW, ABRAHAM H., *Motivation and Personality* (Harper Row, 1954).

MAURES, J. G. (ed.), *Readings in Organisation Theory: Open Systems Approach* (Random House, 1971).

MECHANIC, D., 'Sources of Power of Lower Participants in Complex Organisations', *ASQ* (1967), 7.

MERTON, R. K., *Social Theory and Social Structure* (Free Press, 1957).

MICHELS, R., *Political Parties. A Sociological Study of the Oligarchical Tendencies of Modern Democracy* (Collier, 1962).

MILES, R. E., 'Human Relations or Human Resources ?', *Harvard Business Review* (1965), 43.4, pp. 148–54.

MILIBAND, R., *The State in Capitalist Society* (Weidenfeld & Nicolson, 1969).

MILLER, E. J., 'Territory, Technology and Time. The Internal Differentiation of Complex Production Systems', *Human Relations* (1966), 13.

MILLHAM, S., BULLOCK, R. and CHERRETT, P., 'Social Control in Organisations', *BJS* (1972), 23.4, pp. 406–21.

MILLS, C. WRIGHT, *The Causes of World War III* (Secker & Warbug, 1959).

—— *The Power Elite* (OUP, 1959).

—— *The Sociological Imagination* (OUP, 1959).

MISHAN, E. J., *The Costs of Economic Growth* (Penguin, 1969).

MOUZELIS, N. P., *Organisation and Bureaucracy* (Routledge & Kegan Paul, 1967).

NEUMANN, F., *Behemoth. The Structure and Practice of National Socialism* (Harper, 1966).

NICOLAUS, M., 'The Professional Organisation of Sociology: A View from Below', in Blackburn, R. (ed.), *Ideology in Social Science. Readings in Critical Social Theory* (Fontana, 1972), pp. 45–60.

OSTROGORSKI, M. I., *Democracy and the Organisation of Political Parties* (Anchor, 1964).

PARSONS, T., 'Some Ingredients of a General Theory of Formal Organisation', Litterer, Joseph A. (ed.), *Organisations: Systems Control and Adaptation* (Wiley, 1969), Vol. 2, pp. 197–213.

—— *Structure and Process in Modern Societies* (Free Press, 1960).

PEEL, J. D. Y., *Herbert Spencer. The Evolution of a Sociologist* (Heinemann, 1971).

PERROW, C., 'The Analysis of Goals in Complex Organisations', *ASR* (1961), 26, pp. 854–66.

—— 'Organisational Goals', *International Encyclopaedia of the Social Sciences* (Macmillan, 1968), Vol. 11.

PUGH, DEREK S., 'Modern Organisation Theory: A Psychological and Sociological Study', *Psy. Bulletin* (1966), 21, pp. 235–51.

RAPOPORT, ROBERT N., 'Three Dilemmas in Action Research', *Human Relations* (1970), 23.6.

REIN, MARTIN and MILLER, S. M., 'The Demonstration as a Strategy of Change', Rein, Martin, *Social Policy: Issues of Choice and Change* (Random House, 1970).

ROETHLISBERGER, F. J. and DICKSON, W. J., *Management and the Worker* (Wiley, 1964).

ROY, D., 'Efficiency and "The Fix": Informal Intergroup Relations in a Piece-work Machine Shop', *AJS* (1964), 60, pp. 255–66.

—— 'Quota-restriction and Gold-bricking in a Machine Shop', *AJS* (1952), 57, pp. 427–42.

SCHAPIRO, LEONARD, *Totalitarianism* (Macmillan, 1972).

SCHEIN, EDGAR H., *Organisational Psychology* (Prentice Hall, 1970).

SCHON, DONALD, *Beyond the Stable State* (Temple Smith, 1971).

SCHUMPETER, J., *Capitalism, Socialism and Democracy* (Allen & Unwin, 1943).

SCOTT, WILLIAM G., 'Organisation Theory: An Overview and an A Litterer', Joseph A. (ed.), *Organisations: Structure and Behaviour* (Wiley, 1963), Vol. 1.

SCOTT, W. RICHARD, 'Field Methods in the Study of Organisations', March, James G. (ed.), *Handbook of Organisations* (Rand McNally, 1965), pp. 261–304.

SELZNICK, P., 'Foundations of the Theory of Organisations' Litterer, Joseph A. (ed.) *Organisations: Systems, Control and Adaptation* (Wiley, 1969), Vol. 2, pp. 358–68.

—— *Leadership in Administration* (Harper & Row, 1957).

SILLS, DAVID L., *The Volunteers* (Free Press, 1957).

SILVERMAN, D., *The Theory of Organisations* (Heinemann, 1970).

SIMON, H. A., 'A Behavioural Model of Rational Choice', *Quarterly Journal of Economics* (1955), 69, pp. 99–118.

SIMON, H. A. and MARCH, J. G., *Organisations* (Wiley, 1958).

SPENCER, H., *Principles of Sociology* (Williams & Norgate, 1893).

—— *The Study of Sociology* (Ann Arbor, 1960).

STINCHCOMBE, A. L., *Constructing Social Theories* (Harcourt Brace, 1968).

TANNENBAUM, A. S., *Control in Organisations* (McGraw-Hill, 1968).

TAYLOR, F. W., *Scientific Management* (Harper & Row, 1947).

TERREBERRY, S., 'The Evolution of Organisational Environments', Thomas, John M. and Bennis, Warren G. (eds), *Management of Change and Conflict* (Penguin, 1972).

THOMAS, JOHN M. and BENNIS, WARREN G. (eds), *Management of Change and Conflict* (Penguin, 1972).

THOMPSON, JAMES D., *Organisations in Action* (McGraw-Hill, 1967).

THOMPSON, JAMES D. and MCEWAN, W. J., 'Organisational Goals and Environments: Goal-setting as an Interactive Process', *ASR* (1958), 23, pp. 23–31.

TOFFLER, ALVIN, *Future Shock* (Bodley Head, 1970).

TOWNSEND, R., '*Up the Organisation*' (Hodder-Fawcett, 1971).

TRIST, E. L. and BAMFORTH, K. W., 'Some Social and Psychological Consequences of the Longwall Method of Coal-getting', *Human Relations* (1951) 4, pp. 3–38.

TRIST, E. L., MURRAY, H., HIGGIN, G. W. and POLLOCK, A., *Organisational Choice* (Tavistock, 1963).

TROTSKY, L., *The Revolution Betrayed* (New Park Publications, 1967).

UDY, STANLEY H., 'The Comparative Analysis of Organisations', March, James G. (ed.), *Handbook of Organisations* (Rand McNally, 1965), pp. 678–709.

VICKERS, G., *The Art of Judgment* (Chapman & Hall, 1965).

—— *Freedom in a Rocking Boat* (Allen Lane, 1970).

—— *Value Systems and Social Processes* (Tavistock, 1968).

WEBB, SYDNEY and BEATRICE, *Industrial Democracy* (London, 1911).

WEBER, MAX, 'Bureaucracy' Gerth, H. and Mills, C. W. (eds), *From Max Weber* (Routledge & Kegan Paul, 1948).

—— *Economy and Society* (Bedminster Press, 1968).

—— *The Theory of Social and Economic Organisations* (Free Press, 1964).

WHEELER, HARVEY, 'The Short and Happy Life of a Research Consultantship', Polsby, Nelson W., Dentler, Robert A. and Smith, Paul A. (eds), *Politics and Social Life* (Houghton Mifflin, 1963).

WILLENER, ALFRED, *The Action-Image of Society* (Tavistock, 1970).

WOODWARD, JOAN (ed.), *Industrial Organisation: Behaviour and Control* (OUP, 1970).

—— *Industrial Organisation: Theory and Practice* (OUP, 1965).

—— *Management and Technology* (HMSO, 1958).

SUBJECT INDEX

AUTHOR INDEX

Abeglenn J.C. 71, 205
Ackoff R. 38, 47, 49, 61, 69, 70, 205
Andreski S. 131, 205
Angyal A. 71, 72, 95, 205
Arendt H. 156–8, 205
Argyris C. 117, 205
Aron R. 150, 152, 158, 187, 205

Bamforth K.W. 39, 210
Baritz L. 190, 205
Barkes R.G. 87, 205
Bell D. 197, 205
Benne K.D. 197–9, 205, 206
Bennis W.G. 97, 197, 198, 205, 206, 210
Berger P.L. 176–8
Blackburn R. 194, 209
Blau P. 37, 38, 41, 65, 96, 108, 205
Blauner R. 38, 41–4, 107, 205
Boulding K. 72, 205
Bowers R.V. 78
Brown J.F. 87, 205
Brzezinski Z.K. 150, 152, 207
Buckley W. 94, 205
Bullock R. 118, 209
Burns T. 32, 116, 168, 169, 205

Caplow T. 22, 23, 25, 27, 31, 205
Chein I. 62
Cherrett P. 118, 209
Child J. 82–4, 174, 205
Chin R. 197–9, 205, 206
Chomsky N. 196, 197, 206
Churchman C.W. 40, 94, 206
Cloward R. 200, 206
Cohn-Bendit D. 196, 206
Cohn-Bendit G. 196, 206
Coleman J.S. 163, 208
Crombie A.D. 49, 85, 206
Crozier M. 71, 119, 124, 206

Dahrendorf R. 153, 154, 187, 206

Dawe A. 17, 206
Debray R. 188
Dentler R.A. 193, 211
Dickson W.J. 111, 169–72, 210
Dill W.R. 78, 206
Drucker P. 12, 178–81, 206
Durkheim E. 18, 38, 131–6, 206

Eldridge J.E.T. 44, 135, 206
Emery F.E. 11, 40, 49, 61, 70, 73, 75, 76, 78, 80–2, 94, 116, 205, 206
Engels F. 138, 209
Etzioni A. 14, 24, 25, 27, 33, 37, 38, 45, 46, 51, 89, 123, 206
Evan W.R. 78, 206

Fayol H. 120
Feibleman J. 11, 206
Fishman J.A. 191–3, 207
Flacks R. 195
Florence P.S. 166, 167, 206
Foster M. 197, 199, 206
Fox A. 173, 174, 207
Friedrich C.J. 150, 152, 207
Friend J.W. 11, 206

Galbraith J.K. 83, 106, 181–4, 207
Gans H. 200, 201, 207
Gerth H. 149
Giddens A. 135, 207
Gilbert M. 91, 168
Glaser B.G. 14–16, 207
Goffman E. 45, 52–6, 88, 89, 207
Gouldner A.W. 96, 108, 119, 167–9, 191, 199, 207
Gross N. 191–3, 207
Guetzkow H. 78, 207
Gulick L. 166, 207

Harrison P. 177, 207
Hegel F. 136, 137
Higgin G. 108, 211

216